IMAGES
of Rail

Kansas City Southern Railway

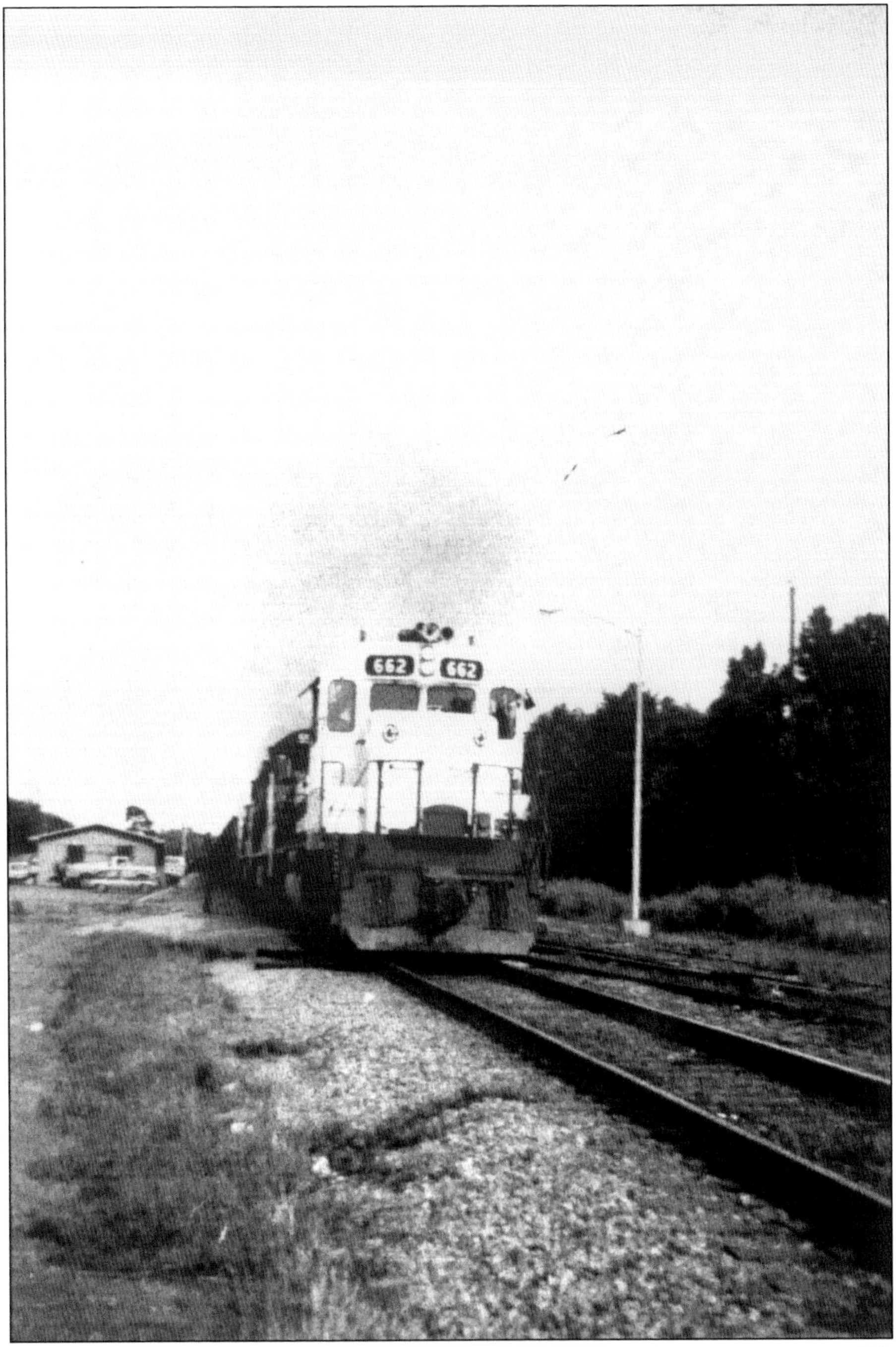

Kansas City Southern Railway freight leaves Hughes Springs, Texas, on its journey toward Dallas. This was part of the Louisiana and Arkansas Railway line. (Courtesy Belinda S. Carter.)

On the cover: A reminder of the original 1940 *Southern Belle*, this executive train is at Roodhouse, Illinois, in December 2007. The holiday express delivers gifts to children up and down the line. The engines are painted in the original *Belle* colors. (Courtesy Gary Coates.)

IMAGES
of Rail

KANSAS CITY SOUTHERN RAILWAY

Thad Hillis Carter

ARCADIA
PUBLISHING

ISBN 978-0-7385-6001-4

Published by Arcadia Publishing
Charleston, South Carolina

Printed in the United States of America

Library of Congress Control Number: 2009925455

For all general information contact Arcadia Publishing at:
Telephone 843-853-2070
Fax 843-853-0044
E-mail sales@arcadiapublishing.com
For customer service and orders:
Toll-Free 1-888-313-2665

Visit us on the Internet at www.arcadiapublishing.com

To Paul Ethan, John Thad, and Henry Francis Xavier

Contents

Acknowledgments

Thanks to Harold K. Vollrath, who has an encyclopedic knowledge of railroad history and especially the Kansas City Southern Railway (KCS), by which he was employed. His photographs grace many railroad volumes, so I am honored to have his wonderful black-and-white photographs included in this work.

Philip Moseley, a longtime KCS employee at DeQueen, Arkansas, offered help in the form of miscellaneous artifacts and a splendid photograph of the last *Belle* at DeQueen. KCS employee Bill Hartwell helped me locate Philip and answered questions for me when I visited him in Ashdown, Arkansas. Thanks to my friend John Reed for providing the menus from KCS dining cars.

Judge Ben Z. Grant helped locate pictures and offered encouragement. He is a playwright and has written about Louisiana governor Huey Long. Ben was also a cousin of Eddie Guinn, locomotive engineer for the KCS about whom I have written.

Longtime friend Don Wriborg drove to DeQuincy, Louisiana, to look for old pictures at the depot museum. Don and I worked in radio 30 years ago and explored the old Kansas City Union Station shortly before much of the trackage was removed.

Glen Roark, retired schoolteacher and scoutmaster, offered beautiful shots of the *Southern Belle* as it exists today. Glen rode the KCS on short school outings from Neosho to Joplin in Missouri and has a collection of memorabilia that he was willing to share.

A dear friend when I lived in northeast Texas was KCS employee Jack McCrary. His widow, Mary Jane McCrary, shared copies of early-20th-century timetables from which I was able to extract valuable historical information.

Thanks to Wayne Kuchinsky for an outstanding story in *Passenger Train Journal* on the KCS *Southern Belle*. Thanks to Gary Coates for his excellent photographs of the *Belle* business train. Gary's "Southern Belle in the Snow" graces the cover of this volume. Thanks to the Joplin Public Library for allowing me to access files and take photocopies of *Southern Belle* materials.

To my wife Belinda, who helped in manuscript preparation, and to our sons John and Paul, who rode trains because their dad wanted to, I thank you. A special thank-you to Harvey at the Neosho Historical Museum. Thanks to a long-departed gentleman known to me as Pop Spencer who worked KCS passenger trains from Heavener, Oklahoma, to Shreveport, Louisiana, and who let a teenage boy get in the way while he went about the performance of his duties.

And last but not least, to Mary Cleveland of the Museum of West Louisiana in Leesville, thank you for the photographs.

INTRODUCTION

From the age of two, the Kansas City Southern Railway (KCS) was a part of my life. Mom and I would board the bus at the KCS depot in Lake Charles, Louisiana. A short, stocky, cheerful man, George Edwards, who smoked a pipe and walked with a limp, took our tickets. We left the depot and headed over the Calcasieu River Bridge to Sulphur, Louisiana. After a few more miles, we crossed the diamond-shaped trackage and parked beside the DeQuincy, Louisiana, depot. There we waited, usually not more than a few minutes, for our train to arrive from Port Arthur, Texas. We were on our way to see family in Springfield, Missouri.

A stop in Leesville, Louisiana, afforded time to cross the street and buy hamburgers from the KCS café. My memories of our ride north of Shreveport, Louisiana, in the early 1950s consist of a streamlined coach and a heavyweight car. We would get off the train at the union depot in Joplin, Missouri, and walk to the Greyhound bus terminal to board for a ride to Springfield. I would tell my cousins Becky and Pamela about the train ride, but they never seemed very interested.

At the age of nine, I remember my mom and dad took me by Continental Trailways bus to Alexandria, Louisiana. After an extended wait in the bus depot, we walked to the KCS depot to await the arrival of the *Southern Belle*. At about 3:00 a.m., the northbound from New Orleans would come off the main line and down the terminal track. Mom and I boarded while Dad helped get our luggage on board. As we backed out of the station onto the main line, I remember seeing Dad on the concrete walkway starting back to the bus terminal.

Other family memories include my aunts May and Helen riding the *Flying Crow* from Kansas City to see Uncle Pam in Lake Charles. They complained about the fares. (I wonder what they would think of 21st-century Amtrak prices?) We took them back to the Lake Charles depot to board the bus for DeQuincy, which by this time was a Chevrolet panel truck.

Grandmother Edge visited by train, and we took her back to the station to return on the northbound. John Leblanc's mother-in-law, Mrs. McClendon, who lived in Texarkana, Arkansas, was also the subject of a visit to the depot. That day the train was late because of a car accident. When it finally arrived, a black GP7 had replaced the E-unit and the consist included an American Flyer coach (actually an Osgood Bradley coach built in the 1930s, but the nickname stuck). The tail car was either the *Good Cheer* or the *Hospitality* reduced from *Southern Belle* service to operating on the Shreveport-to-Port Arthur train.

In my 15th year, it was decided I was old enough to travel by myself to see Aunt May and Uncle Herb in Kansas City. An E8 diesel pulling a railway express car, heavyweight railway post office (RPO), streamlined coach, and observation car made up our train that day. In Shreveport, I waited at the union station for the New Orleans train. Coming up the middle of the street was a short three-car consist of a baggage car, coach, and ex–New York Central Railroad observation car repainted in the KCS color scheme. After some switching, our two trains became one, minus the *Good Cheer* observation, and we headed off through the maze of switch tracks for the Deramus yard and on toward Kansas City. I wanted to ride the sleeper *Arthur Stilwell* that had been added at Shreveport but did not have the extra $15 for overnight fare.

My trips on KCS passenger trains ended in 1969 with a round-trip on the *Southern Belle* from Alexandria, Louisiana, to Kansas City and back. The Pullman car was missing, and the E-unit had been painted white with yellow trim. For some reason, the train was crowded, but the car attendant told me they often left Shreveport with only five or six passengers aboard.

A few months later, the KCS exited the passenger train market due to loss of RPO contracts. The only other time I rode the KCS was in 1978 when one of my church members offered me a ride on the turn from Leesville to Zwolle, Louisiana. I was pastor of the United Methodist church at Hornbeck, Louisiana, and Eddie Guinn was a longtime employee of the KCS. He started on the steam engines and eventually had enough seniority to operate the passenger trains from Port Arthur to Leesville.

One Sunday after church, Eddie told me to wait at the Fisher, Louisiana, depot that afternoon for the local freight from Leesville. I climbed aboard the SW1500, and the crew switched cars at Fisher then headed to Many, Louisiana, followed by more switching in a light rain, and then back toward Fisher. The good-natured crew rode in the cab as we bounced and jolted along back to Fisher. I got off the train, waved good-bye to the crew, and ended 26 years of riding the KCS.

The 1880s saw Kansas City, Missouri, in the midst of a change from a frontier trading post town to a thriving commercial settlement. Located in the fertile Midwest, Kansas City was in a position to supply the food demands of cities in the industrial East.

A successful businessman from the East, Arthur Stilwell, moved to Kansas City in 1886. Stilwell's grandfather had been a packet boat operator on the Erie Canal. He had listened to his granddad's tales of possibilities in the transportation industry and became intrigued with the idea of building a railroad.

On a Monday afternoon in 1889, two men met at the Missouri-Kansas-Texas Trust Company on Wyandotte Street in Kansas City. E. L. Martin, a director of the bank and former mayor of Kansas City, discussed the possible earnings potential of a belt line railroad to connect the 20 railroads that entered Kansas City. He had not been able to raise the money, but he did have the charter.

With Martin was Stilwell, who had a record of being able to raise large sums of money. He had experience in selling annuity contracts and raising funds for building and loan associations but not much railroad experience.

Martin asked Stilwell, "Do you think there'd be any trouble raising this money in Philadelphia?"

"Why should there be?" replied Stilwell in an assuring voice. "Those Philadelphia investors want their money to work for them." He grinned and continued, "I have a hunch money'll work fast in a belt line railroad around a growing town like this one."

Stilwell and Martin left for Philadelphia the next day but not before Stilwell had satisfied himself that work on the railroad could start just as soon as the money had been raised. "That should be by Friday, at the latest," he said to Martin.

"How do you expect to get the capital so quick?" inquired Martin. "Surely you don't intend to ask the Philadelphia directors of the Guardian Trust Company to use its capital to build a railroad?"

On the way to Philadelphia, Stilwell outlined his plans for financing Martin's belt line scheme. He would issue $1 million in bonds and $2 million in common stock. The bonds were to be sold at $666 per $1,000 bond with 20 shares of common stock as a bonus. The plan worked. In Philadelphia, Stilwell took Martin to visit some of the rich stockholders of Missouri-Kansas-Texas Trust, and before the next Friday, as he had anticipated, $180,000 in cash was made available to start the belt line. Known as the Kansas City Suburban Belt Railroad, it was one of the earliest predecessors of KCS.

These were the opening moves in several money-raising campaigns that allowed Stilwell to put together the financial structure of the KCS. In six years, he raised about $25 million.

Initially the line served as a hauler for meat and grain. Stilwell continued to raise money and was able to expand the line, looking to haul coal located in mines to the south at Hume, Missouri. Stilwell and Martin decided to build to Pittsburg, Kansas, then on to Joplin, the site of a large lead-and-zinc-mining field.

By 1889, the Kansas City, Nevada and Fort Smith Railroad was in business. Stilwell was already dreaming of building the line as far as the Gulf of Mexico but kept the secret between himself and his wife.

The railroad continued to expand. Mathias Splitlog was chief owner of 51 miles of railroad from Joplin to Sulphur Springs, Arkansas. The Wyandotte chief owned what was believed to be a rich gold and silver mine. The mine proved to be a fake, and Splitlog derived his income from hauling timber over the Kansas City, Fort Smith and Southern Railway.

Splitlog realized he had been taken advantage of and decided to sell his line to Stilwell for a mere $50,000. The line had cost the chief and a fellow investor $100,000.

Stilwell wanted to extend his railroad from Sulphur Springs through western Arkansas, but the grade was too stiff. He decided to move south through the Cherokee, Creek, and Choctaw Nations and on into Texarkana and Shreveport. This effort was aided by financing from Holland. Stilwell appealed to a commodity broker in Amsterdam and raised $3 million.

Stilwell acquired timberland running 30 miles along the right-of-way south of Sulphur Springs. That profitable investment provided capital to help build the KCS through the Ozark Mountains.

The Texarkana and Fort Smith line ran 20 miles north from Texarkana to Little River, Arkansas, and had been purchased by the Kansas City, Pittsburg and Gulf Railroad. Combined with the Splitlog road, the line had right-of-way from Kansas City to Texarkana, located on the Arkansas-Texas state line.

Fred Hornbeck was hired by Stilwell to look after the offering of free town sites to newcomers. Hornbeck, a resident of Kansas City, was a real estate man who went ahead of the actual railroad construction, bought large tracts of land, and then sold the land at a profit.

Stillwell's partner, Martin, resigned as president of the two railroad companies, and Stilwell became president at the young age of 32.

Stilwell thought that heading south to the Gulf of Mexico made sense. After transporting goods by rail, the remainder of the journey eastward could be made by sea. He continued to push southward. He planned to end his railroad at Shreveport, a river port town, and use other railroads to transport freight to Houston, Galveston, Texas, and New Orleans.

However, Stilwell continued to push south toward the gulf. Hollanders were let in on the ground floor of some of the town site promotions as a result of the $3 million bond issue.

Stilwell was intent on ending his railroad at the well-established port city of Galveston. However, due to a dream, he decided to build a city in the swampy area of Sabine Lake, only seven miles from the gulf, and link the city with the gulf by canal. This harbor would provide protection against the hurricanes of the Gulf Coast. Against opposition from entrenched area developers, Stilwell built Port Arthur and its ship canal, which became one of the country's leading ports. A short time later, Galveston was destroyed by a hurricane. Stilwell had been right.

In April 1900, the KCS became a corporate entity. At the same time, Stilwell was forced out. A bit of good luck occurred with the discovery of oil near Beaumont, Texas, in 1901. The Spindletop field produced an oil refinery center and related industries and provided new revenue for the KCS.

One

Early History of the Railroad

The Louisiana and Arkansas Railway Company (L&A) was originally a logging railroad built by William Buchanan, timber baron, around 1898. With additional rail construction, plus the purchase of other small lines, Buchanan's railroad reached Winnfield, Louisiana, in May 1902. That was the year the L&A line was organized. The extension to Hope, Arkansas, was finished in June 1903. It reached Alexandria, Louisiana, in 1906.

The Louisiana Railway and Navigation Company purchased the property of the Shreveport and Red River Valley Railroad with the intention of completing construction of the line to New Orleans. By April 14, 1907, this service had been inaugurated.

On April 1, 1923, a branch of the Missouri-Kansas-Texas Railroad (also known as the Katy), between the Louisiana-Texas line, was secured.

The Louisiana Railway and Navigation Company and the L&A line were purchased by Harvey Couch, utility executive, and his associates in 1928. The two lines were reorganized into the Louisiana and Arkansas Railway and Navigation Company.

In 1930, the corporate name of the Louisiana Railway and Navigation Company of Texas was changed to the Louisiana, Arkansas and Texas Railway Company. This line was extended to Dallas on July 1, 1932. It was then purchased by and became part of the Louisiana and Arkansas Railway Company in 1939.

The New Orleans connection of the Kansas City Southern Railway (KCS) is at Shreveport, Louisiana, over the rails of the L&A line. The KCS obtained control of the L&A by acquisition of its capital stock in 1939.

From 1900 to 1940, the KCS devoted itself to increasing markets along its lines. L. F. Loree, chairman, led the railroad operations and contributed to the growth of the railroad. It was during this period that the Louisiana and Arkansas Railway Company was acquired by the KCS, opening up new markets for the latter railroad in New Orleans and Baton Rouge and Dallas.

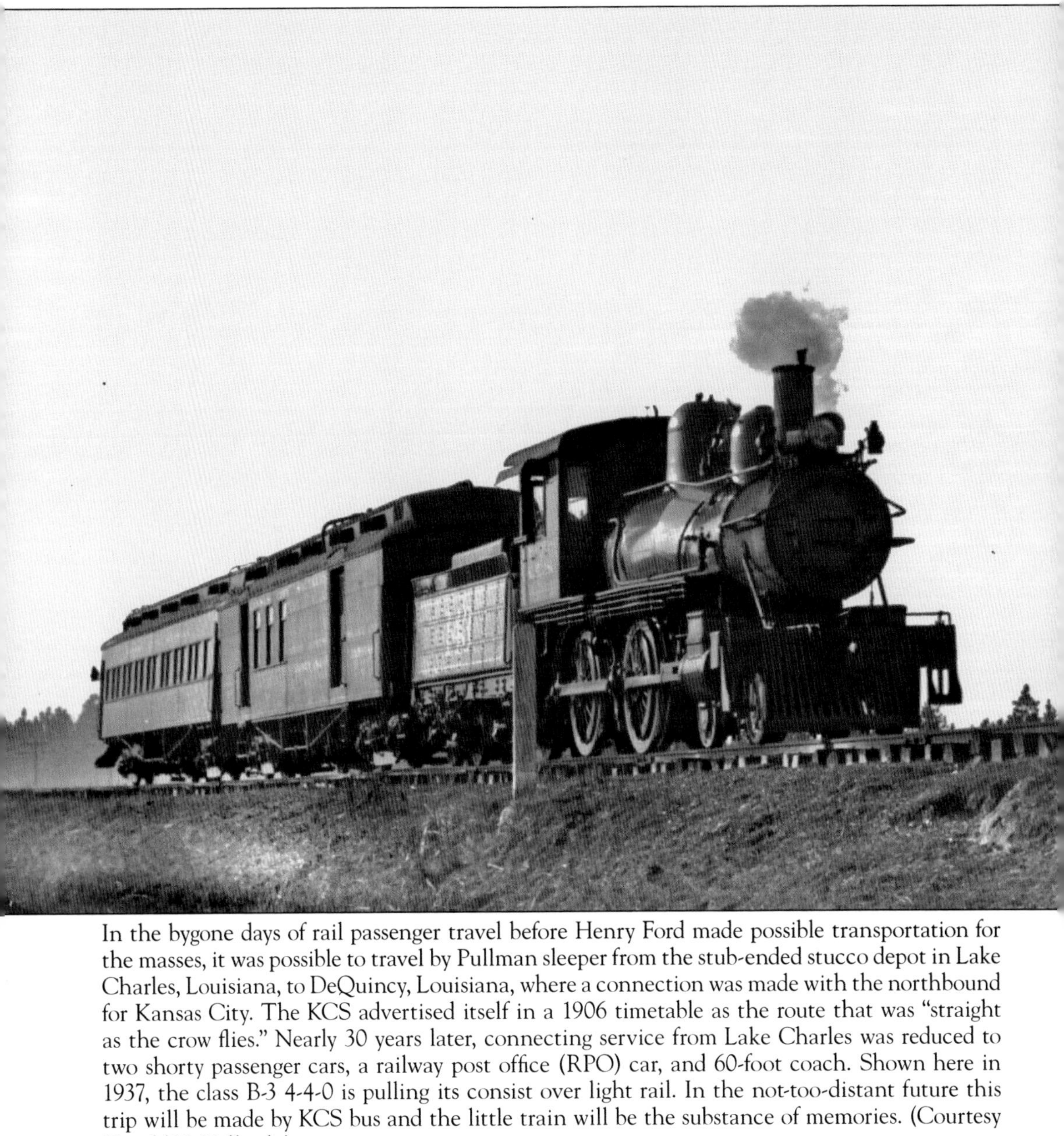

In the bygone days of rail passenger travel before Henry Ford made possible transportation for the masses, it was possible to travel by Pullman sleeper from the stub-ended stucco depot in Lake Charles, Louisiana, to DeQuincy, Louisiana, where a connection was made with the northbound for Kansas City. The KCS advertised itself in a 1906 timetable as the route that was "straight as the crow flies." Nearly 30 years later, connecting service from Lake Charles was reduced to two shorty passenger cars, a railway post office (RPO) car, and 60-foot coach. Shown here in 1937, the class B-3 4-4-0 is pulling its consist over light rail. In the not-too-distant future this trip will be made by KCS bus and the little train will be the substance of memories. (Courtesy Harold K. Vollrath.)

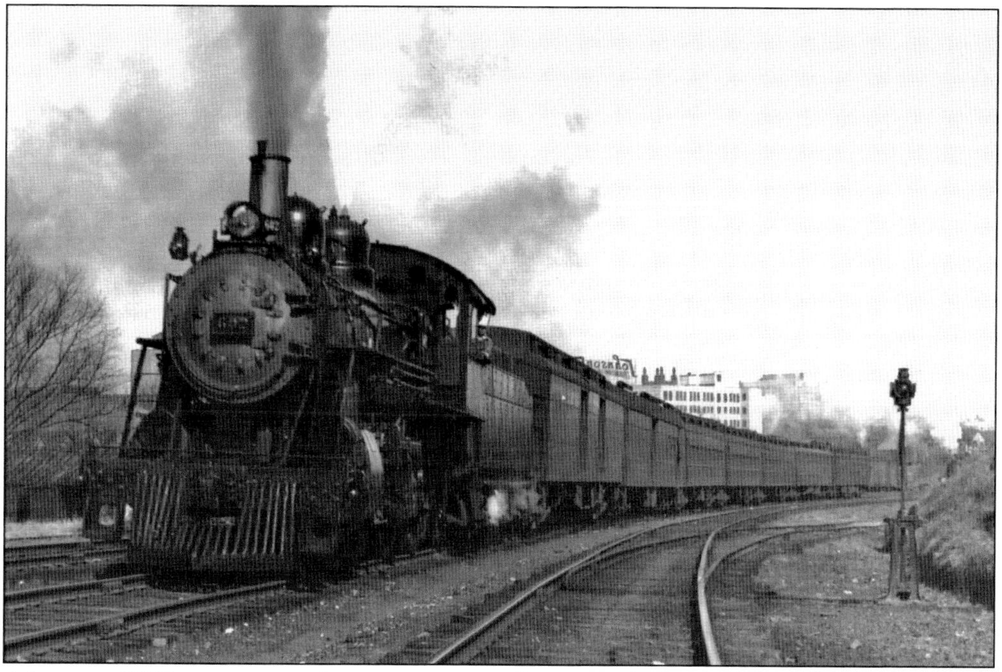

A long-ago KCS steam-powered passenger train of heavyweight design departs for its destination. Note the Harriman RPO car in the consist. These cars were used until the KCS lost its mail contract shortly before the discontinuance of its passenger service. (Courtesy Harold K. Vollrath.)

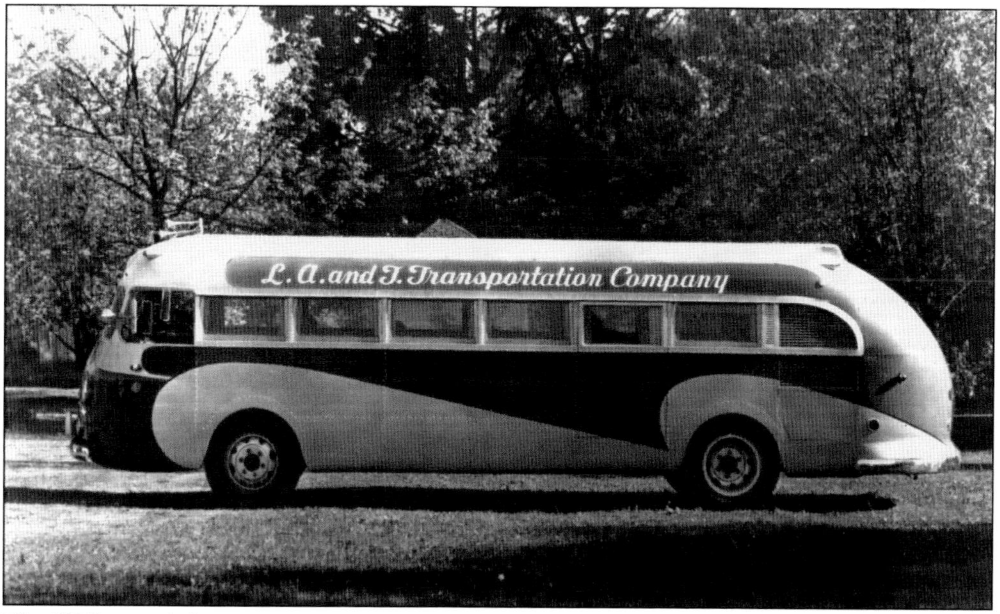

The KCS provided connections to its passenger trains by using bus service from Lake Charles to DeQuincy, Sallisaw to Fort Smith, Arkansas, and Clarence, Louisiana, to Winnfield for trains No. 9 and No. 10. This Louisiana, Arkansas and Texas Railway Company transport motor coach photographed at Shreveport, Louisiana, in 1940 is representative of buses used into the early 1950s. Lake Charles-to-DeQuincy bus service was provided by a school bus and finally by a panel truck until the connecting train was discontinued in 1968. (Courtesy Harold K. Vollrath.)

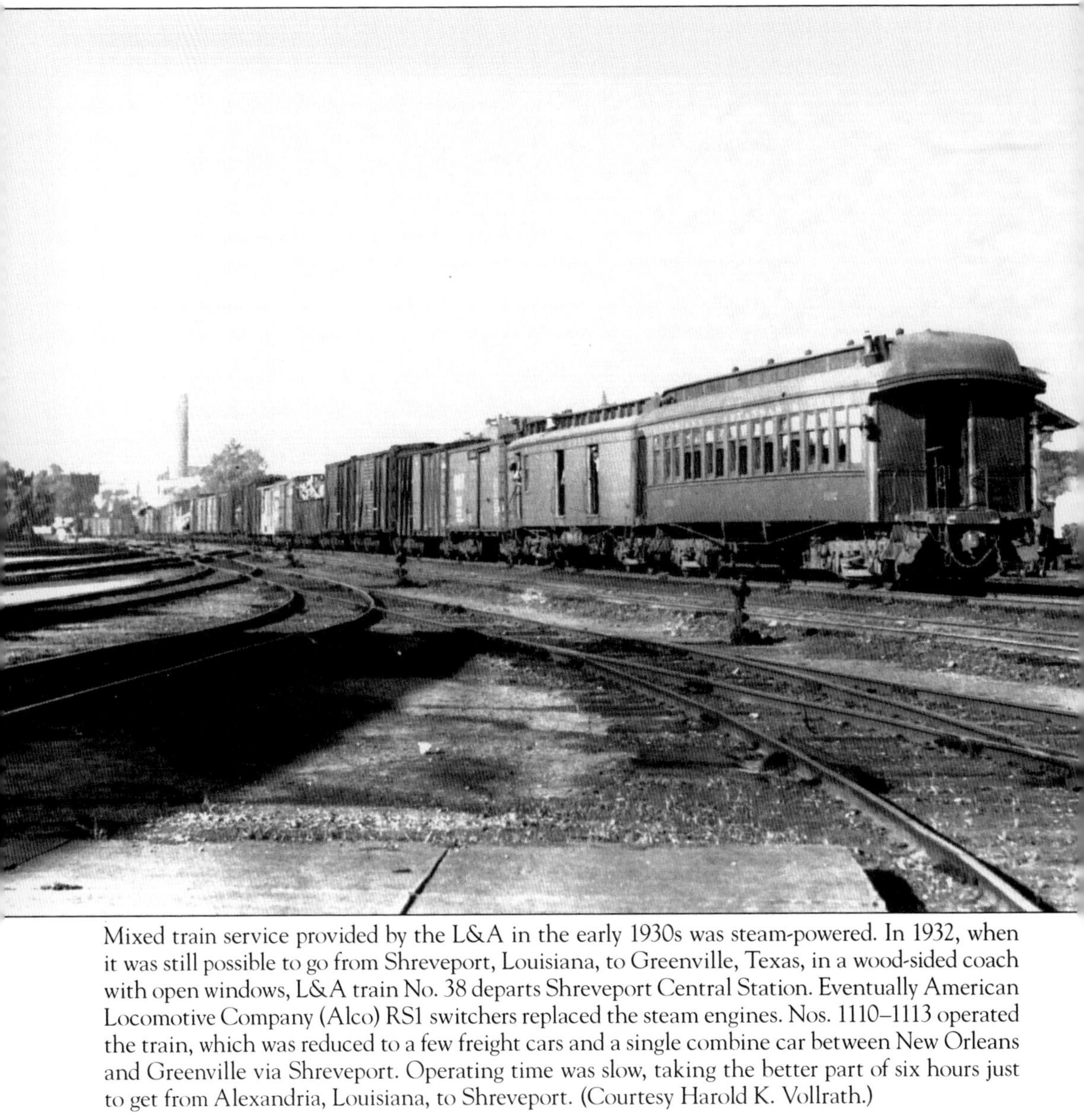

Mixed train service provided by the L&A in the early 1930s was steam-powered. In 1932, when it was still possible to go from Shreveport, Louisiana, to Greenville, Texas, in a wood-sided coach with open windows, L&A train No. 38 departs Shreveport Central Station. Eventually American Locomotive Company (Alco) RS1 switchers replaced the steam engines. Nos. 1110–1113 operated the train, which was reduced to a few freight cars and a single combine car between New Orleans and Greenville via Shreveport. Operating time was slow, taking the better part of six hours just to get from Alexandria, Louisiana, to Shreveport. (Courtesy Harold K. Vollrath.)

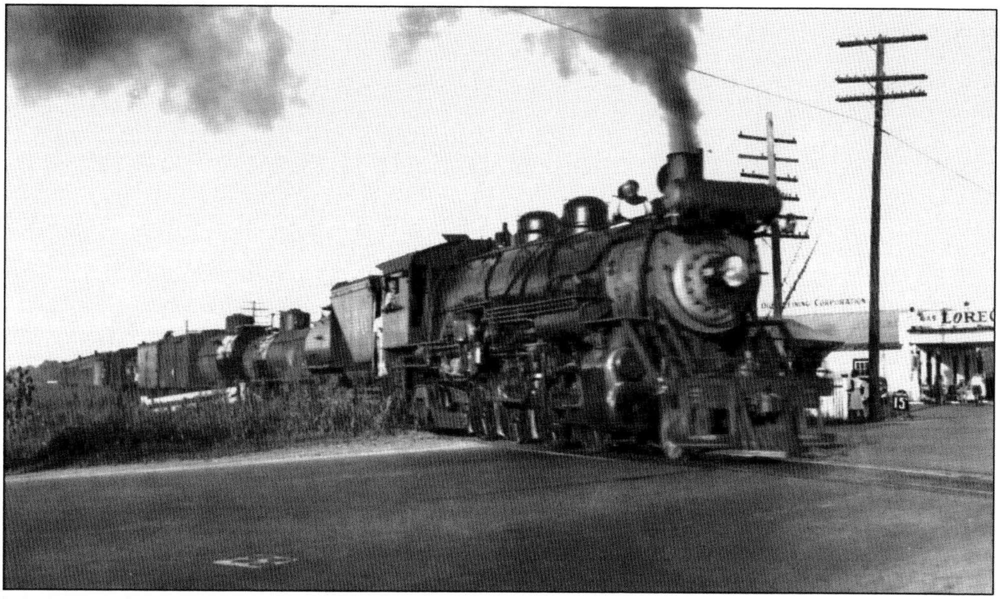

L&A mixed train No. 38 is close to Hughes Springs, Texas, in 1935. Today's train is powered by a 1927 Baldwin Locomotive Works engine and has three passenger cars in tow. (Courtesy Harold K. Vollrath.)

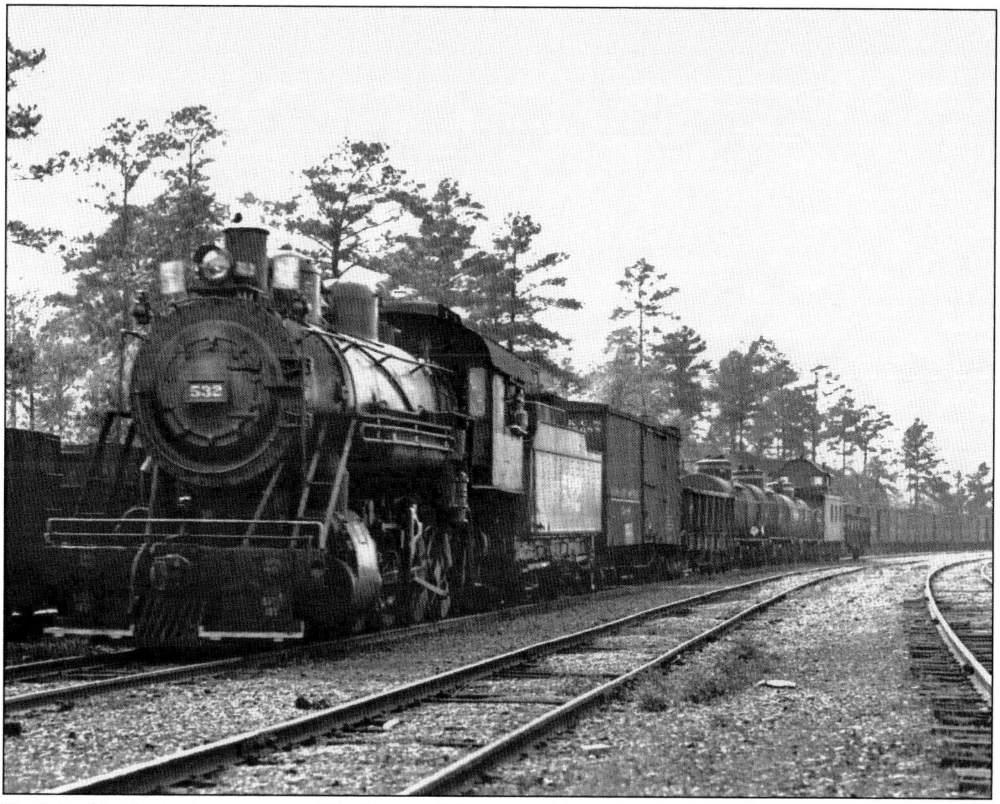

Built by Baldwin Locomotive Works in 1907, class E-3 No. 532 is busy hauling revenue freight near Shreveport in 1932. (Courtesy Harold K. Vollrath.)

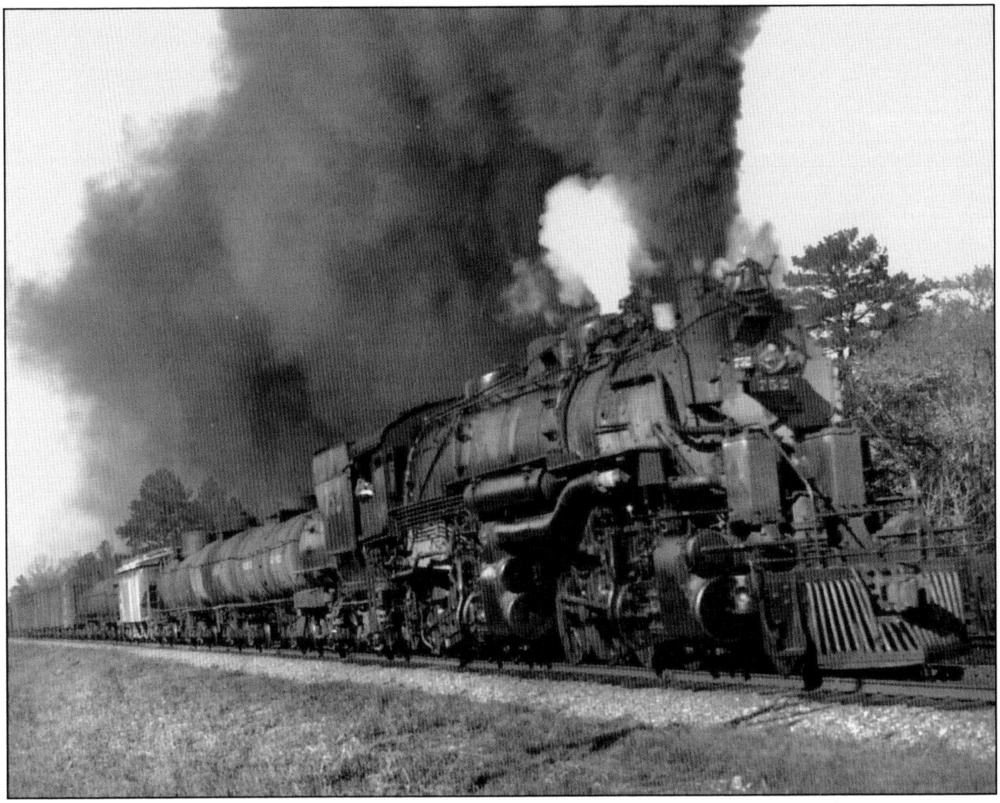

KCS class G-1 No. 752, built by Alco in 1918, gets up steam in April 1946 in southern Louisiana. (Courtesy Harold K. Vollrath.)

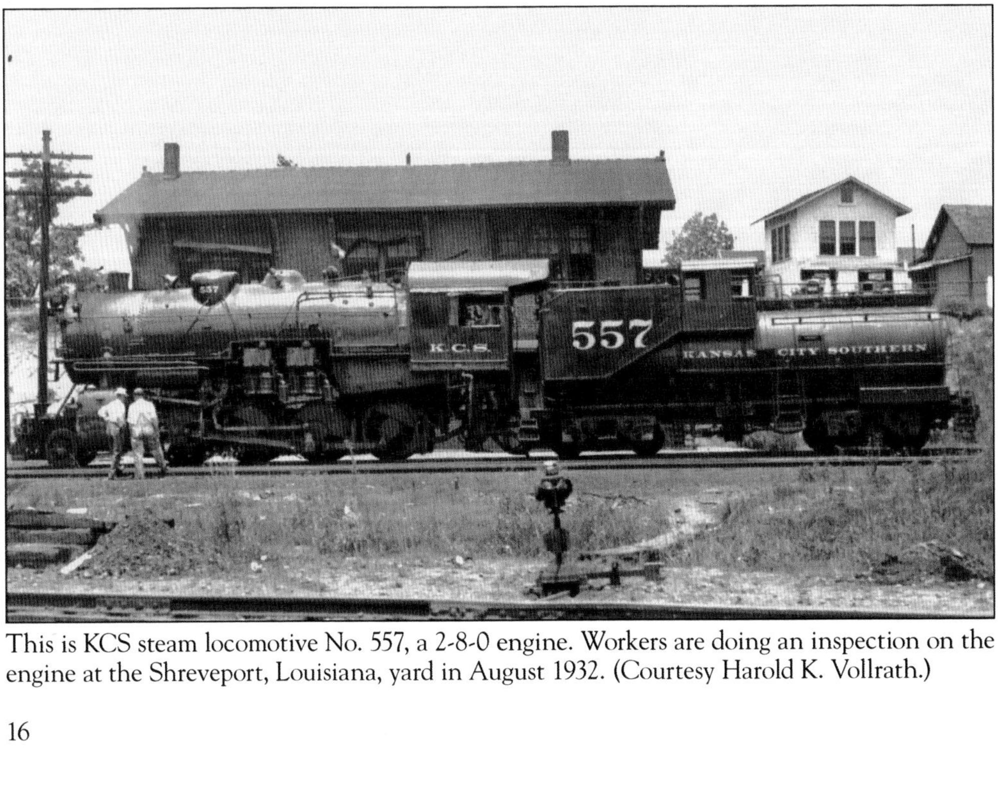

This is KCS steam locomotive No. 557, a 2-8-0 engine. Workers are doing an inspection on the engine at the Shreveport, Louisiana, yard in August 1932. (Courtesy Harold K. Vollrath.)

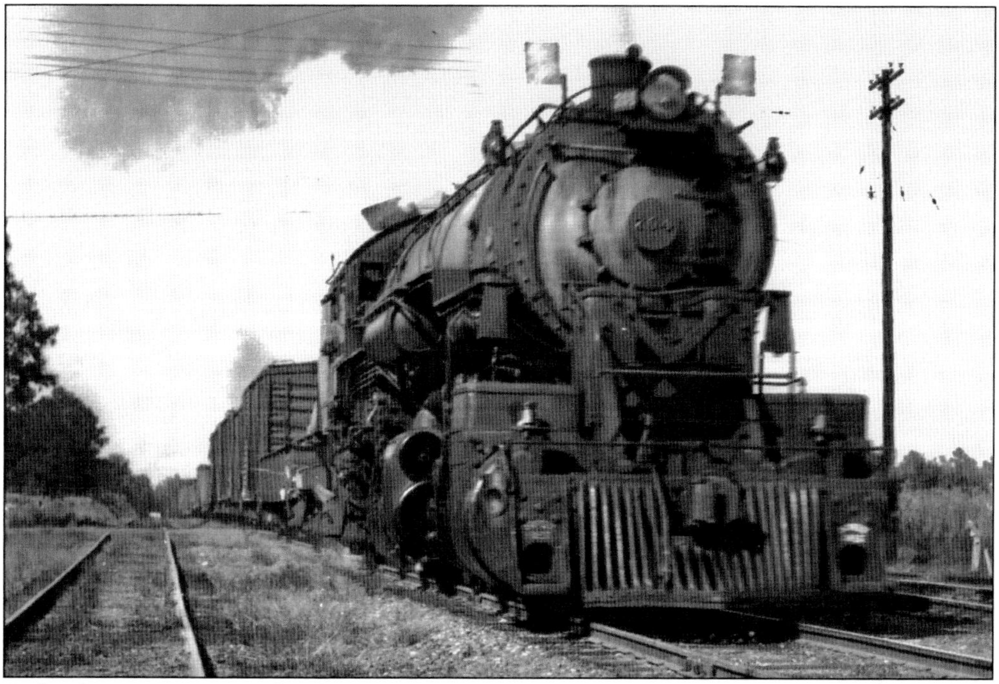

Cedar Grove, Louisiana, plays host to KCS No. 704, one of 12 of its class in service on the KCS. (Courtesy Harold K. Vollrath.)

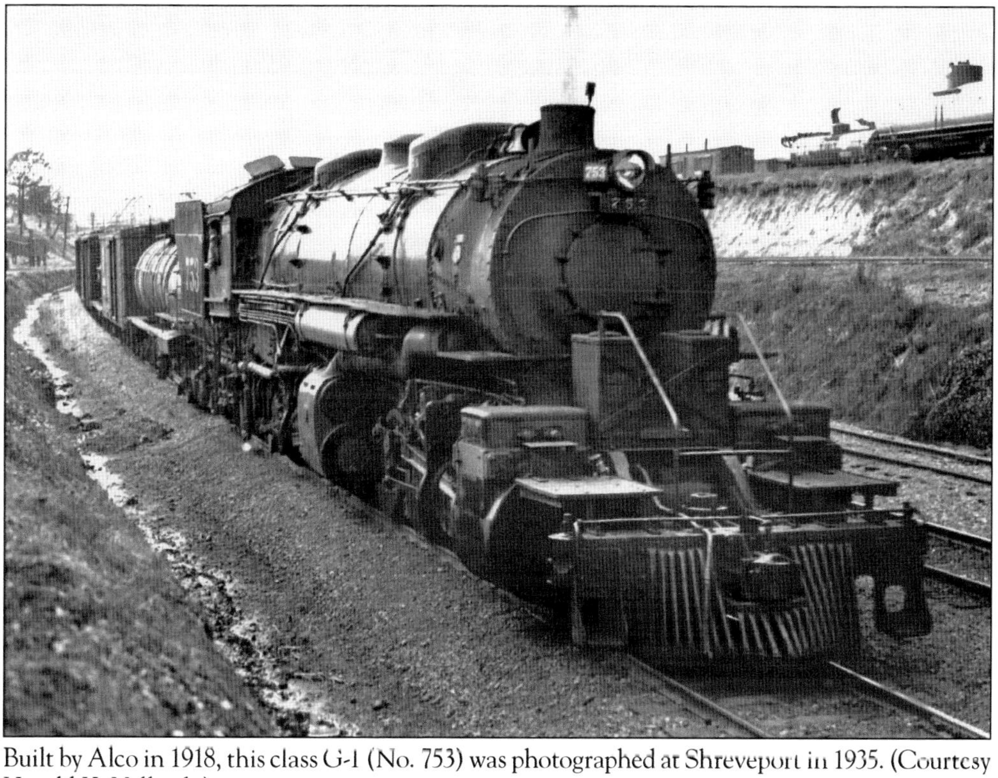

Built by Alco in 1918, this class G-1 (No. 753) was photographed at Shreveport in 1935. (Courtesy Harold K. Vollrath.)

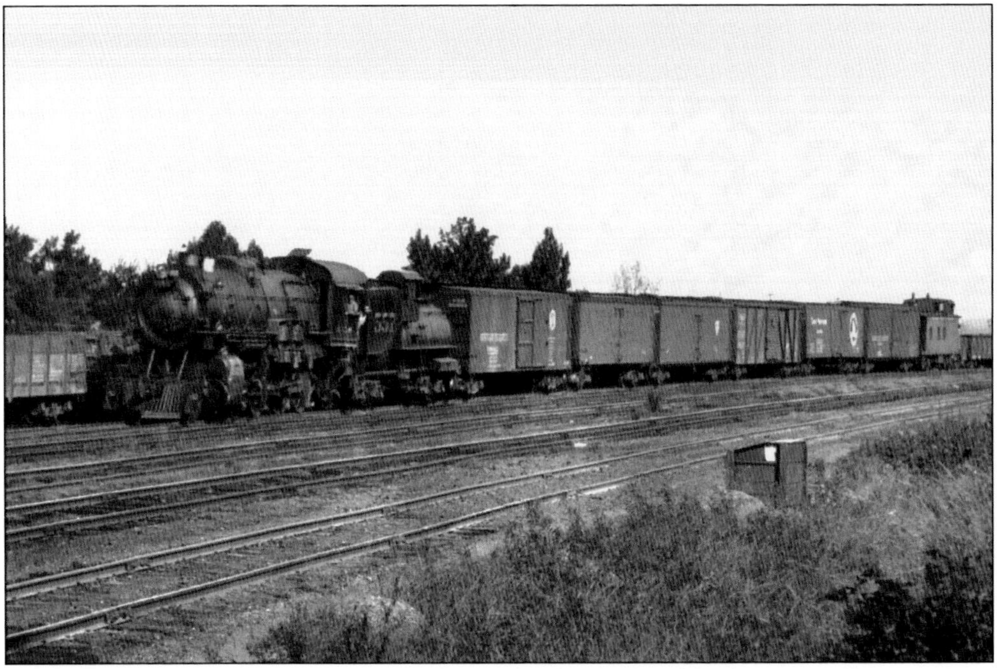

No. 557, equipped with a doghouse on the tender for the head brakeman, pulls six revenue cars, including wood-sided reefers, near Shreveport, Louisiana, in 1935. (Courtesy Harold K. Vollrath.)

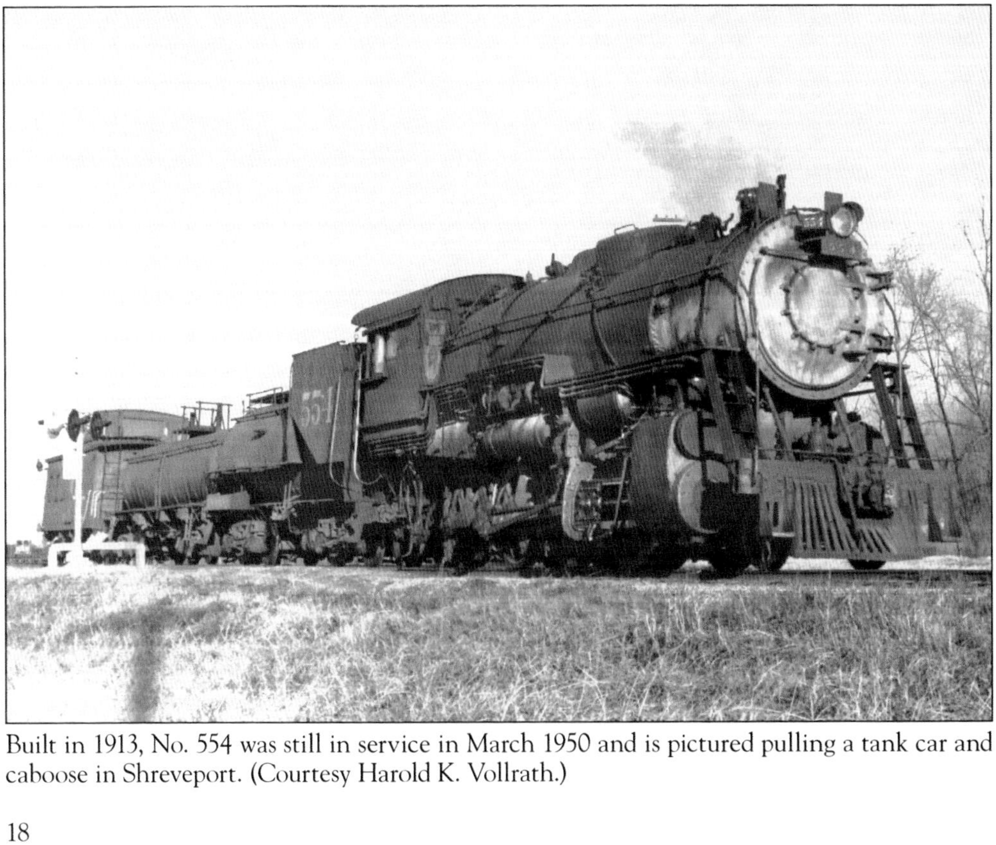

Built in 1913, No. 554 was still in service in March 1950 and is pictured pulling a tank car and caboose in Shreveport. (Courtesy Harold K. Vollrath.)

Two

LATER YEARS

In 1941, William N. Deramus II was selected as president of the railroad. While Deramus II was head of the KCS, passenger service was improved and the railroad was dieselized. In 1961, Deramus's son William N. Deramus III succeeded him while Deramus II remained as chairman until 1965.

The younger Deramus had served as president of the Chicago Great Western Railway and the Missouri-Kansas-Texas Railroad (the Katy) before assuming the presidency. Father and son were instrumental in forming Kansas City Southern Industries in 1962. The railroad then became a subsidiary of the newly formed holding company.

In 1973, Thomas S. Carter became president of the railroad and went to work rehabilitating the line to accommodate the heavy coal trains. He was very successful, and the KCS was able to fulfill its contractual obligations and deliver the coal and handle increased piggyback business.

In 1986, yet another Deramus, William N. Deramus IV, became president of the KCS, continuing the tradition of Deramus family involvement in the railroad for 84 of its first 100 years.

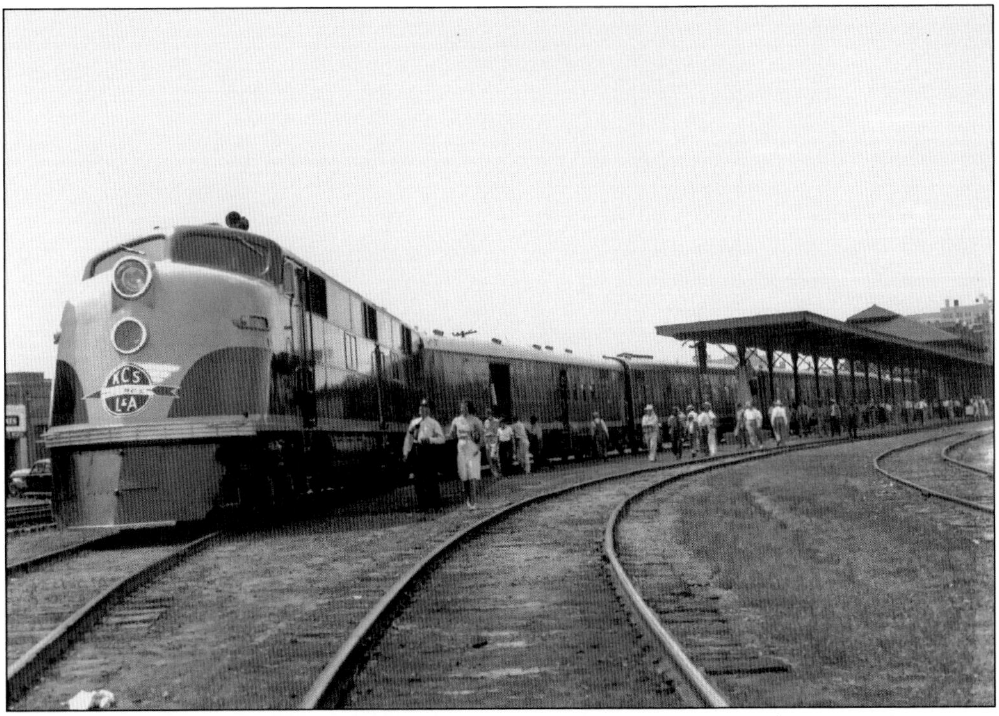

Here is the new *Southern Belle* train set on exhibit at the central station in Shreveport, Louisiana, in 1940. The KCS joined other railroads that had begun streamlining their passenger trains also. (Courtesy Harold K. Vollrath.)

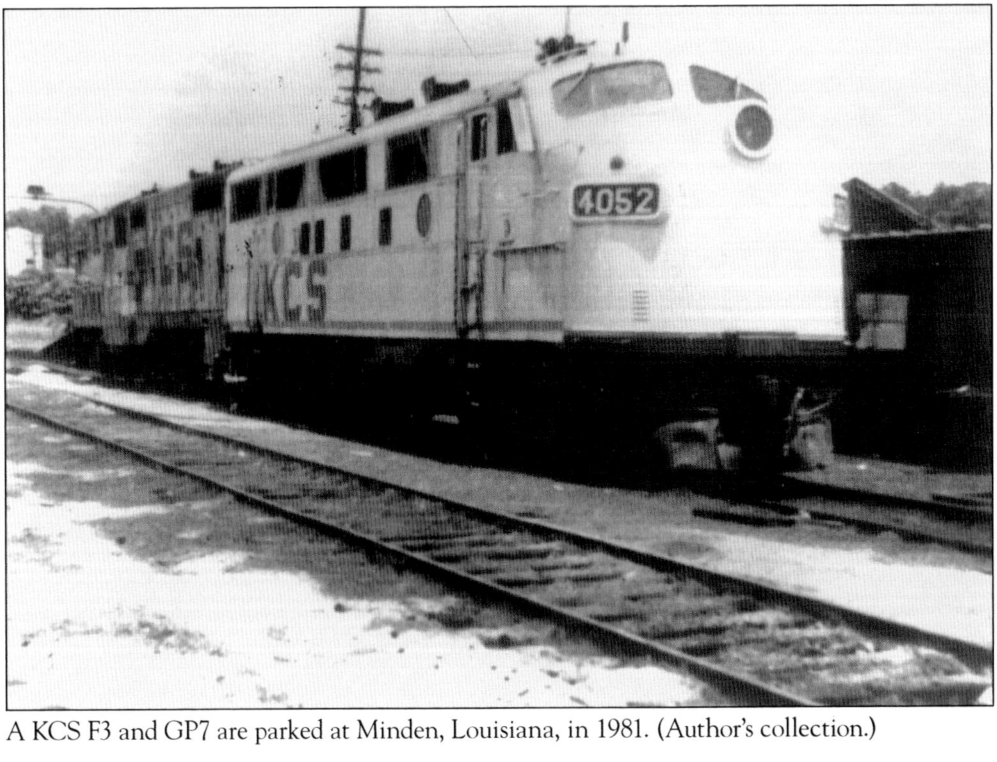

A KCS F3 and GP7 are parked at Minden, Louisiana, in 1981. (Author's collection.)

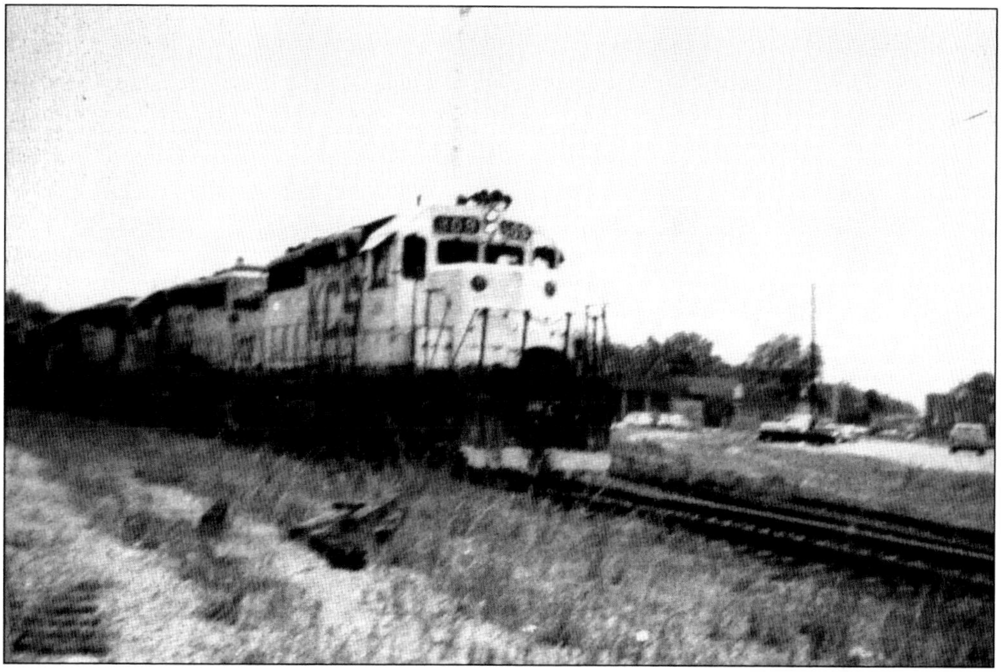

KCS SD40s are parked at DeQuincy, Louisiana, in the early 1970s. These locomotives were built by General Motors and represent the second generation of diesel power on the KCS railroad. (Author's collection.)

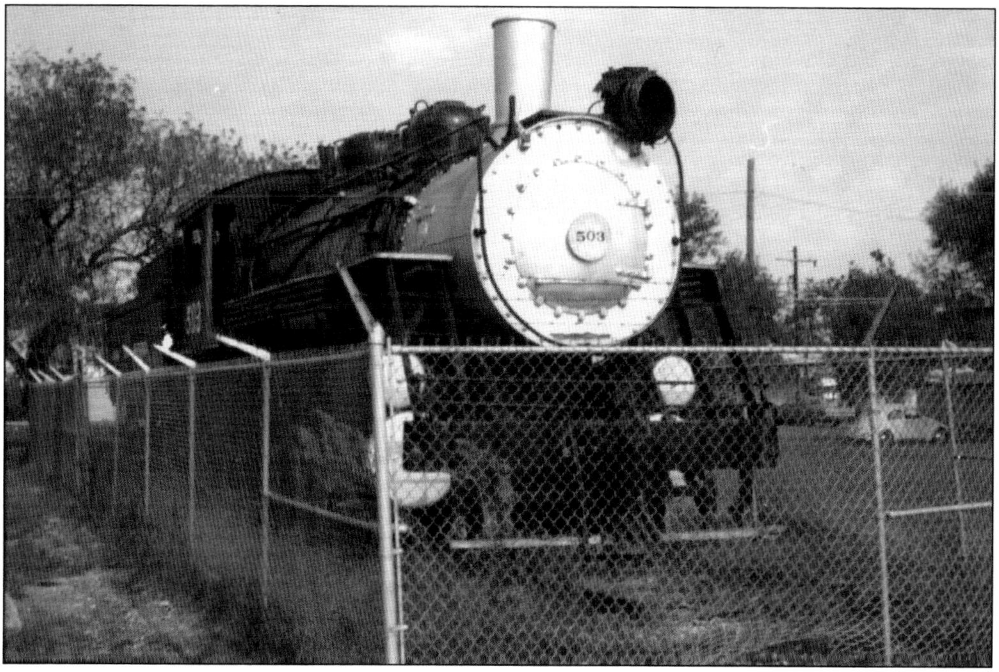

A KCS steam engine is in the park at Port Arthur, Texas, in 1973. (Author's collection.)

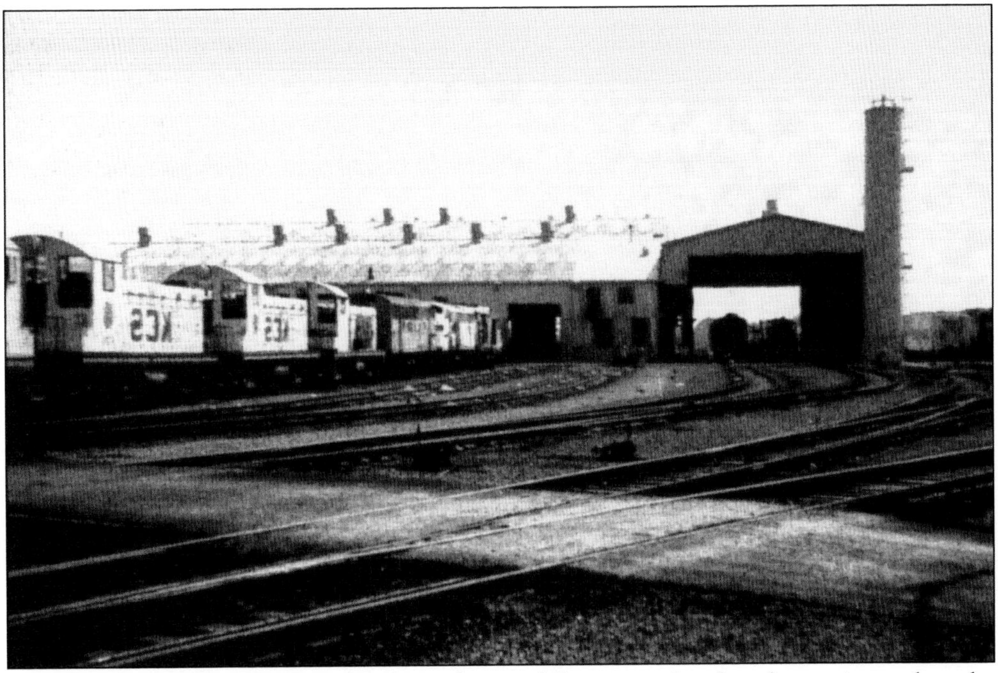

A long string of first-generation diesel switchers and F-units are lined up for service work at the Deramus yard in Shreveport, Louisiana, in the early 1980s. The yard switchers represent some of the first diesels used on the KCS. (Courtesy Belinda S. Carter.)

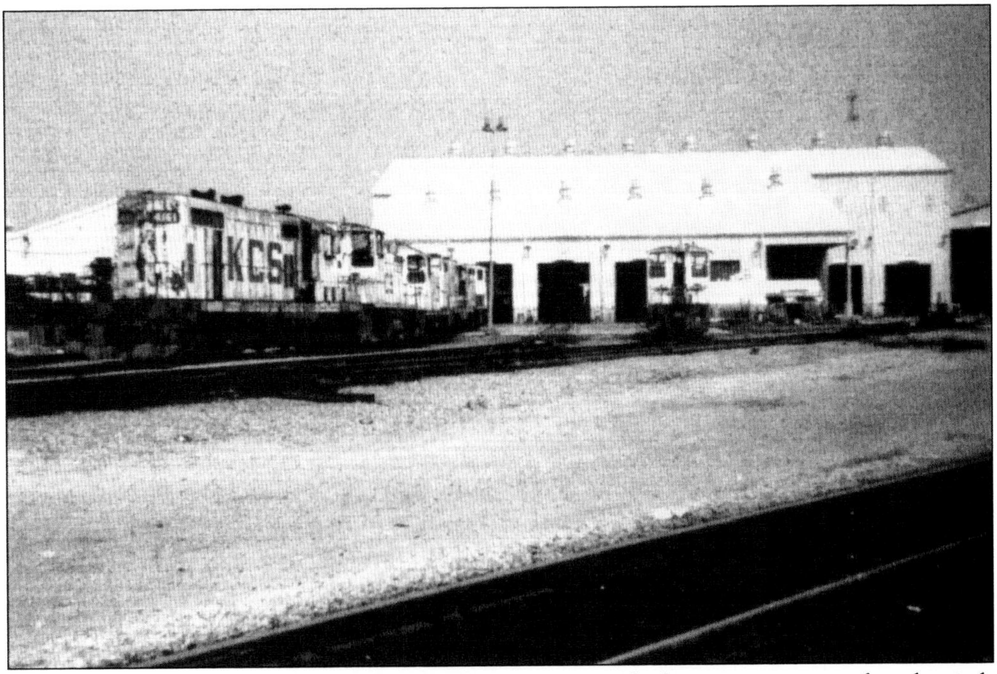

An old GP7 diesel locomotive used in freight service is parked next to a group of yard switch engines at the Deramus yard in Shreveport in 1982. (Courtesy Belinda S. Carter.)

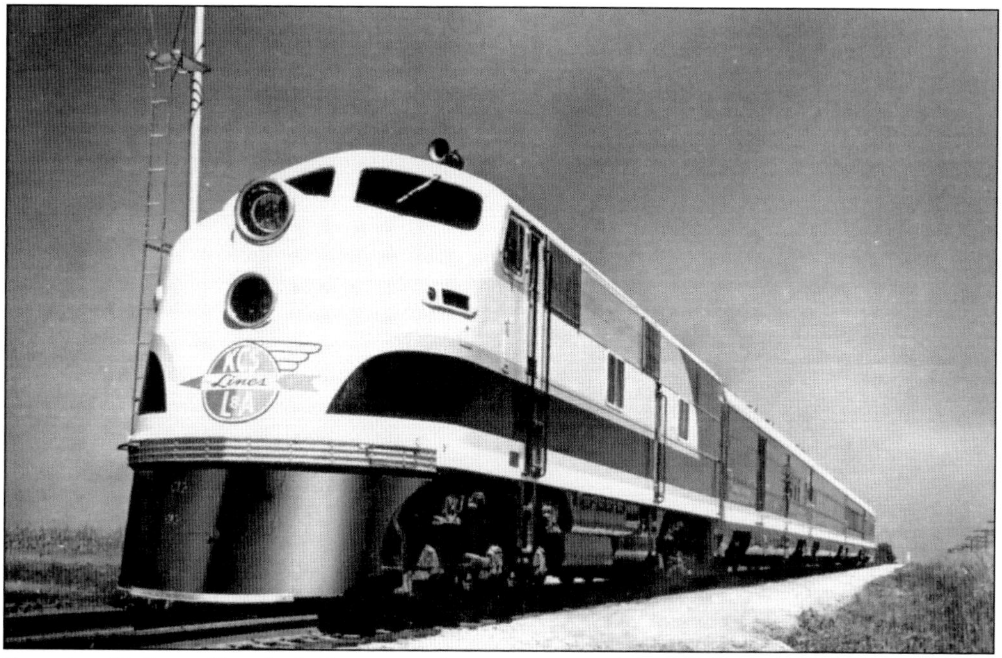

Featuring Pullman-Standard Company aluminum streamlined cars, the 1940 KCS *Southern Belle* is posed for a publicity shot. The Kansas City–New Orleans daily train featured sleeping car and dinner service. The *Southern Belle* was the railroad's attempt at competing with other lines in entering the "streamliner" market. (Courtesy Harold K. Vollrath.)

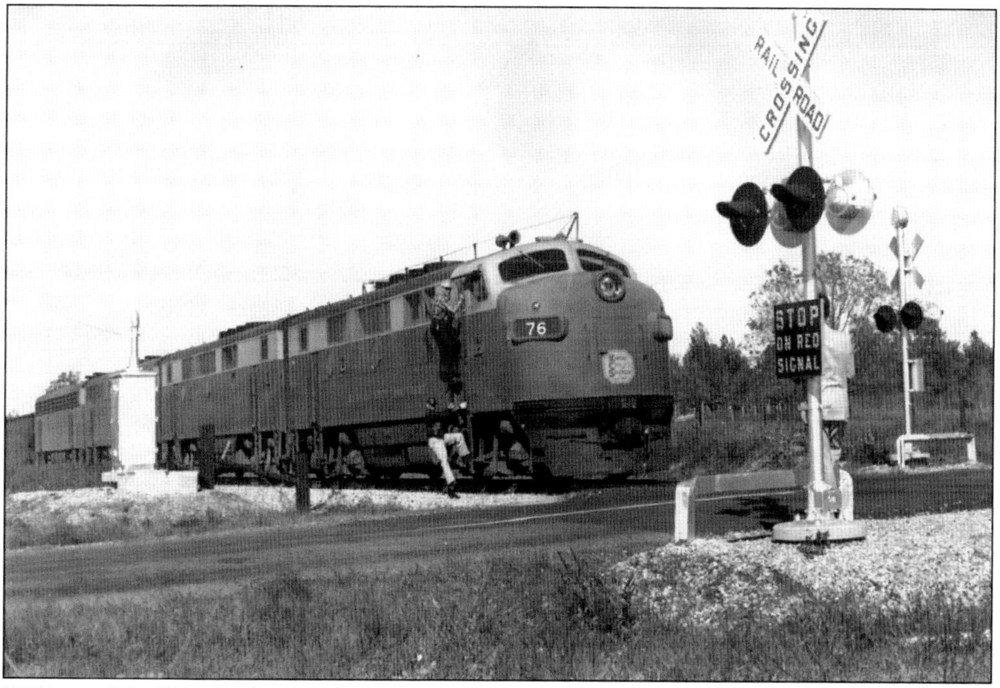

KCS train No. 76 is at Blanchard, Louisiana, as a crew prepares to board in October 1956. These are first-generation F3 units built by the Electro-Motive Division (EMD) of General Motors. Note the well-dressed gentleman standing behind the signal. (Courtesy Harold K. Vollrath.)

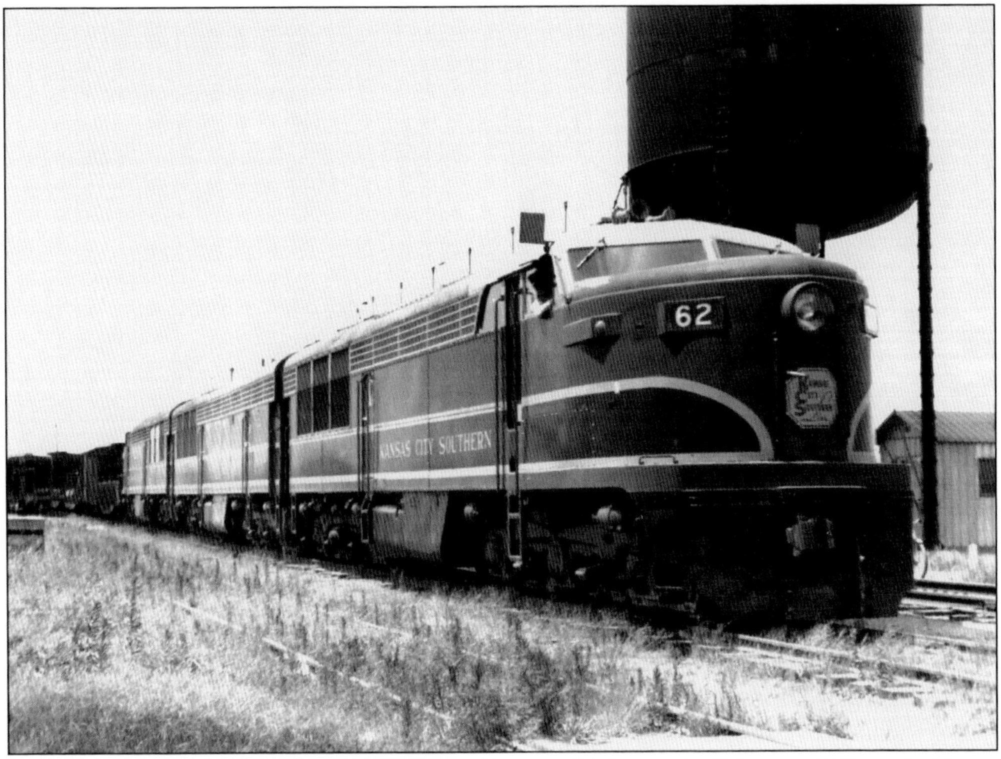

No. 62, a Fairbanks-Morse engine, is seen at Spiro, Oklahoma, in February 1951, probably on train No. 41. Notice the presence of radio antenna equipment on the locomotive. (Courtesy Harold K. Vollrath.)

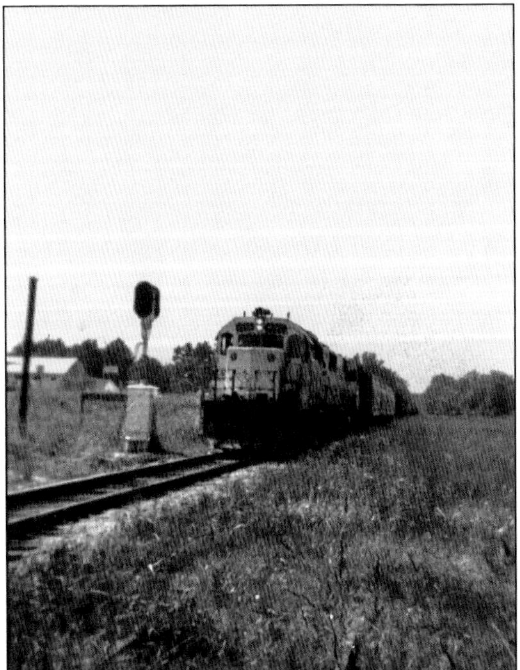

A KCS freight is at Hornbeck, Louisiana, in 1981. (Author's collection.)

EMD SD40s line up near Hughes Springs, Texas, on the L&A line for this 1983 photograph. Traffic has increased considerably on this line in the last few years with the MidSouth line east of Shreveport, Louisiana, belonging to the KCS. Through service is provided from Dallas to Meridian, Mississippi, and points east. (Courtesy Belinda S. Carter.)

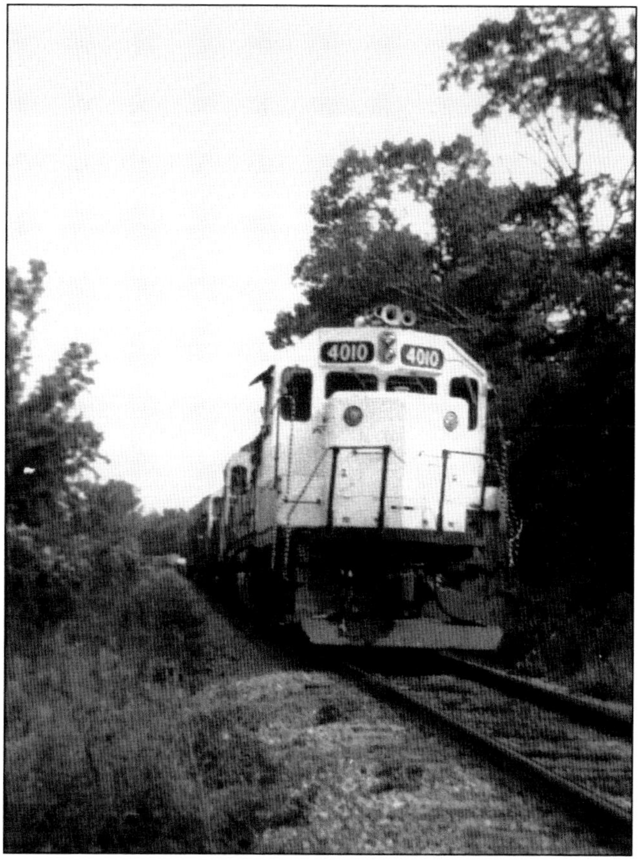

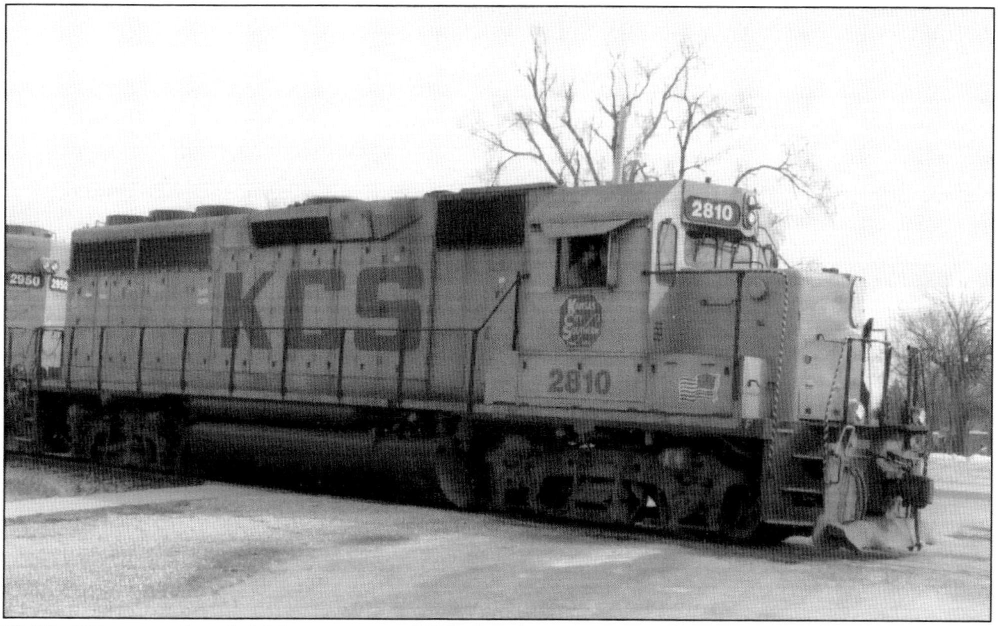

EMD GP series diesel 2810 powers a KCS freight on its journey to Kansas City. (Courtesy Belinda S. Carter.)

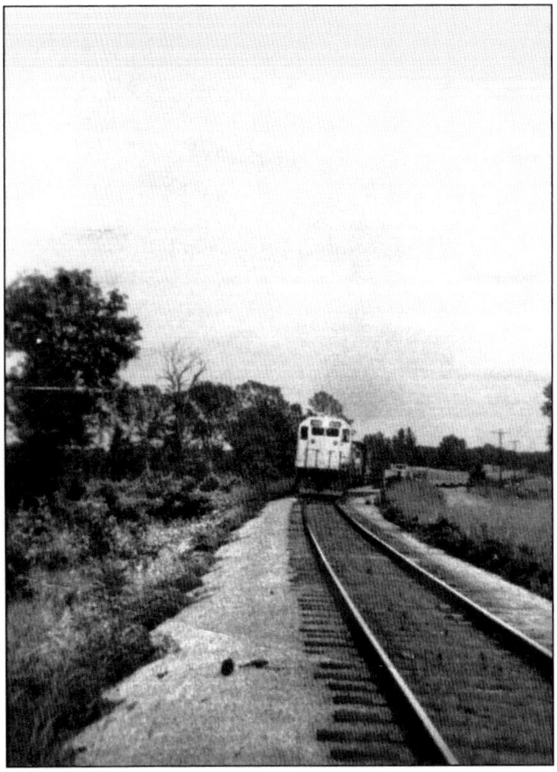

A KCS freight sporting second-generation diesels rounds a curve on its journey to Kansas City. (Author's collection.)

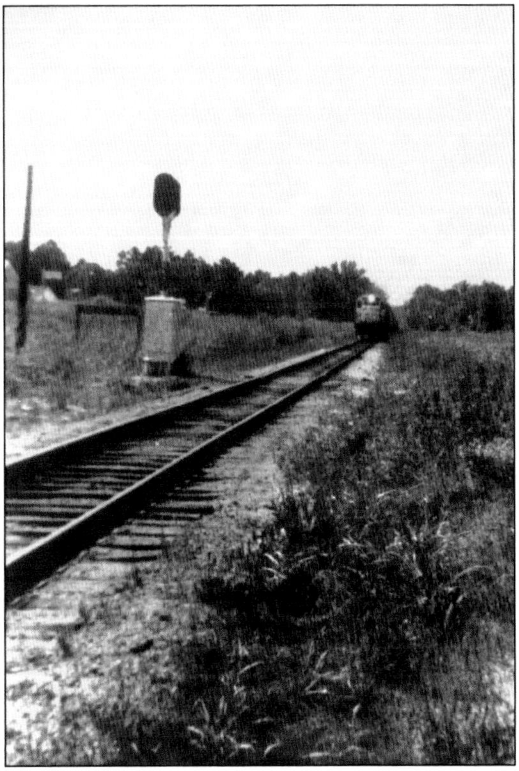

Notice the well-worn roadbed in this shot as a freight bound for Shreveport, Louisiana, heads for the crossing at Hornbeck, Louisiana. (Author's collection.)

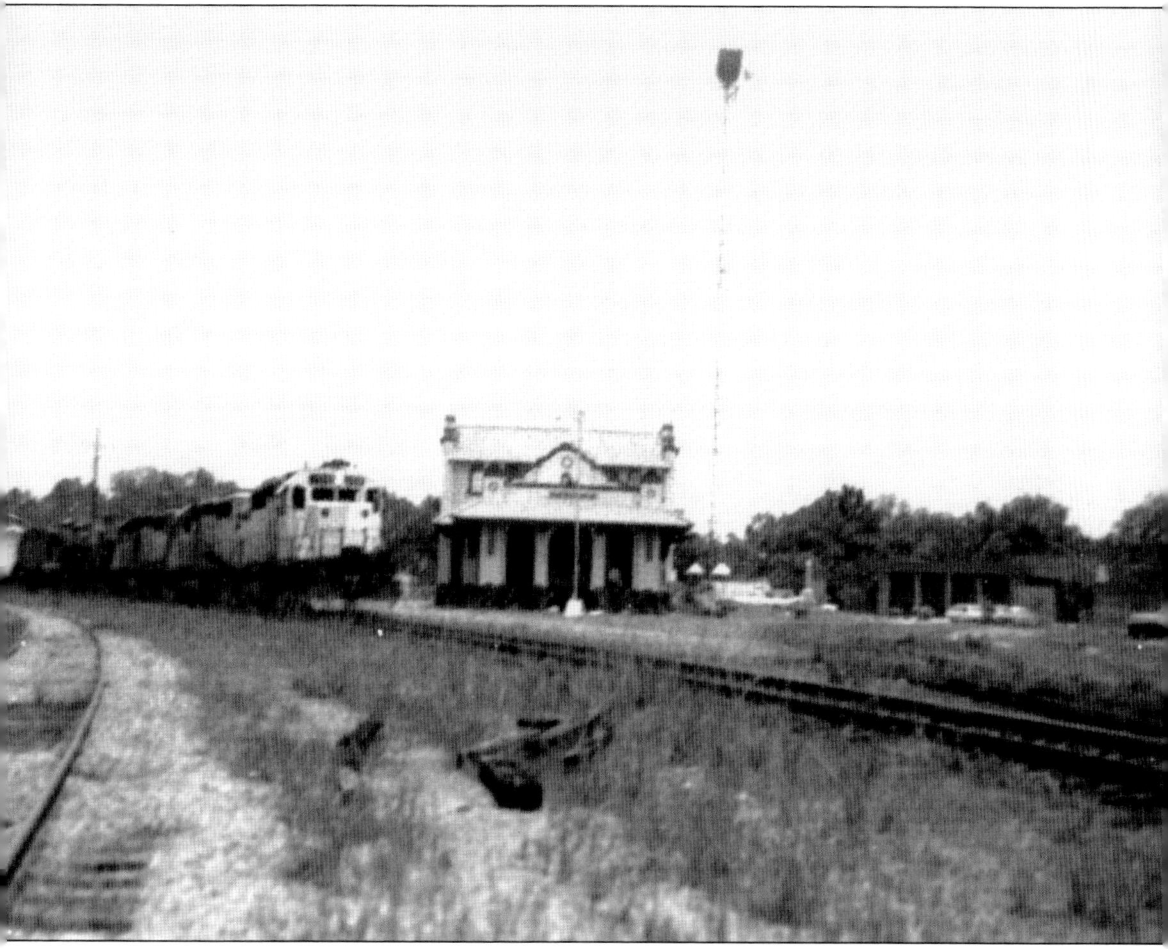

Stopping for its picture in front of the DeQuincy, Louisiana, station, a freight bound for Port Arthur, Texas, waits for clearance to proceed on its journey. (Courtesy Belinda S. Carter.)

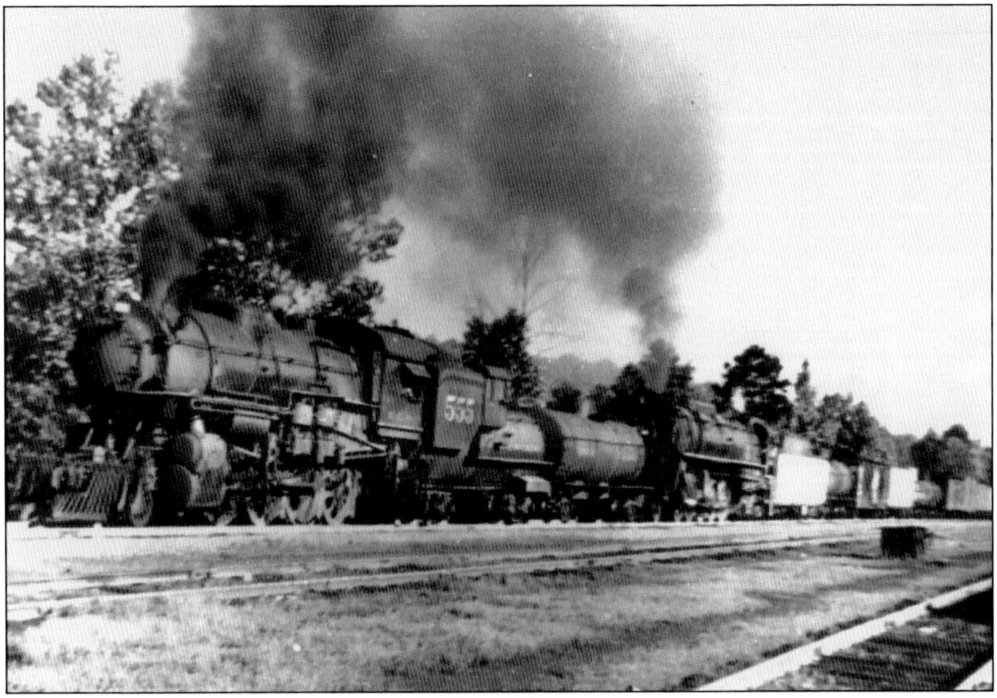

Complete with a Vanderbilt tender on the first unit, No. 555 leads a doubleheader during wartime. Notice the patriotic insignia on the second tender. (Courtesy Philip L. Moseley.)

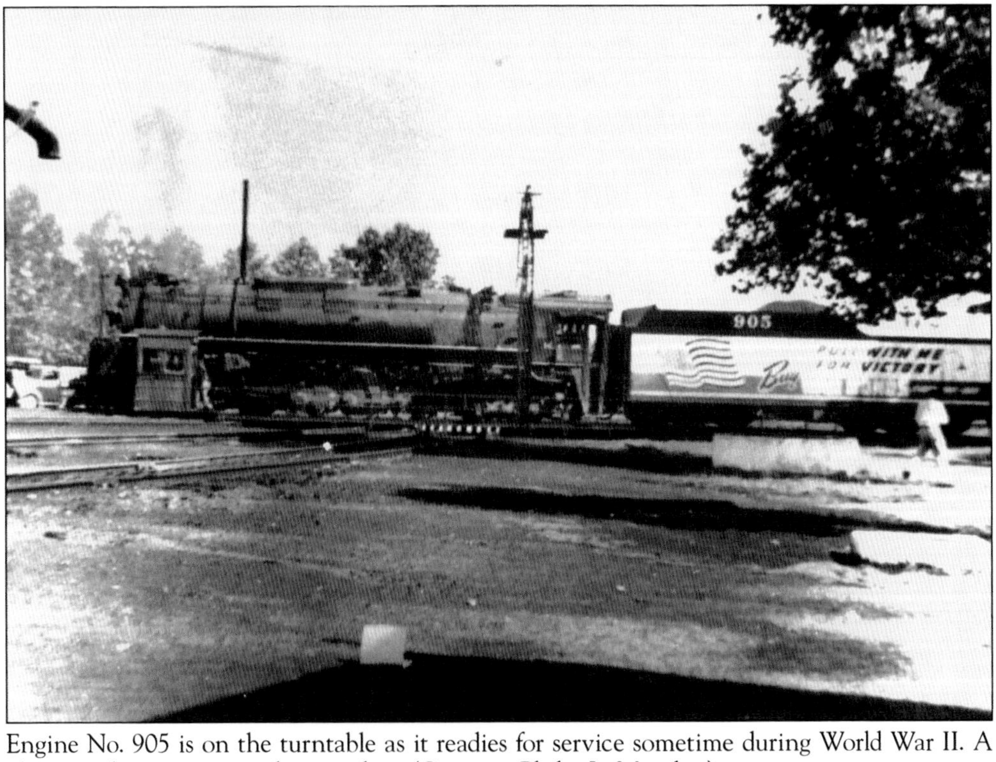

Engine No. 905 is on the turntable as it readies for service sometime during World War II. A photographer attempts a close-up shot. (Courtesy Philip L. Moseley.)

Three

Steam Memories on the Kansas City Southern

The KCS had an unusual motive power roster. In 1912, the railroad purchased 12 0-6-6-0 Mallets. These locomotives were intended for use in freight service. Then in 1918, a series of 2-8-8-0 engines numbered 750–756 were delivered from Alco in Schenectady, New York. These engines proved themselves by pulling long trains on stiff grades and were superior to the 0-6-6-0s. Then in 1924, the KCS purchased 10 additional 2-8-8-0s from Alco. These engines were used in pulling drag freights, to which they proved well-suited.

In 1937, the KCS took delivery of 10 Lima Locomotive Works 70-inch drivered blockbusters. Half of these engines were oil burners. These engines allowed for heavier cargo loads and faster speeds. These Texas types were used on the Northern Division running manifest freights from Kansas City to DeQueen, Arkansas. J class 2-10-4s were double-headed with Mallets between Heavener, Oklahoma, and DeQueen. Nine of the earlier Mallets purchased went to the scrap heap by 1937. KCS 0-6-6-0s were still operating from Shreveport, Louisiana, to Port Arthur, Texas. They also served as helper units from Watts, Oklahoma, to Neosho, Missouri, and between Heavener and Mena, Arkansas.

The KCS used 10-wheelers and Americans for lighter passenger train work. Main line service was the domain of the 800-series Pacifics. Alco supplied engine Nos. 800–810 in 1912 and 1919. These engines featuring 75-inch drivers were eventually upgraded for continued performance on the line. The Pacifics not only operated in passenger service on the *Flying Crow*, they also worked on freight duty.

Handling the bulk of KCS passenger trains were the 600s. They were built by Baldwin Locomotive Works in 1903 and later upgraded to provide additional operating power. These 4-6-0s continued to be improved and maintained for passenger operations.

The last American types worked Lake Charles, Louisiana, to DeQuincy, Louisiana, on the *Flying Crow* connection until it was replaced by bus service in the late 1930s.

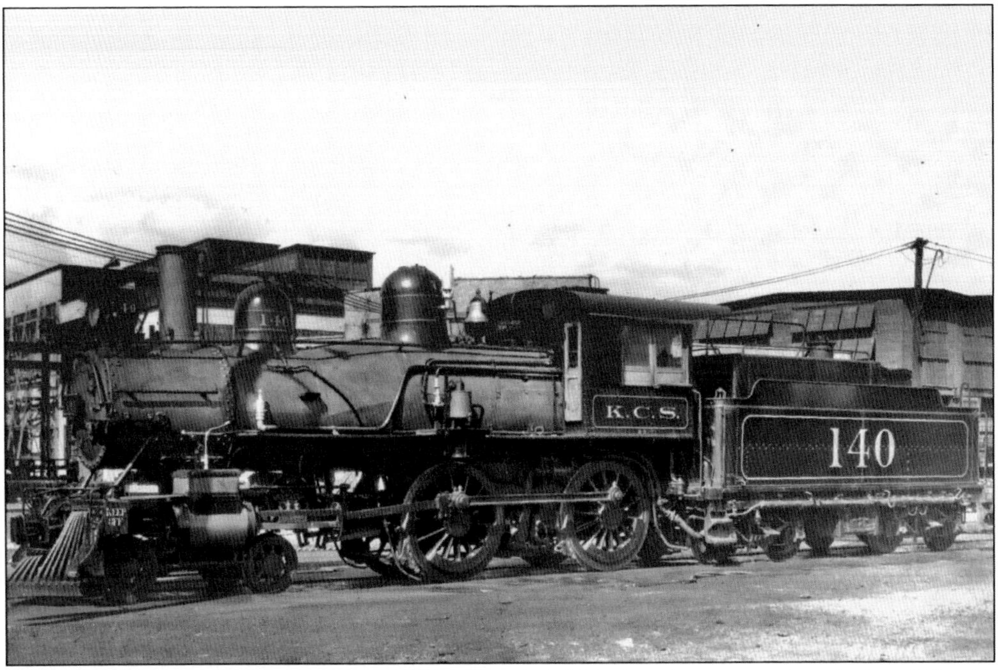

KCS No. 140 was an ex–Kansas City, Pittsburg and Gulf Railroad steam engine. A class B-3 built in 1893, it is shown at Shreveport, Louisiana, in 1931. (Courtesy Harold K. Vollrath.)

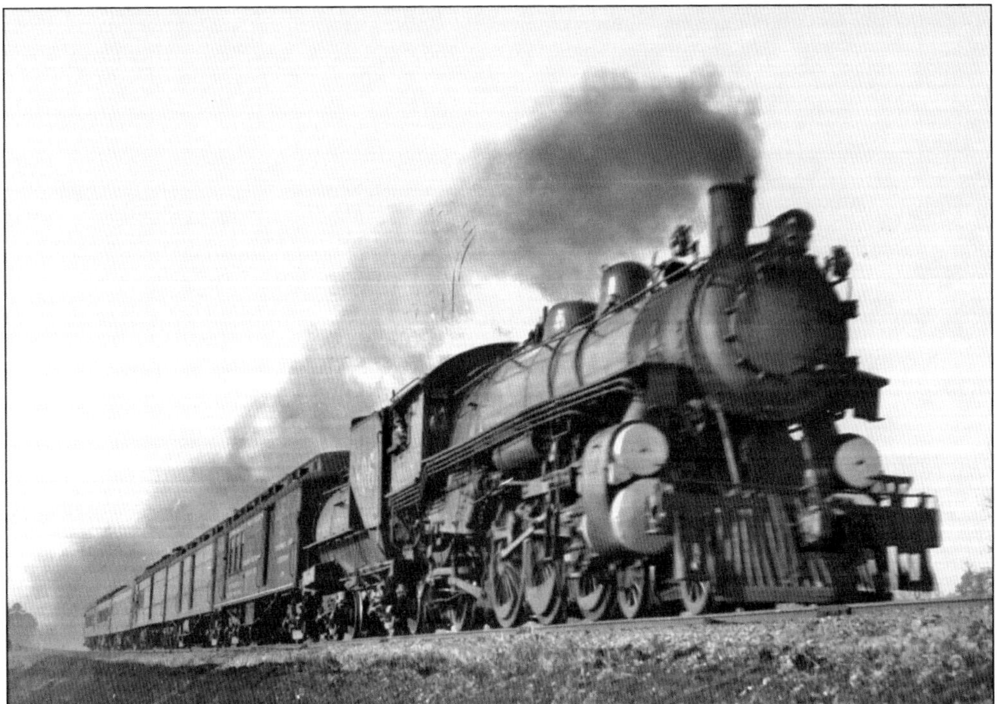

KCS passenger train No. 15, the *Flying Crow*, rolls through Blanchard, Louisiana, in May 1938. Two years later, the streamlined *Southern Belle* ran over this same route. (Courtesy Harold K. Vollrath.)

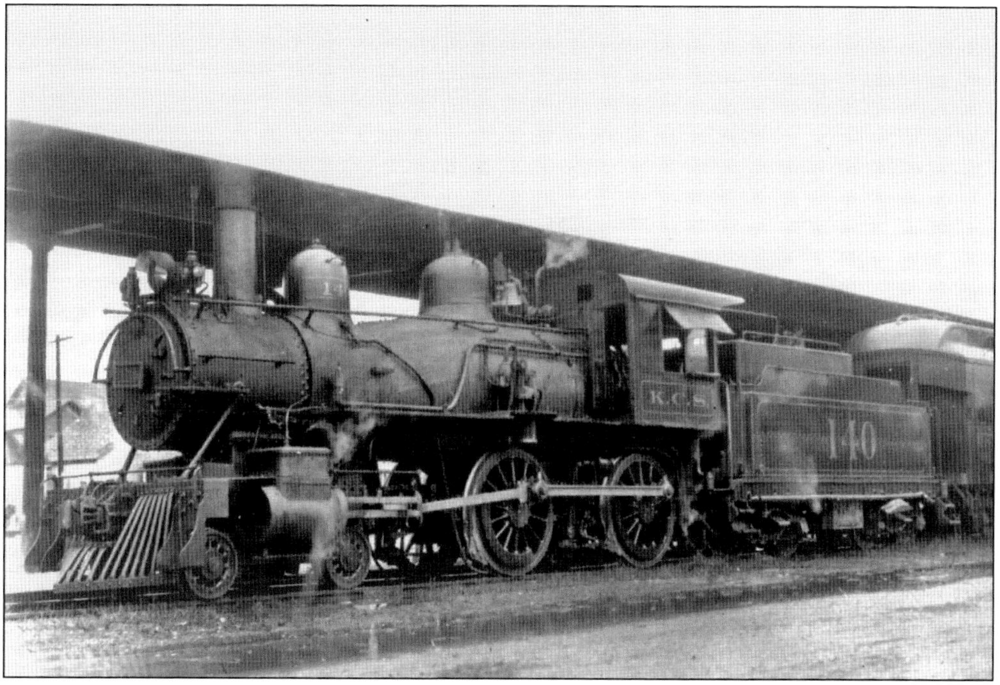

Ex–Kansas City, Pittsburg and Gulf engine No. 140 is parked at the Lake Charles, Louisiana, stub-ended terminal in 1934. This engine pulled a passenger train to DeQuincy, Louisiana, until the 1940s. (Courtesy Harold K. Vollrath.)

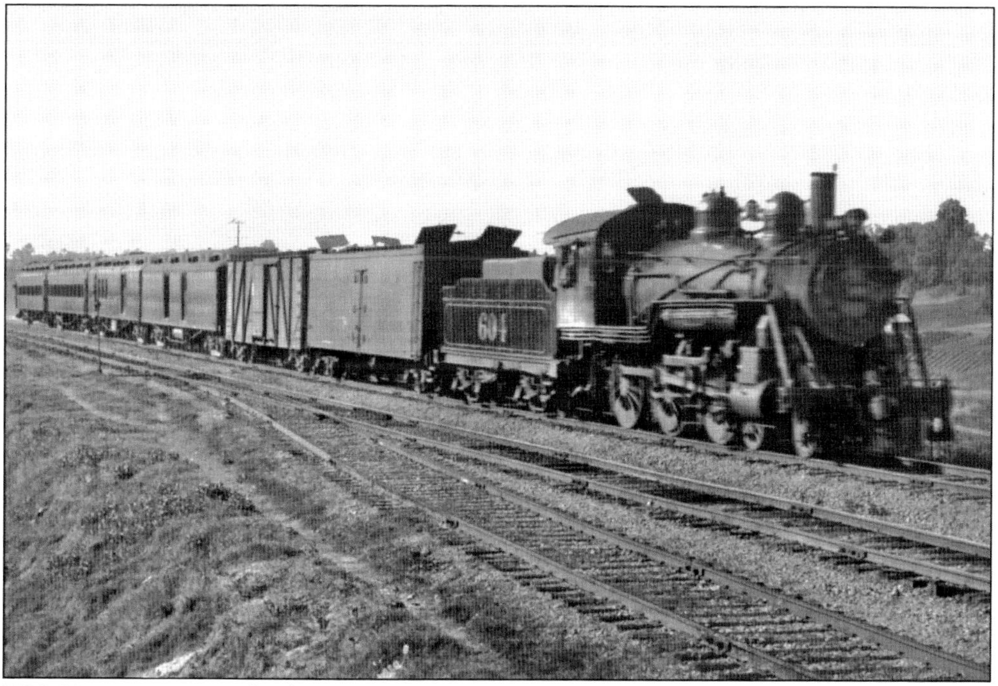

KCS No. 16 is in north Shreveport, Louisiana, in January 1934. Powered by steam engine No. 604, the train's consist includes a refrigerator car loaded with perishables for overnight delivery. (Courtesy Harold K. Vollrath.)

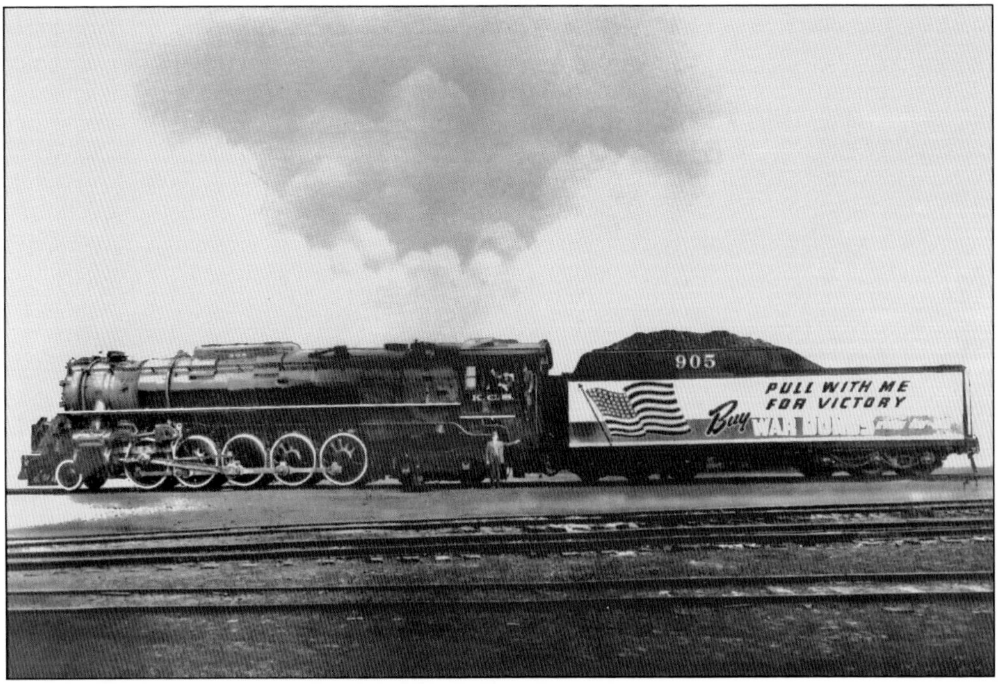

Engine No. 905, with its tender decorated to support the war effort, is pictured at Kansas City in 1942. The locomotive was built by Lima Locomotive Works in 1937. (Courtesy Harold K. Vollrath.)

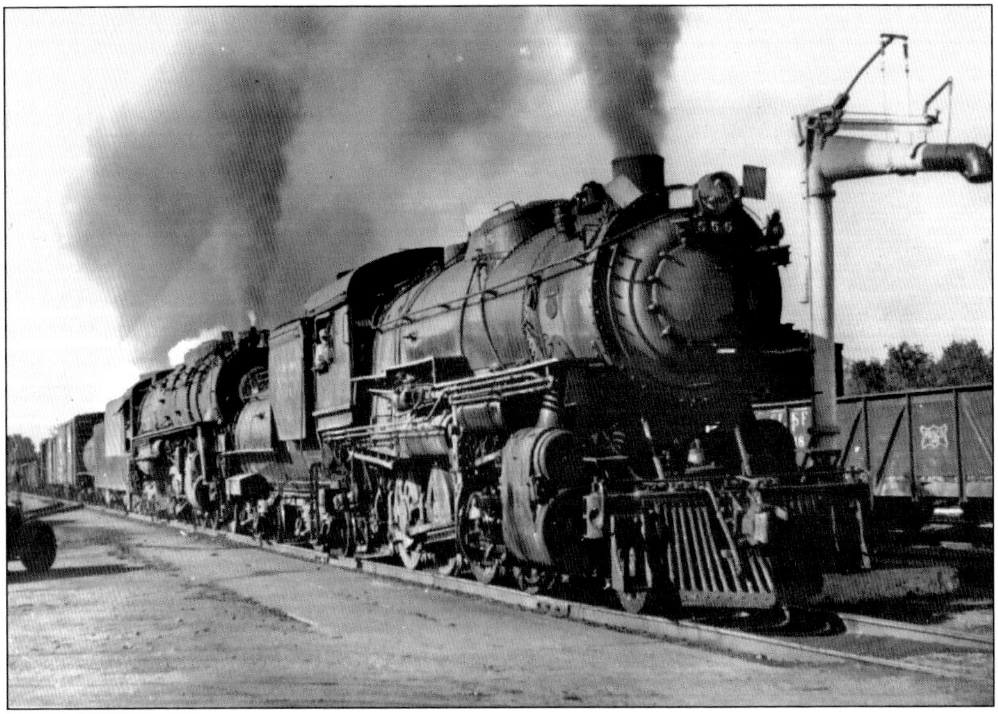

KCS No. 555 and No. 905 double-head a freight through Neosho, Missouri, in April 1942. (Courtesy Harold K. Vollrath.)

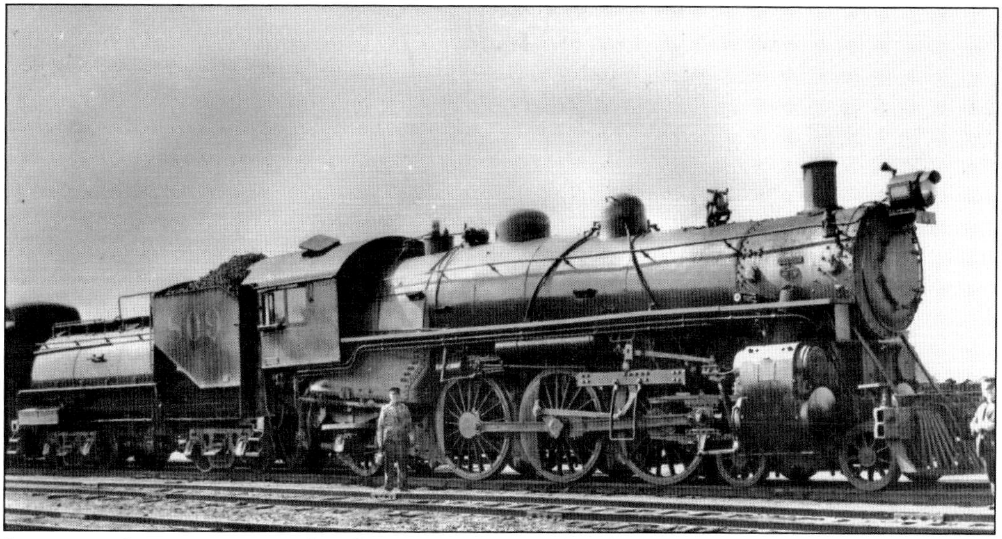

In an era when passenger railroading was a matter of pride for even smaller carriers like KCS, a recently delivered class H-1 locomotive, a 4-6-2 road engine, is the subject of lavish attention by the company employees as it prepares to go over the road at the allowable speed. (Courtesy KCS archives.)

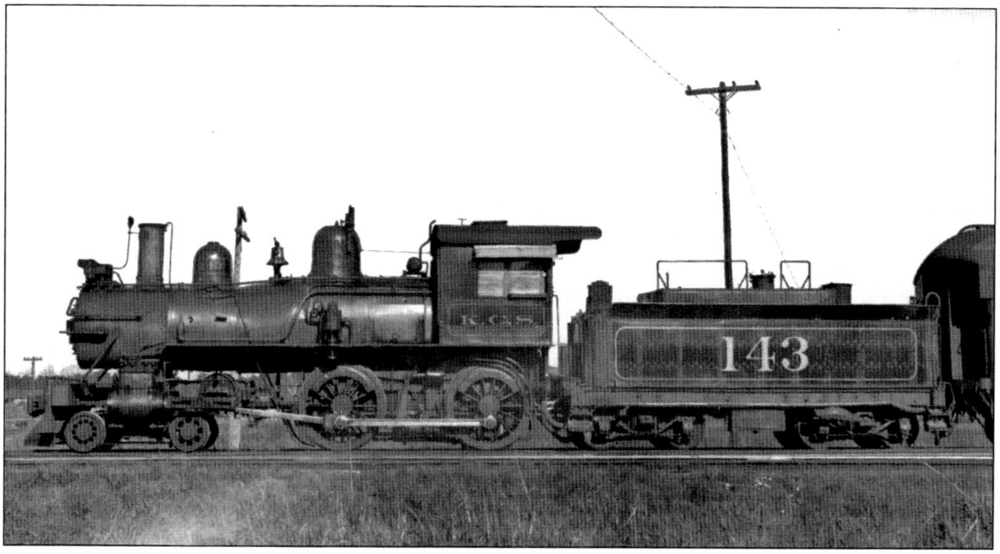

Here is KCS steam engine No. 143, a former Kansas City, Pittsburg and Gulf Railroad engine, near DeQuincy, Louisiana, in February 1937. The engine is more than 40 years old and still active in passenger service. (Courtesy Harold K. Vollrath.)

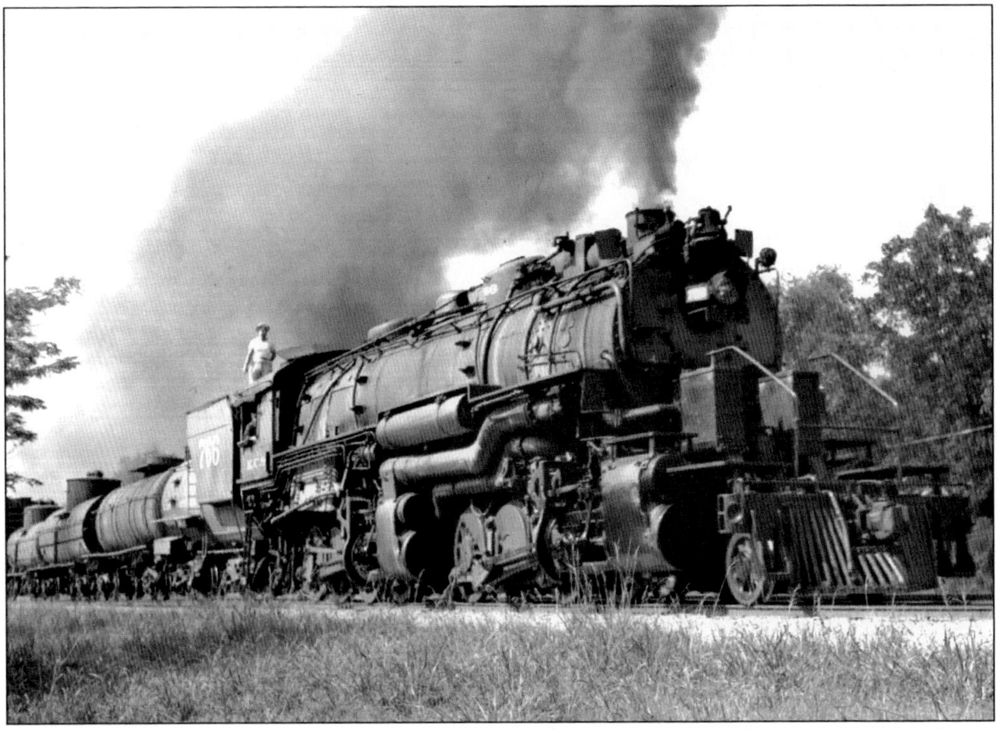

KCS No. 766, one of 10 locomotives purchased for freight service and built by Alco in 1924, is shown heading toward Shreveport, Louisiana, in September 1949. (Courtesy Harold K. Vollrath.)

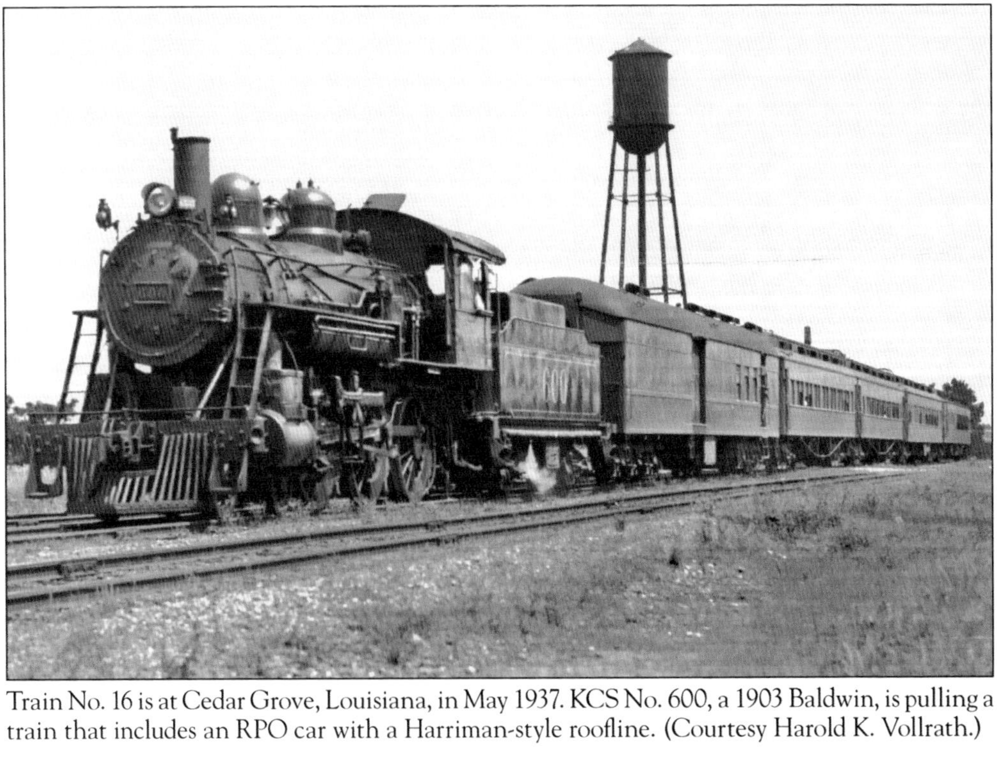

Train No. 16 is at Cedar Grove, Louisiana, in May 1937. KCS No. 600, a 1903 Baldwin, is pulling a train that includes an RPO car with a Harriman-style roofline. (Courtesy Harold K. Vollrath.)

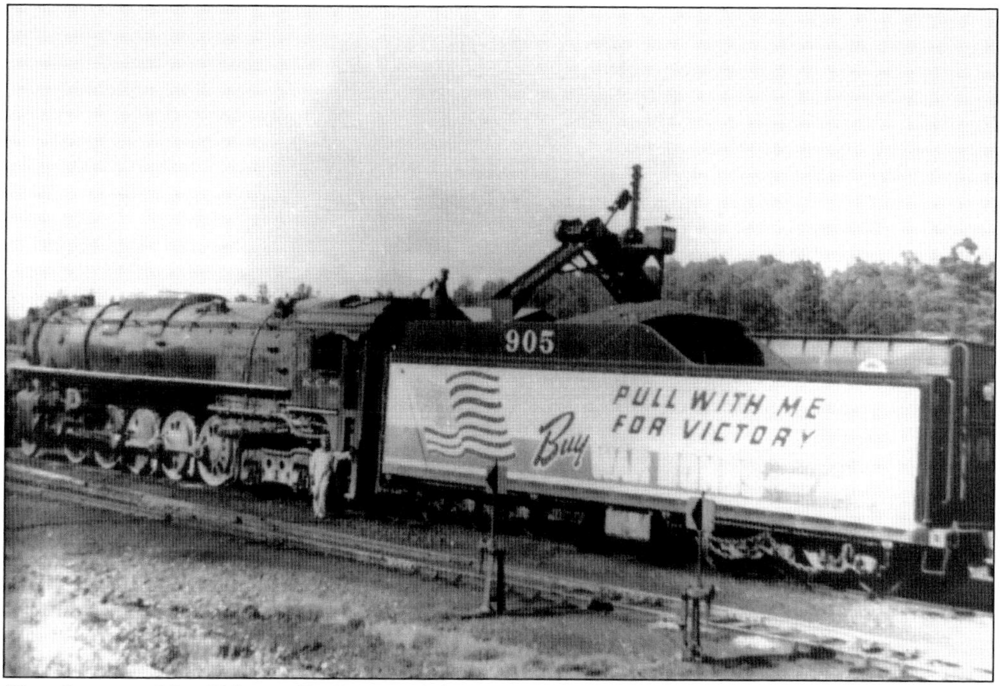

Class J engine No. 905 is at DeQueen, Arkansas, in 1943 taking on coal as it serves in the war effort. (Courtesy Philip L. Moseley.)

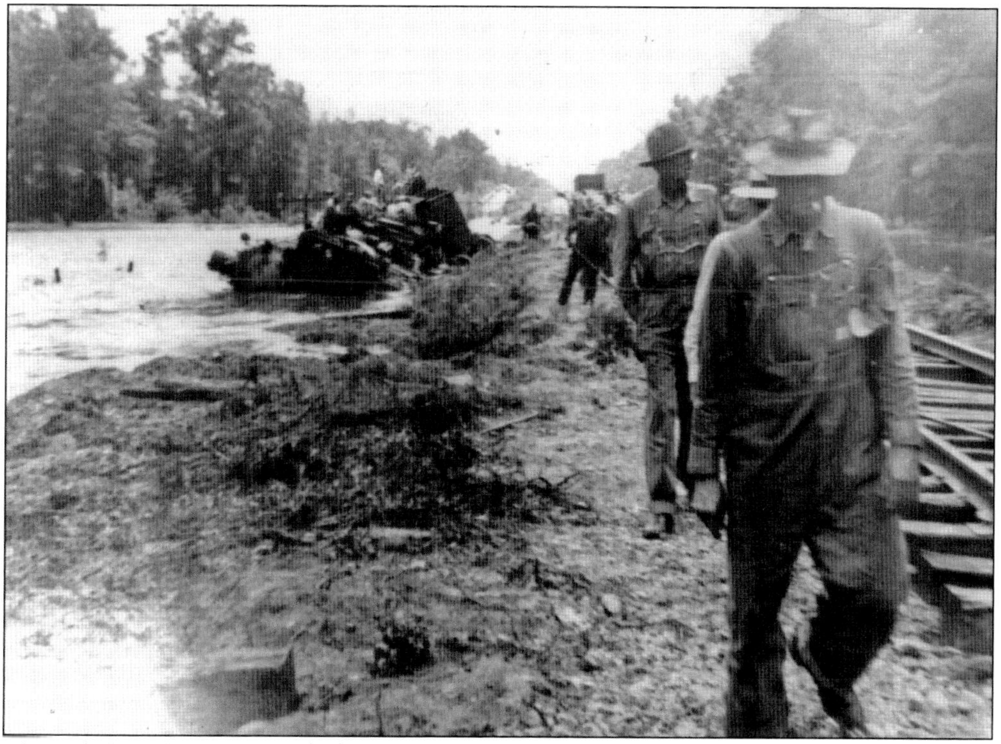

This is believed to be a wreck that resulted from a washout at Flat Creek Bridge just south of Winthrop, Arkansas, in 1943. (Courtesy Philip L. Moseley.)

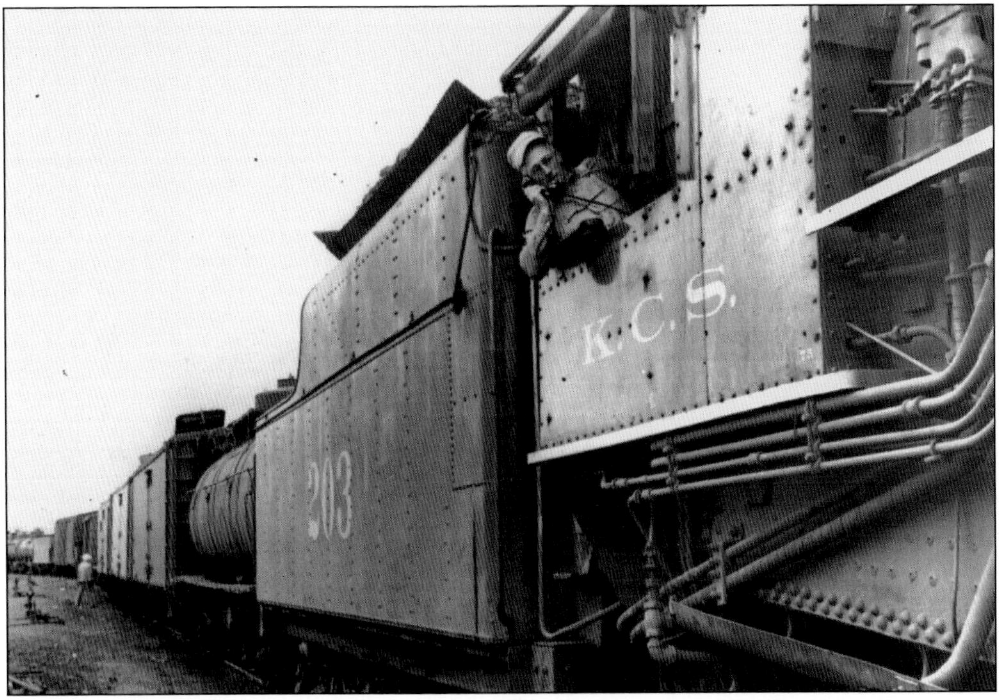

Engineer Troy Shirk sits proudly in the cab of this 2-10-2 steam engine. Boasting the latest in railroad communication, he is using a Motorola radio telephone no doubt to receive orders from the conductor. The year is 1948, and soon these steam engines will be replaced by diesel power. (Courtesy Harold K. Vollrath.)

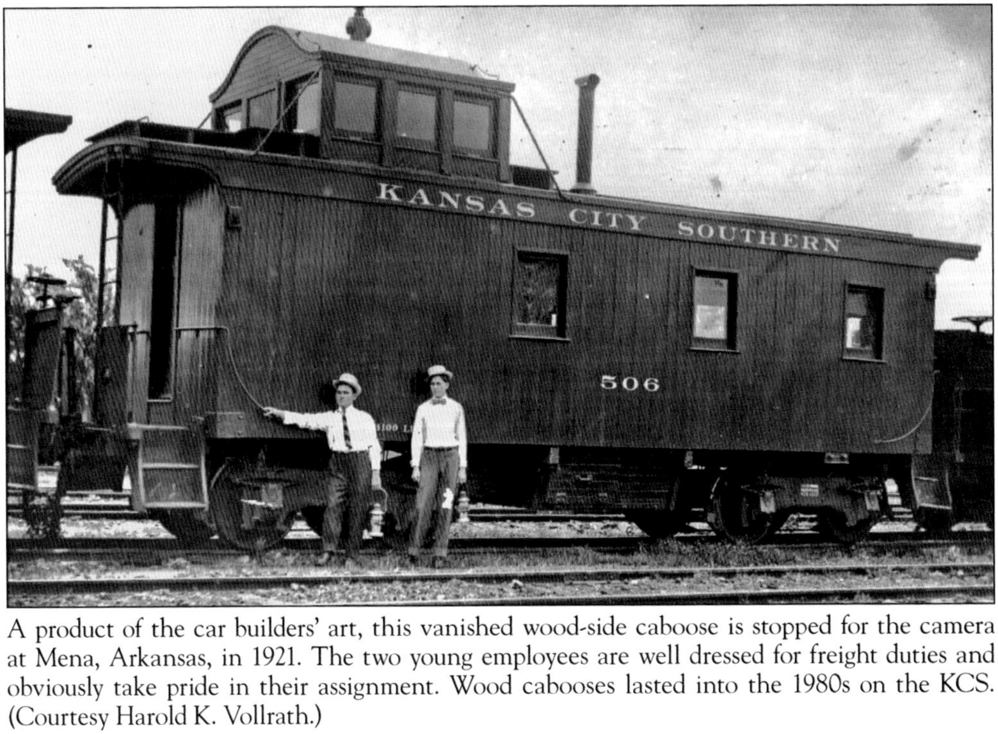

A product of the car builders' art, this vanished wood-side caboose is stopped for the camera at Mena, Arkansas, in 1921. The two young employees are well dressed for freight duties and obviously take pride in their assignment. Wood cabooses lasted into the 1980s on the KCS. (Courtesy Harold K. Vollrath.)

Four

Passenger Trains on the Kansas City Southern

By the early 1900s, trains were running from Kansas City to Independence, Missouri. Trains on the roster included Nos. 1 and 2 (Kansas City to Port Arthur, Texas), Nos. 3 and 4 (Kansas City to Shreveport, Louisiana), and service going from Beaumont, Texas, to Port Arthur and from Heavener, Oklahoma, to Fort Smith, Arkansas. Passenger service was provided from Heavener to Waldron, Arkansas, as early as 1903 on the Arkansas Western Railroad.

In 1928, the *Flying Crow* went into service between Kansas City and Port Arthur. This train took the place of trains Nos. 1 and 2 and, through the Depression-era 1930s, provided the bulk of passenger service. Nos. 3 and 4 were gone from the timetable by 1933, having ended their run as a mixed train. The KCS was attempting to advertise itself as being "straight as the crow flies," so the *Flying Crow* was the name given to its premier passenger service.

In 1939, two EMD E3s went into service pulling the *Flying Crow*. These units were actually intended for service on the soon-to-debut *Southern Belle*, a streamliner, which would operate between Kansas City and New Orleans.

The first *Southern Belle* left the union station in Kansas City for a publicity tour on August 23, 1940, at 9:00 a.m. Executive Pete Couch, president of the KCS, and executive vice president William N. Deramus II were accompanied by officials of the Pullman-Standard Company and the Aluminum Company of America (ALCOA). Other dignitaries included Norris Goff of Mena, Arkansas. Goff, who was known as Abner Peabody on the radio comedy team of Lum and Abner, brought his family from Hollywood to ride to Mena on the *Belle*'s inaugural run. On September 2, 1940, the *Southern Belle* began regular service to the public.

The year 1948 saw streamlined Pullman car service on the *Southern Belle*. Prior service had been provided by the Pullman-Standard Company in the form of rebuilt heavyweight sleepers. Some of the former heavyweight sleepers were later used for day coach service from Shreveport to Port Arthur.

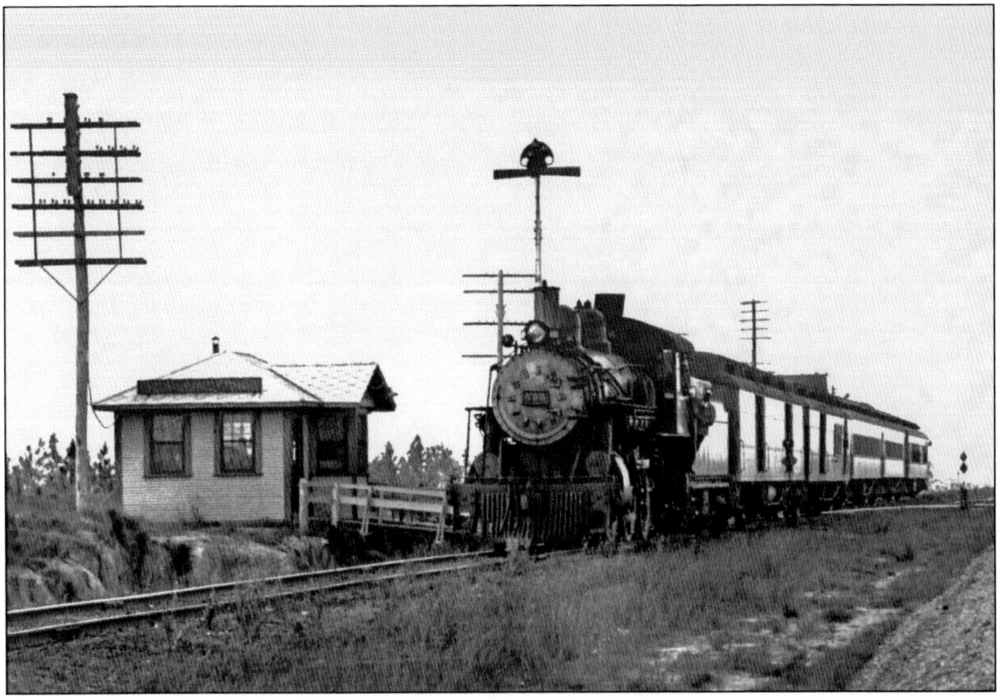

A KCS passenger train in DeQuincy, Louisiana, in September 1931 is pulled by a Baldwin steam locomotive built in 1903. The crew poses for a picture in this long-ago scene. (Courtesy Harold K. Vollrath.)

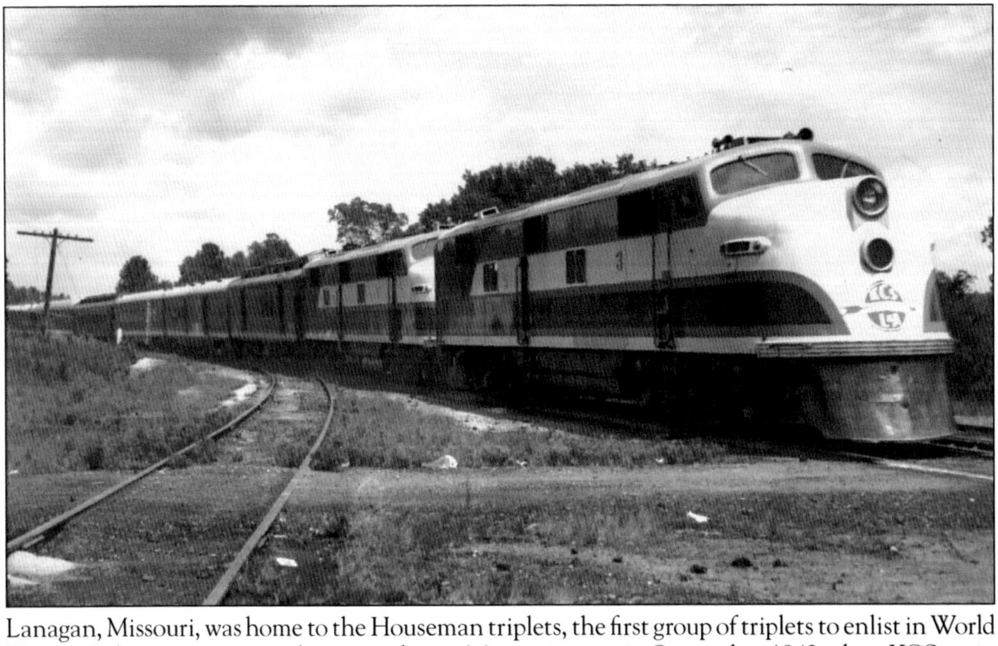

Lanagan, Missouri, was home to the Houseman triplets, the first group of triplets to enlist in World War II. Otherwise, it was a sleepy southwest Missouri town in September 1942 when KCS train No. 1, the *Southern Belle*, broke the silence at 50 miles per hour. The train is swollen to six cars with the addition of the heavyweight mail car and the heavyweight coach. The coach was added to accommodate military travelers and short-distance riders. (Courtesy Harold K. Vollrath.)

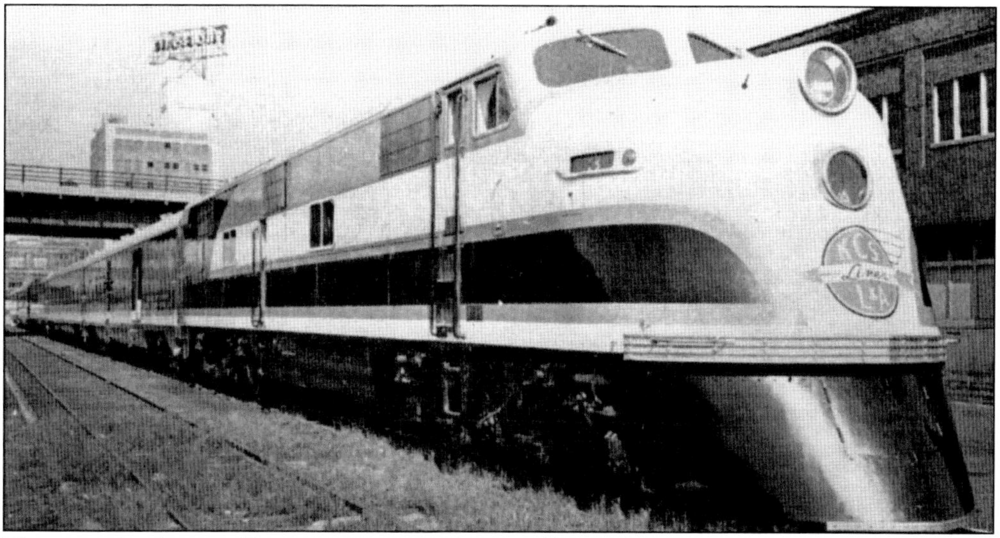

The new *Southern Belle* streamliner sits for a publicity shot at Kansas City in 1940. The streamlined train has one heavyweight Pullman car in its consist. Streamlined sleepers did not make their debut on the *Belle* until after World War II. (Courtesy KCS archives.)

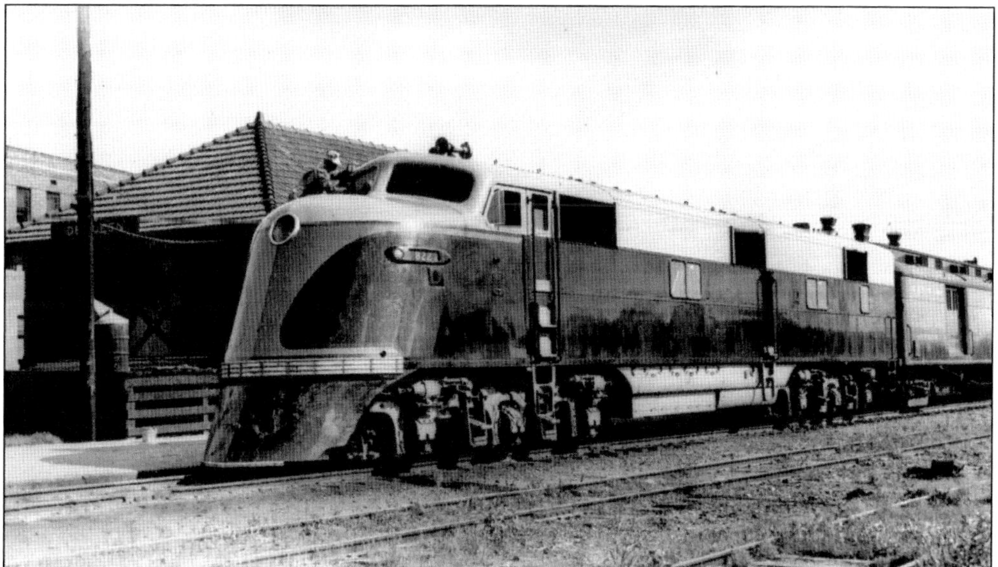

Stopped at DeQueen, Arkansas, in July 1939, the EMD demonstrator gets a clean windshield. Pulling train No. 15, this engine was later repainted and numbered 21. The first diesel to be purchased by the KCS, it operated nearly 25 years and was scrapped at Pittsburg, Kansas, in 1964. (Courtesy Harold K. Vollrath.)

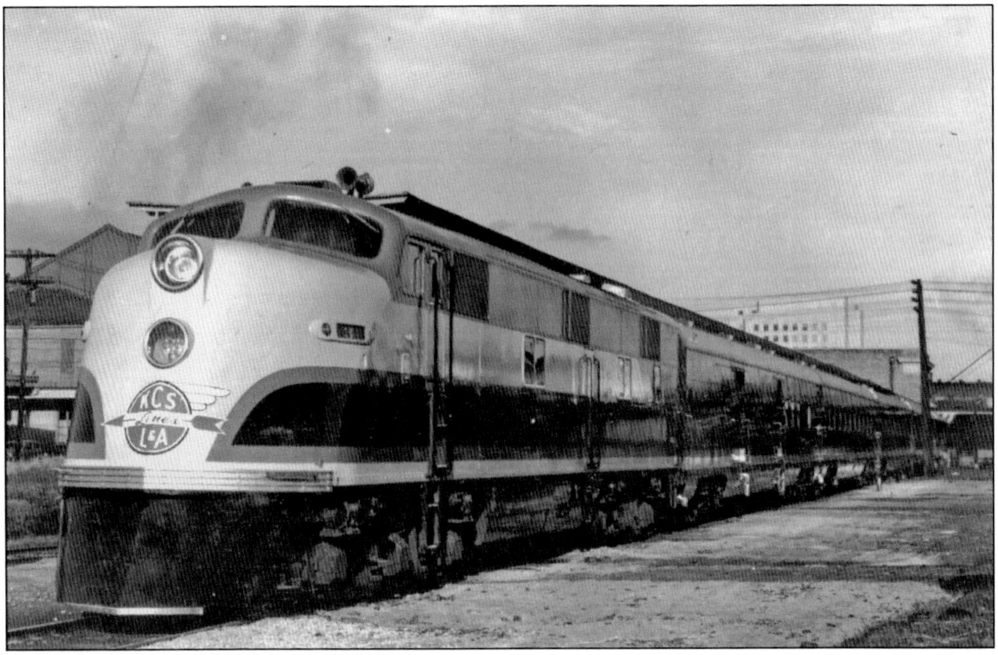

Dr. Norman L. Nunn, a serviceman in the U.S. Army Air Forces who rode the *Southern Belle*, commented, "It was in Louisiana that I fell in love with a Southern Belle, not a lady but a train. I boarded in Shreveport and got off in Neosho, Missouri. It was a pleasure to watch through the wide windows as the landscape slid by while we clicked along from Shreveport to Neosho. The food was delicious, not just because of the contrast with army chow. Fifty-six years have passed since I was discharged from the army. I still remember the Southern Belle as one sweetheart of a train." (Courtesy Harold K. Vollrath.)

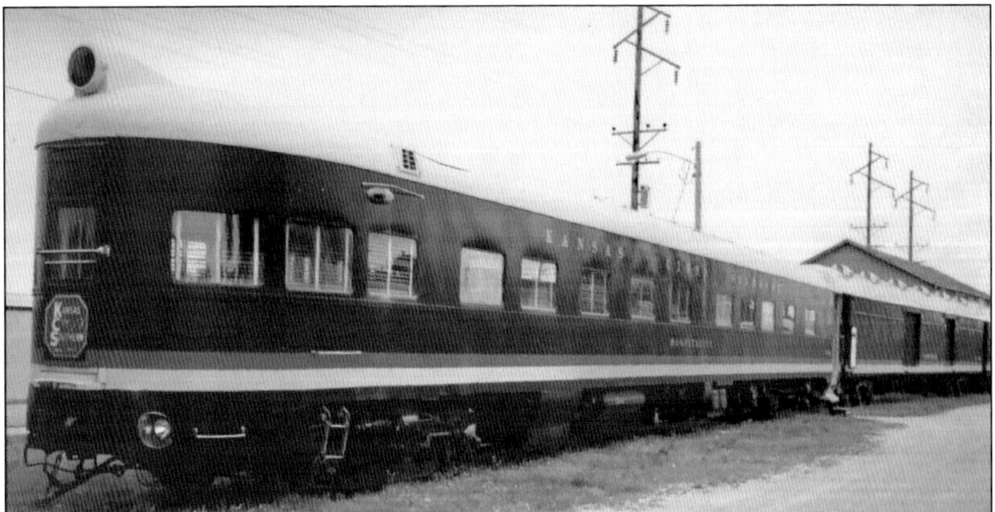

Round-ended observation cars were used on KCS passenger trains. Built by Pullman-Standard Company in 1940, the *Shreveport* was renamed the *Hospitality* and finished its days in service on the line from Shreveport, Louisiana, to Port Arthur, Texas. After retirement in 1968, it was acquired by the Smoky Hill Historical Society in Belton, Missouri. Sister car *Good Cheer* went to the Gulf Coast Chapter of the National Railway Historical Society in Houston. (Courtesy Glen Roark.)

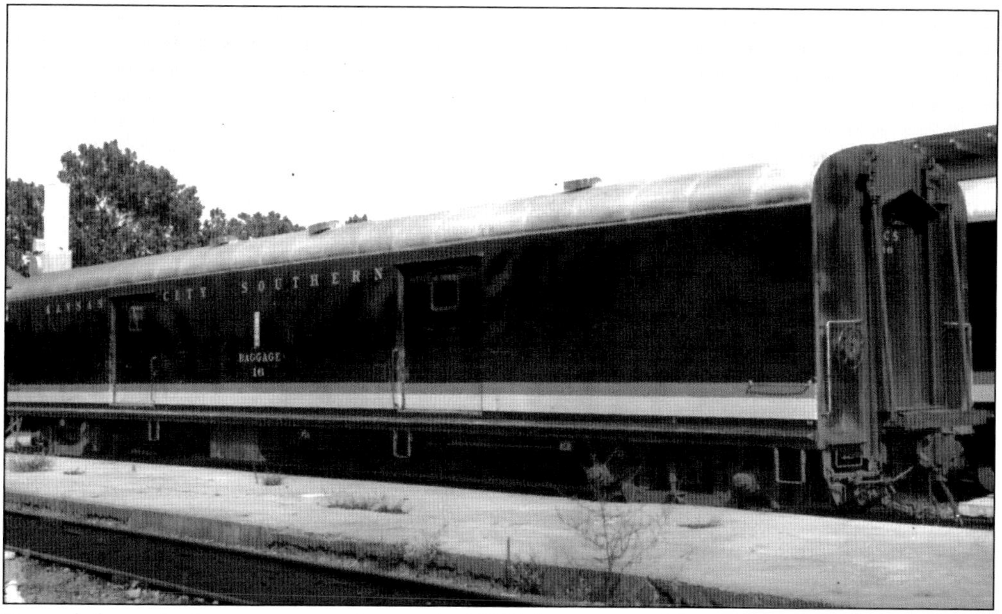

Toward the end of passenger service on the KCS, baggage car No. 16 awaits an assignment at the Shreveport Union Station. This car was built by the Pullman-Standard Company for the Santa Fe Railway in the 1950s and acquired by KCS in 1964. At a time when many railroads used heavyweight head-end equipment with their streamliners, the KCS was still streamlined. (Courtesy Harold K. Vollrath.)

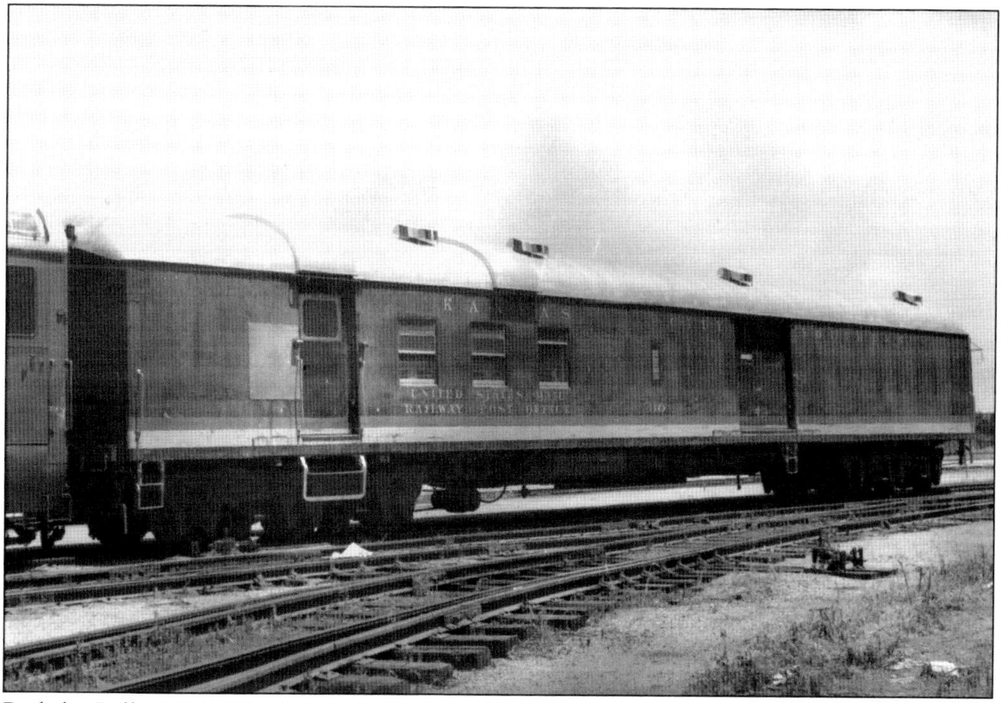

Built by Pullman-Standard in 1931, RPO car No. 30 saw service on most KCS passenger runs over the years. Today the car is used by the Midland Railway, a tourist operation running from Baldwin City, Kansas, to Norwood, Kansas. (Author's collection.)

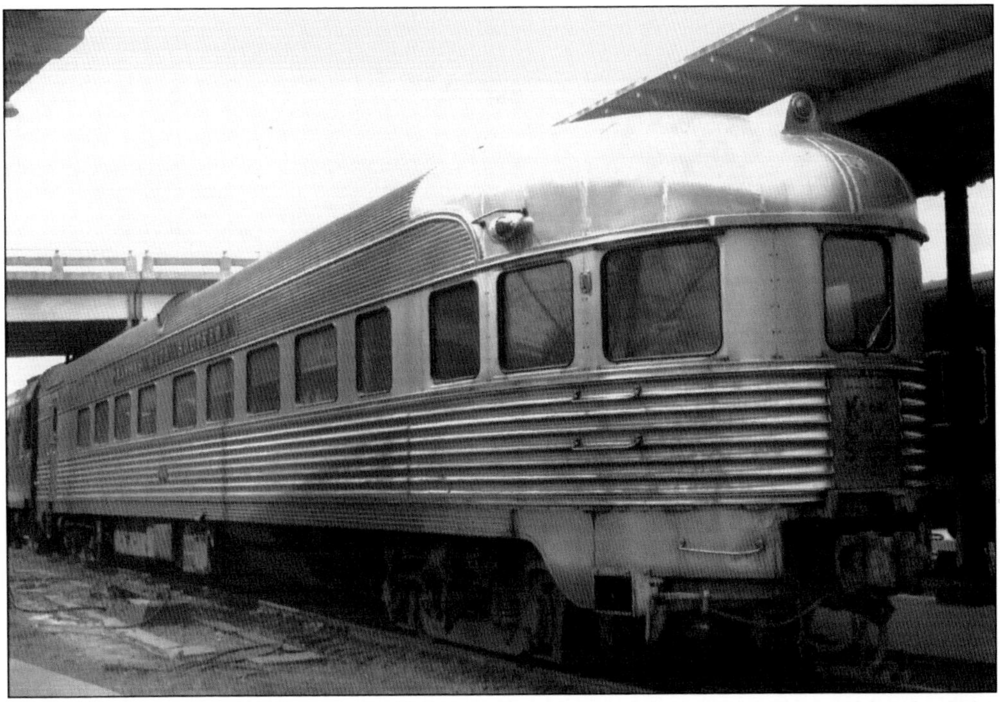

Here is a former New York Central Railroad observation car that was acquired by the KCS in 1959. These cars were used for food service and graced the tail end of the *Southern Belle*, until it was discontinued in 1969. The car was eventually painted KCS colors. (Courtesy Harold K. Vollrath.)

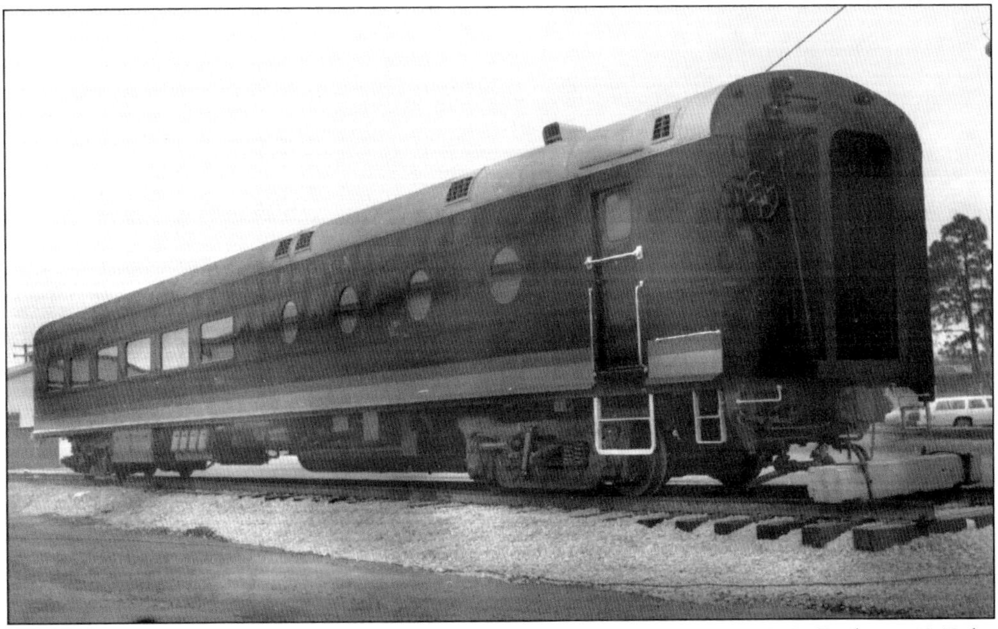

A KCS diner sits at the Deramus yard in Shreveport, Louisiana, in 1982. Built in 1948 by American Car and Foundry, it operated in service on the *Southern Belle* until it was replaced by ex–New York Central observation cars. (Courtesy Harold K. Vollrath.)

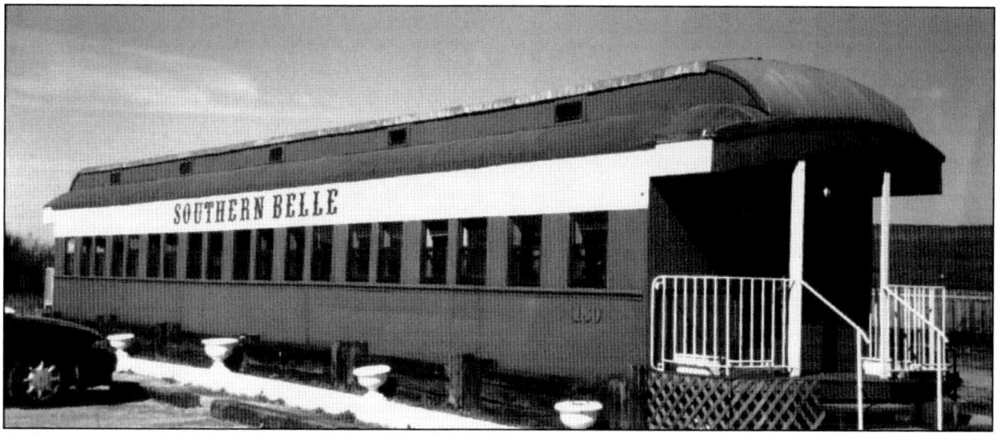

A former KCS coach is a restaurant in Heavener, Oklahoma. (Courtesy John Hillis Carter.)

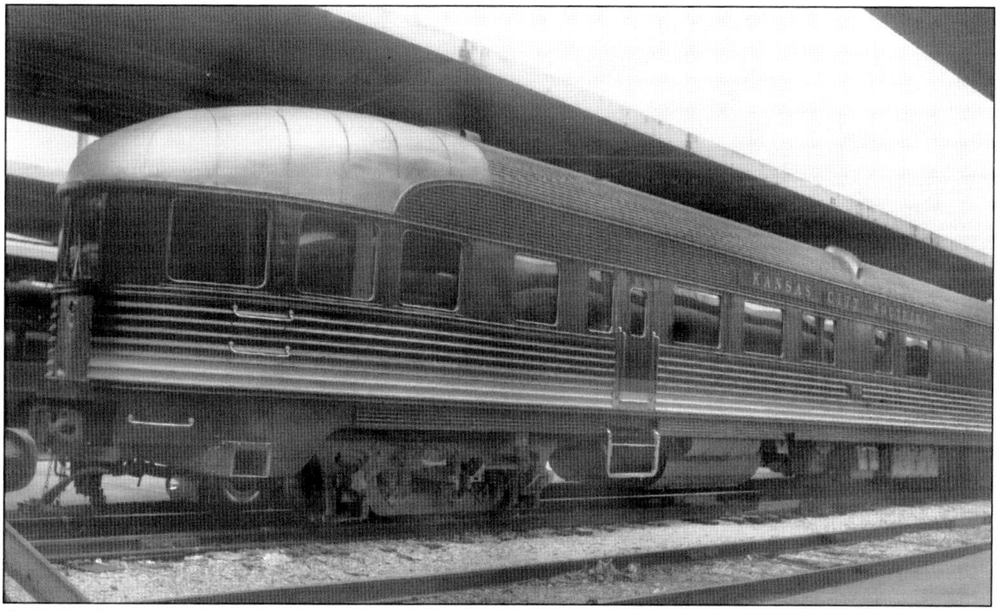
A KCS observation car is parked at the Shreveport station near the end of its career. (Courtesy Harold K. Vollrath.)

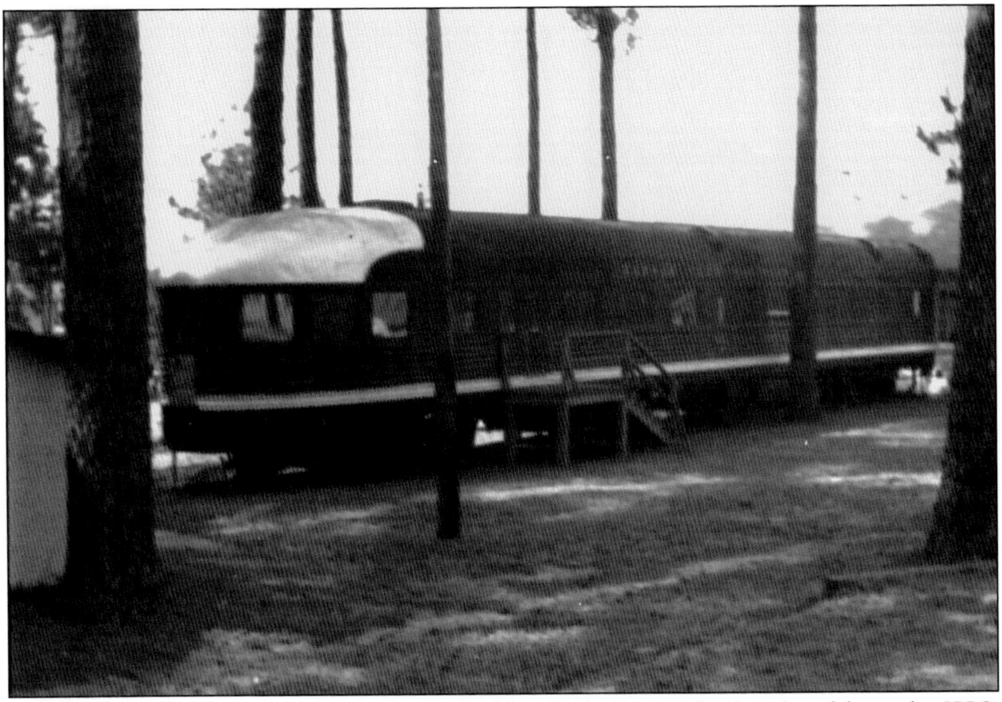

Following its use in passenger service on the New York Central Railroad and later the KCS, this observation car has found a home at a lumber company in Winnfield, Louisiana. (Courtesy Belinda S. Carter.)

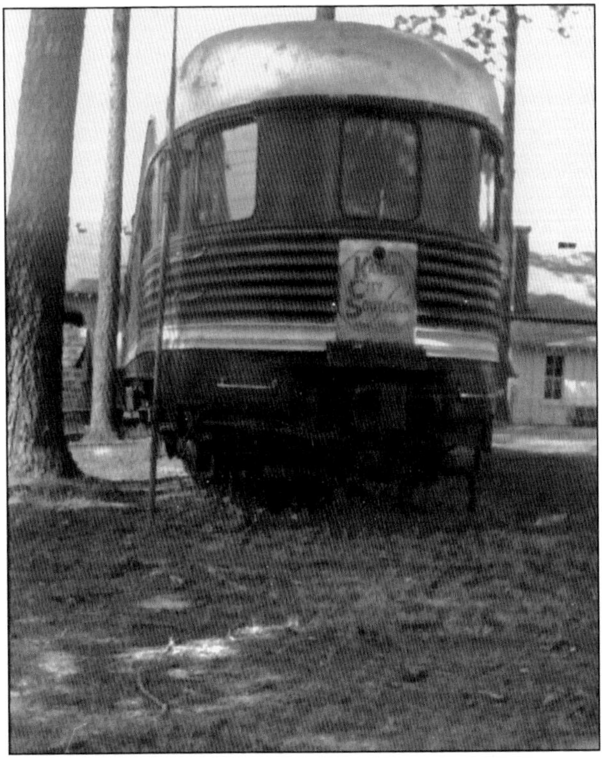

This former New York Central observation car was photographed at Winnfield. The car, purchased by the KCS in 1959, eventually ended up between a row of pine trees in Winnfield. Louisiana-Pacific purchased the car for company parties. (Courtesy Belinda S. Carter.)

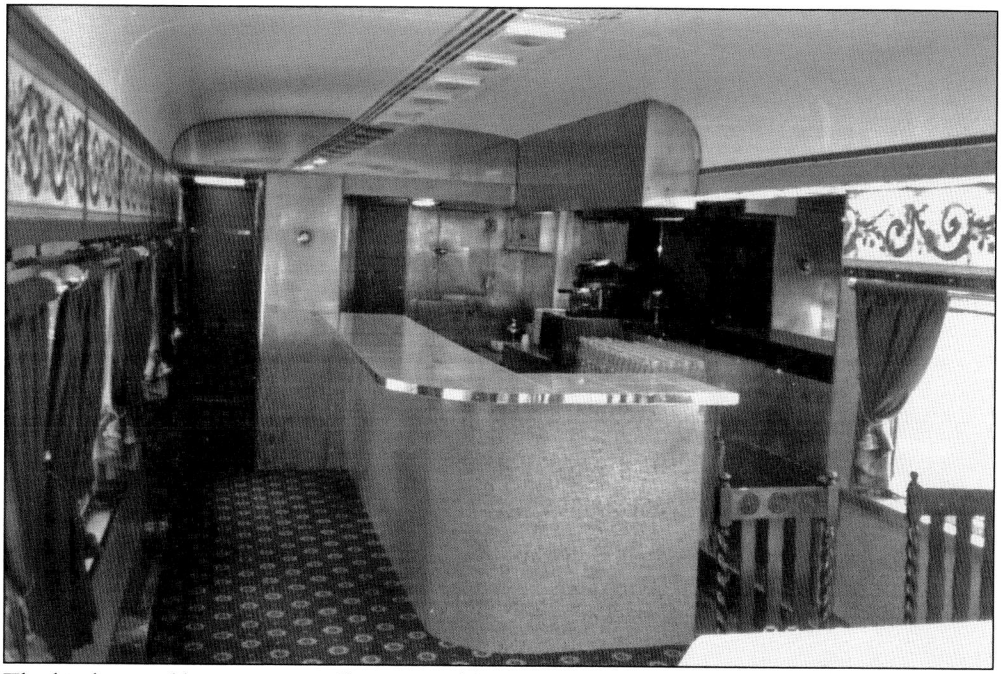

The kitchen and bar area was still intact and brought back memories of $1.55 ham steak dinners when photographed at Jackson, Louisiana. (Courtesy John Reed.)

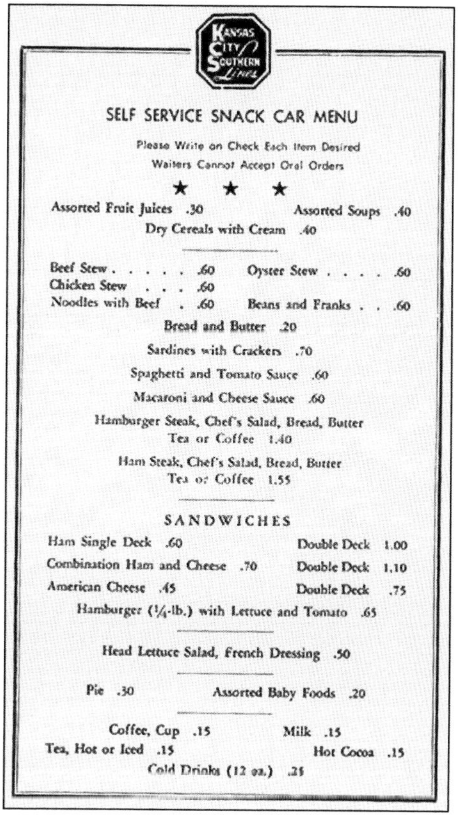

Kansas City Southern Lines

SELF SERVICE SNACK CAR MENU

Please Write on Check Each Item Desired
Waiters Cannot Accept Oral Orders

★ ★ ★

Assorted Fruit Juices .30 — Assorted Soups .40
Dry Cereals with Cream .40

Beef Stew . . . . . .60 — Oyster Stew 60
Chicken Stew 60
Noodles with Beef . .60 — Beans and Franks . . .60
Bread and Butter .20
Sardines with Crackers .70
Spaghetti and Tomato Sauce .60
Macaroni and Cheese Sauce .60
Hamburger Steak, Chef's Salad, Bread, Butter
Tea or Coffee 1.40
Ham Steak, Chef's Salad, Bread, Butter
Tea or Coffee 1.55

SANDWICHES

Ham Single Deck .60 — Double Deck 1.00
Combination Ham and Cheese .70 — Double Deck 1.10
American Cheese .45 — Double Deck .75
Hamburger (¼-lb.) with Lettuce and Tomato .65

Head Lettuce Salad, French Dressing .50

Pie .30 — Assorted Baby Foods .20

Coffee, Cup .15 — Milk .15
Tea, Hot or Iced .15 — Hot Cocoa .15
Cold Drinks (12 oz.) .25

Here is one of the final café observation car menus used in food service on the KCS. Dining service was provided in the former New York Central observation cars that brought up the rear of KCS passenger trains. (Courtesy Philip L. Moseley.)

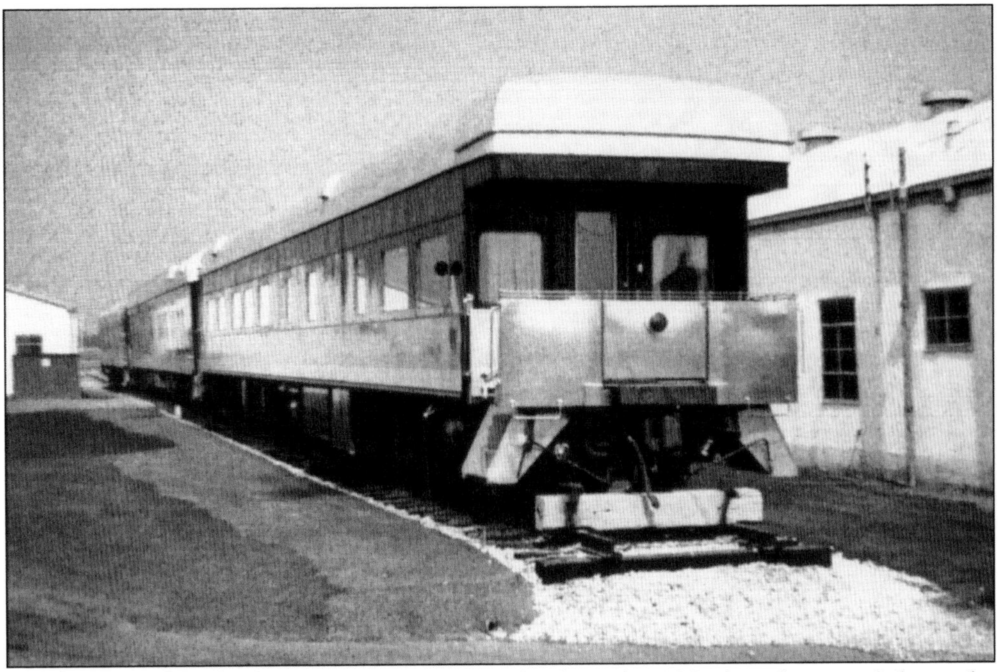

After being rebuilt, this private car was used by officials on the KCS when they traveled over the line for business and inspections. The car is parked at Shreveport, Louisiana, in the early 1980s. (Courtesy Belinda S. Carter.)

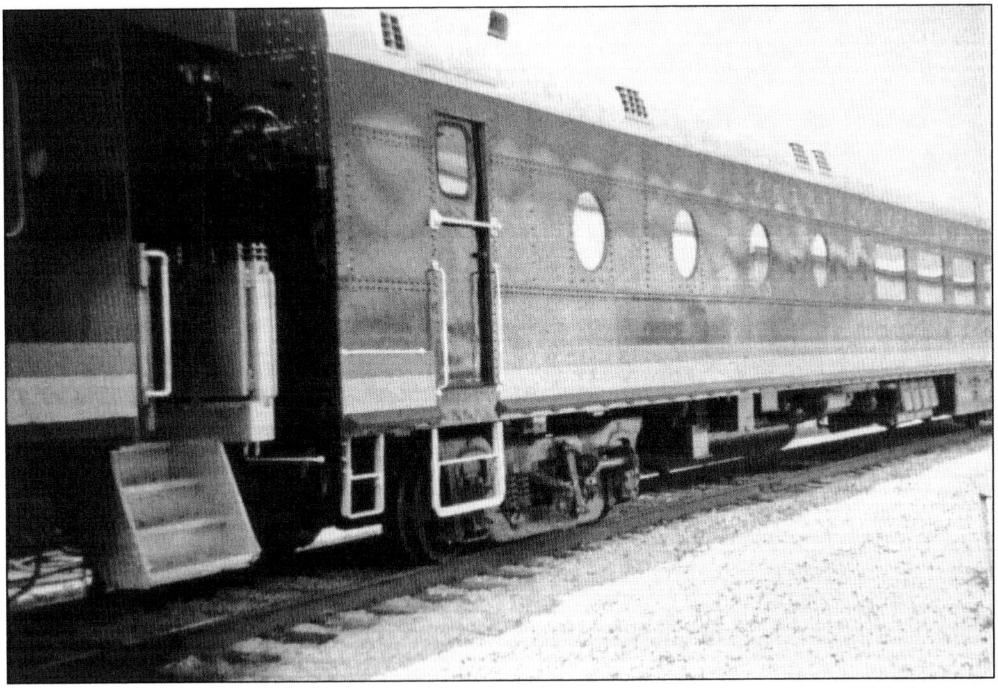

A former dining car from the original *Southern Belle* is pictured in service on a KCS business train at Shreveport. The porthole windows and door indicate the kitchen area where the meals were prepared. (Courtesy Belinda S. Carter.)

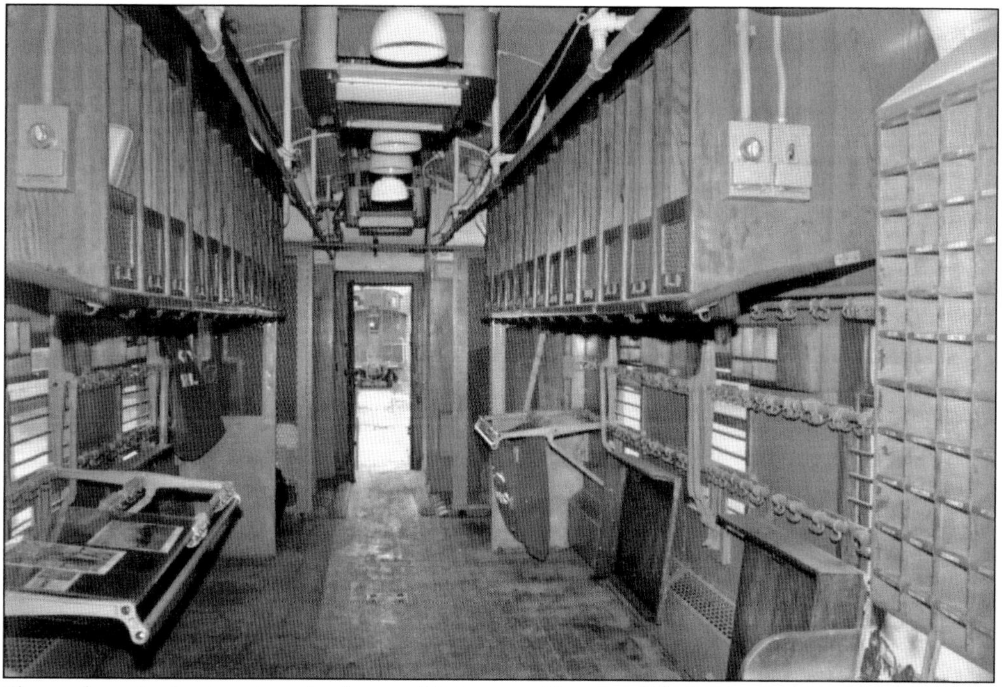

Shown here is the interior of a former KCS post office car. While the trains were going from town to town, the post office crews sorted mail and dropped off mailbags at small towns where the train was not scheduled to stop. (Author's collection.)

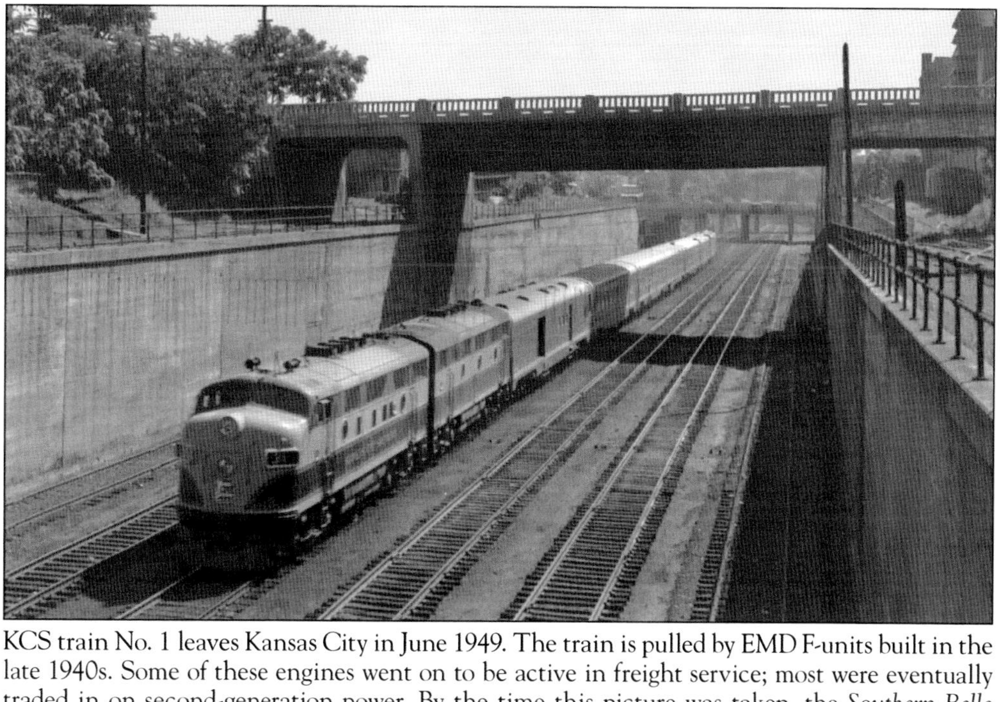

KCS train No. 1 leaves Kansas City in June 1949. The train is pulled by EMD F-units built in the late 1940s. Some of these engines went on to be active in freight service; most were eventually traded in on second-generation power. By the time this picture was taken, the *Southern Belle* had a 14-roomette, 4-double-bed-room sleeping car and was equipped with a full dining car. (Courtesy Harold K. Vollrath.)

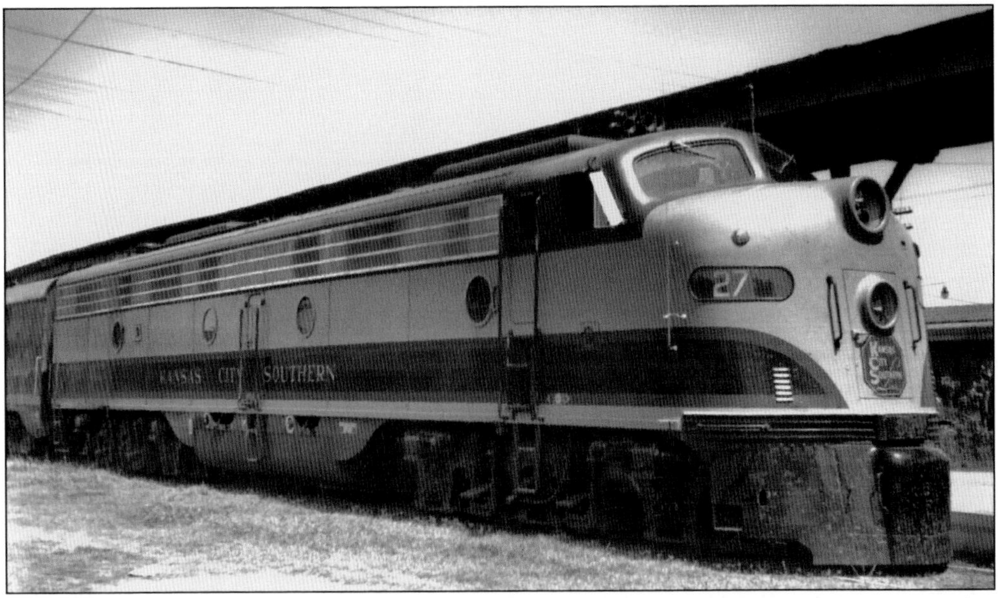

KCS No. 27, an EMD E8 unit, heads up the *Southern Belle* at New Orleans in June 1952. This photograph was taken at the Rampart Street station, built in 1924 by William Edenborn's Louisiana Railway and Navigation Company. (Courtesy Harold K. Vollrath.)

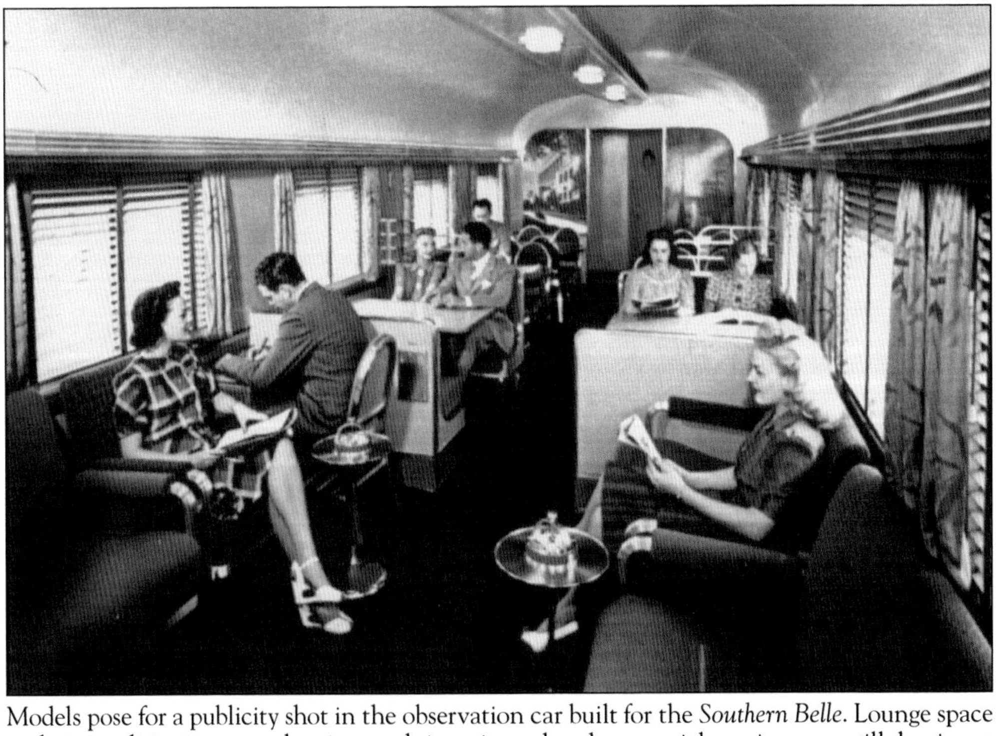

Models pose for a publicity shot in the observation car built for the *Southern Belle*. Lounge space and air-conditioning were drawing cards in a time when heavyweight trains were still dominant and windows were raised to let in fresh air, which also allowed smoke from the steam engine to enter. (Courtesy KCS archives.)

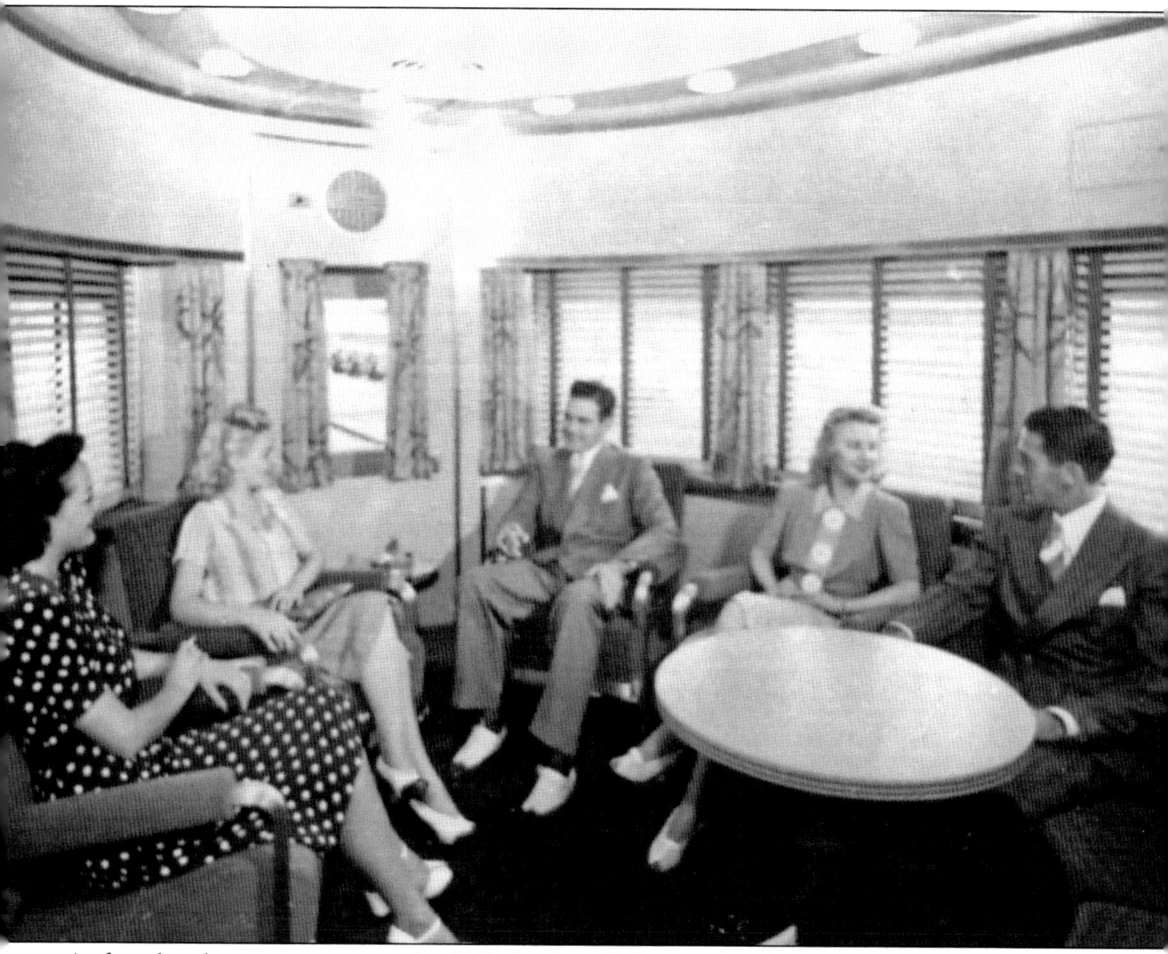

At first the observation cars on the 1940 *Southern Belle* served as lounge and diner. With the introduction of full diners after World War II, the cars were remodeled to serve as lounge cars. Eventually the cars operated from Kansas City to Shreveport, Louisiana. After being removed from the *Southern Belle*, they were used as snack cars on train Nos. 15 and 16. (Courtesy KCS archives.)

THE KANSAS CITY SOUTHERN RAILWAY LINES
Passenger Traffic Department

Shreveport, La., December 19, 1957

File...............D-285

cc - File 285/1

ALL K.C.S. - L.& A. TICKET AGENTS
ALL K.C.S. - L.& A. PASSENGER CONDUCTORS
ALL PASSENGER DEPARTMENT REPRESENTATIVES
ALL GENERAL AND COMMERCIAL AGENTS
ALL DEPARTMENT HEADS

(NOT FOR PUBLIC INFORMATION UNTIL FRIDAY NOON, DECEMBER 20, 1957)

EFFECTIVE 12:01 AM January 12, 1958, we will make major passenger train schedule changes which will effect all of our service with the exception of Trains 3 and 4 and the operation of the Shreveport-St. Louis Sleeper. The new schedules are attached.

It will be noted that the present "Southern Belle" schedule is to be discontinued. Present Trains 9 and 10 with minor schedule changes, will become Trains 1 and 2, the "Southern Belle". Present Trains 15 and 16 will have minor changes between Kansas City and Port Arthur and these trains will be extended through between Shreveport and New Orleans, designated as Trains 9 and 10 between these points.

Trains 1 and 2, the "Southern Belle", will have a 14 Roomette 4-Double Bedroom Sleeper and Diner-Lounge Car (Bar service south of Shreveport) between Kansas City and New Orleans in addition to providing through chair cars. Tavern-Lounge-Observation car will be provided between Kansas City and Shreveport.

Trains 15-9 and 16-10 will have a 14 Roomette 4 Double Bedroom Sleeper and Diner-Lounge Car between Kansas City and New Orleans in addition to providing through chair cars between these points. Through chair cars will also be provided on Trains 15 and 16 between Kansas City and Port Arthur making it unnecessary for coach passengers to change trains at Shreveport.

The new folders will be forwarded just as quickly as they are received from the printers.

Please see that all concerned are fully advised of these change.

S. A. WATSON
Passenger Traffic Manager

An interoffice memorandum is shown in this copy from KCS files. The memorandum announces train schedule changes that were coming soon. A new public timetable would be printed to let the general public know about the changes. (Courtesy Philip L. Moseley.)

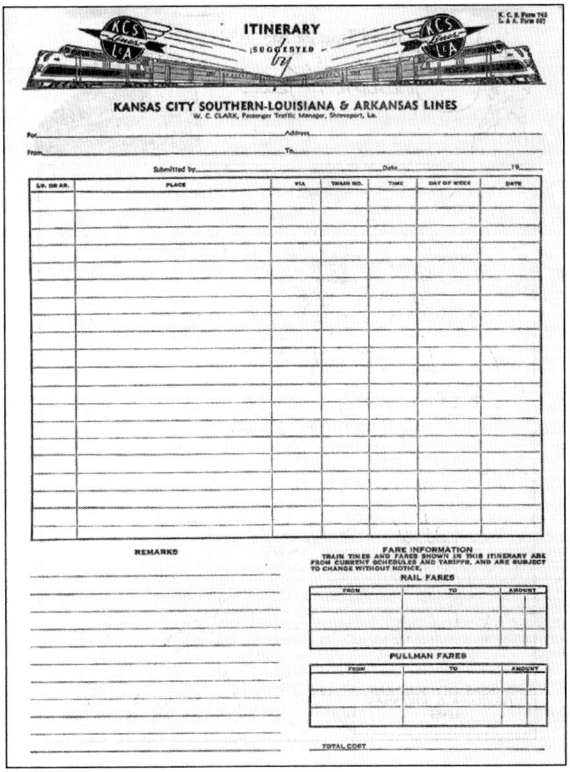

In the days when travelers kept an itinerary of where they were going on their trips and what stops they planned to make, the KCS made these itinerary forms available for planning out a trip. (Courtesy Philip L. Moseley.)

THE KANSAS CITY SOUTHERN RAILWAY LINES
Passenger Traffic Department

PROPOSED PASSENGER TRAIN SCHEDULES

EFFECTIVE JANUARY 12, 1958

(Read Down) TRAIN NO. 15-9	TRAIN NO. 1			(Read Up) TRAIN NO. 2	TRAIN NO. 10-16
9:30PM	10:00AM	Lv. Kansas City, Mo.	Ar.	7:45PM	7:20AM
a		Lv. Grandview, Mo.	Lv.		a
b		Lv. Cleveland, Mo.	Lv.		b
b		Lv. Lisle, Mo.	Lv.		b
b		Lv. Drexel, Mo.	Lv.		6:11AM
b		Lv. Merwin, Mo.	Lv.		b
b		Lv. Amsterdam, Mo.	Lv.		b
b		Lv. Amoret, Mo.	Lv.		b
11:10PM		Lv. Hume, Mo.	Lv.		b
b		Lv. Stotesbury, Mo.	Lv.		b
b		Lv. Richards, Mo.	Lv.		b
b		Lv. Mulberry, Kan.-Mo.	Lv.		b
12:20AM	12:15PM	Lv. Pittsburg, Kans.	Lv.	5:20PM	4:50AM
1:05AM	12:55PM	Lv. Joplin, Mo.	Lv.	4:35PM	4:00AM
1:45AM	1:35PM	Lv. Neosho, Mo.	Lv.	4:01PM	3:20AM
f 1:55AM	f 1:45PM	Lv. McElhany(Ft.Crowder)	Lv.	f 3:42PM	f 3:01AM
f 2:00AM		Lv. Goodman, Mo.	Lv.		f 2:56AM
f 2:10AM		Lv. Anderson, Mo.	Lv.		f 2:43AM
f 2:15AM		Lv. Lanagan, Mo.	Lv.		f 2:35AM
2:25AM	f 2:12PM	Lv. Noel, Mo.	Lv.	f 3:14PM	2:25AM
f 2:33AM		Lv. Sulphur Spgs. Ark.	Lv.		f 2:13AM
f 2:43AM		Lv. Gravette, Ark.	Lv.		f 2:05AM
f 2:52AM		Lv. Decatur, Ark.	Lv.		f 1:55AM
f 3:00AM		Lv. Gentry, Ark.	Lv.		f 1:49AM
3:15AM	2:53PM	Lv. Siloam Spgs., Ark.	Lv.	2:35PM	1:38AM
f 3:25AM		Lv. Watts, Okla.	Lv.		f 1:25AM
f 3:35AM	e	Lv. Westville, Okla.	Lv.	e	f 1:12AM
f 3:55AM	e	Lv. Stilwell, Okla.	Lv.	e	f12:52AM
h		Lv. Bunch, Okla.	Lv.		h
h		Lv. Marble City, Okla.	Lv.		h
4:50AM	4:10PM	Lv. Sallisaw, Okla.	Lv.	1:20PM	12:20AM
		Bus Service			
5:45AM	5:05PM	Ar. Fort Smith, Ark.	Lv.	12:25PM	11:25PM
3:40AM	3:15PM	Lv. Fort Smith, Ark.	Ar.	2:15PM	1:15AM
4:50AM	4:10PM	Lv. Sallisaw, Okla.	Ar.	1:20PM	12:20AM
g		Lv. Redland, Okla.	Lv.		g
5:20AM	f 4:35PM	Lv. Spiro, Okla.	Lv.	f12:52PM	11:50PM
h		Lv. Panama, Okla.	Lv.		h
5:50AM	4:55PM	Lv. Poteau, Okla.	Lv.	f12:35PM	11:29PM
f 6:00AM	f 5:04PM	Lv. Howe, Okla.	Lv.	f12:27PM	f11:18PM
6:20AM	5:15PM	Lv. Heavener, Okla.	Lv.	12:20PM	11:10PM
f 6:42AM		Lv. Page, Okla.	Lv.		f10:34PM
7:20AM	6:15PM	Lv. Mena, Ark.	Lv.	11:20AM	10:05PM
f 7:35AM		Lv. Hatfield, Ark.	Lv.		f 9:47PM
f 7:41AM		Lv. Cove, Ark.	Lv.		f 9:40PM
f 7:48AM		Lv. Vandervoort, Ark.	Lv.		f 9:34PM
f 7:58AM		Lv. Wickes, Ark.	Lv.		f 9:25PM
f 8:14AM		Lv. Gillham, Ark.	Lv.		f 9:10PM
8:40AM	7:30PM	Lv. DeQueen, Ark.	Lv.	10:10AM	8:55PM
8:53AM	d	Ar. Neal Springs, Ark.	Lv.	d	8:31PM
		Bus Service			
9:15AM	d	Ar. Horatio Ark.	Lv.	d	8:10PM
8:30AM	d	Lv. Horatio Ark.	Ar.	d	8:[illegible]PM
8:53AM	d	Lv. Neal Springs, Ark.	Ar.	d	8:31PM
f 9:01AM		Lv. Winthrop, Ark.	Lv.		f8:21PM
f 9:09AM		Lv. Allene, Ark.	Lv.		f8:13PM
f 9:16AM		Lv. Wilton, Ark.	Lv.		f8:04PM
9:26AM	f 8:12PM	Lv. Ashdown, Ark.	Lv.	f 9:26AM	7:55PM
9:55AM	8:45PM	Ar. Texarkana, Ark.-Tex	Lv.	9:00AM	7:25PM
10:10AM	9:00PM	Lv. Texarkana, Ark.-Tex	Ar.	8:45AM	7:10PM
f10:38AM		Lv. Bloomburg, Tex.	Lv.		f6:32PM
f10:43AM		Lv. Ravanna, Ark.	Lv.		f6:24PM
f10:51AM		Lv. Rodessa, La.	Lv.		f6:16PM
11:03AM	f 9:46PM	Lv. Vivian, La.	Lv.	f 7:58AM	6:07PM
f11:13AM		Lv. Oil City, La.	Lv.		f5:55PM
f11:18AM		Lv. Mooringsport, La.	Lv.		f5:49PM
11:55AM	10:30PM	Ar. Shreveport, La.	Lv.	7:15AM	5:[illegible]PM

Here is a 1958 train schedule letting riders know what new schedules the KCS trains will be operating on. (Courtesy Philip L. Moseley.)

NO. 9	NO. 1			TRAIN NO. 2	TRAIN NO. 10
12:20PM	11:00PM	Lv. Shreveport, La.	Ar.	6:45AM	4:30PM
1:24PM		Lv. Coushatta, La.	Lv.		3:18PM
f 1:45PM		Lv. Campti, La.	Lv.		f 2:57PM
f 1:53PM		Lv. Clarence, La.	Lv.		f 2:49PM
f 2:11PM		Lv. Montgomery, La.	Lv.		f 2:33PM
2:32PM		Lv. Colfax, La.	Lv.		2:15PM
	11:57PM	Lv. Minden, La.	Lv.	5:45AM	
	f12:27AM	Lv. Castor, La.	Lv.	f 5:09AM	
	1:20AM	Lv. Winnfield, La.	Lv.	4:15AM	
3:05PM	2:25AM	Ar. Alexandria, La.	Lv.	3:00AM	1:40PM
3:15PM	2:35AM	Lv. Alexandria, La.	Ar.	2:35AM	1:35PM
3:52PM	3:12AM	Lv. Mansura, La.	Lv.	1:55AM	1:00PM
f 4:11PM		Lv. Simmesport, La.	Lv.		f12:41PM
5:40PM	5:05AM	Lv. Baton Rouge, La.	Lv.	12:10AM	11:20AM
f 6:08PM	f 5:28AM	Lv. Gonzales, La.	Lv.	f11:30PM	f10:48AM
f 6:41PM	f 6:02AM	Lv. LaPlace, La.	Lv.	f10:51PM	f10:14AM
c 6:47PM		Lv. Norco, La.	Lv.		c10:07AM
7:12PM	6:37AM	Lv. Carrollton Ave., La.	Lv.	10:11PM	9:40AM
7:30PM	7:00AM	Ar. New Orleans, La.	Lv.	10:00PM	9:30AM

TRAIN NO. 15			TRAIN NO. 16
12:35PM	Lv. Shreveport, La.	Ar.	4:45PM
f 1:08PM	Lv. Frierson, La.	Lv.	f 4:04PM
f 1:13PM	Lv. Kingston, La.	Lv.	f 3:59PM
1:28PM	Lv. Mansfield, La.	Lv.	3:46PM
f 1:43PM	Lv. Benson, La.	Lv.	f 3:28PM
f 1:50PM	Lv. Converse, La.	Lv.	f 3:19PM
f 1:57PM	Lv. Noble, La.	Lv.	f 3:12PM
2:04PM	Lv. Zwolle, La.	Lv.	3:06PM
2:20PM	Lv. Many, La.	Lv.	2:50PM
f 2:32PM	Lv. Fisher, La.	Lv.	f 2:41PM
f 2:37PM	Lv. Florien, La.	Lv.	f 2:37PM
f 2:51PM	Lv. Hornbeck, La.	Lv.	f 2:26PM
f 3:00PM	Lv. Anacoco, La.	Lv.	f 2:17PM
3:25PM	Lv. Leesville, La.	Lv.	2:05PM
3:55PM	Lv. DeRidder, La.	Lv.	1:23PM
f 4:16PM	Lv. Singer, La.	Lv.	f 1:02PM
4:33PM	Ar. DeQuincy, La.	Lv.	12:45PM
	Bus Service		
5:25PM	Ar. Lake Charles, La.	Lv.	11:50AM
4:33PM	Lv. DeQuincy, La.	Ar.	12:45PM
f 4:54PM	Lv. Starks, La.	Lv.	f12:23PM
f 5:01PM	Lv. Ruliff, Tex.	Lv.	f12:15PM
f 5:10PM	Lv. Mauriceville, Tex.	Lv.	f12:05PM
5:35PM	Ar. Beaumont, Tex.	Lv.	11:45AM
5:45PM	Lv. Beaumont, Tex.	Ar.	11:35AM
f 6:00PM	Lv. Nederland, Tex.	Lv.	f11:16AM
6:25PM	Ar. Port Arthur, Tex.	Lv.	11:00AM

EXPLANATION OF SIGNS

a - Trains will stop on flag to pick up or discharge revenue passengers to or from Pittsburg or beyond.

b - Trains will stop on flag to pick up or discharge revenue passengers to or from Kansas City or beyond and to or from Pittsburg or beyond.

c - Trains will stop on flag for revenue passengers to or from Shreveport or beyond when advance request is made to agent.

d - Trains will stop on flag to pick up or discharge revenue passengers to or from Spiro or beyond and to or from Texarkana or beyond with tickets from or to Horatio. Ark.

e - Trains will stop on flag to pick up or discharge revenue passengers to or from Siloam Springs or beyond and to or from Sallisaw or beyond.

f - Flag stop to pick up or discharge revenue passengers.

g - Trains will stop on flag to pick up or discharge revenue passengers to or from Kansas City or beyond.

h - Trains will stop on flag to pick up or discharge revenue passengers to or from Siloam Springs or beyond and to or from Heavener or beyond.

NOTICE

TRAINS 3 AND 4 BETWEEN HOPE, ARK., AND SHREVEPORT, LA., WILL CONTINUE TO OPERATE ON PRESENT SCHEDULES.

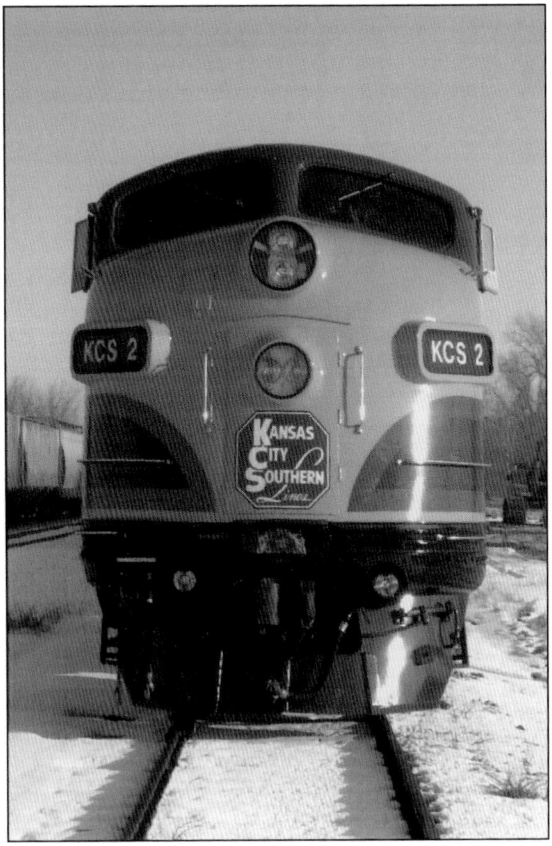

Appearing like a diesel that pulled the *Southern Belle*, a closer look shows this unit is part of the business train that operates on today's KCS. The difference can be seen in the ditch lights, these were not part of the engines in the 1960s. (Courtesy of Gary Coates.)

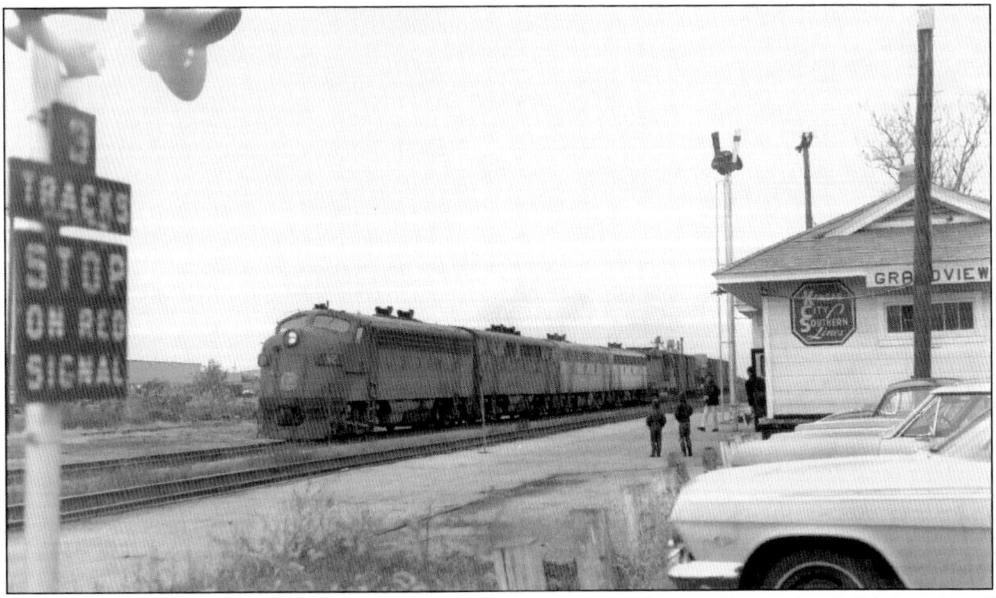

An EMD F7 unit diesel is waiting for the final train No. 1, *Southern Belle*, on the *Belle*'s last day of operation. This photograph was taken at Grandview, Missouri, on November 2, 1969. (Courtesy of Harold K. Vollrath.)

When credit cards were becoming popular, the railroads issued a rail travel card so that riders could charge their trips and pay for them later. This advertisement was part of a KCS timetable. (Courtesy Philip L. Moseley.)

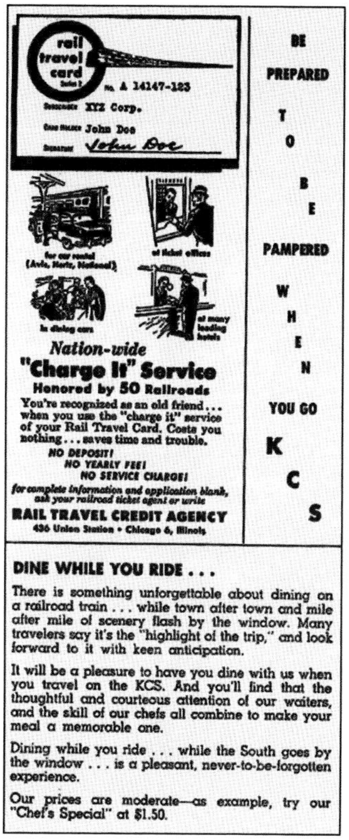

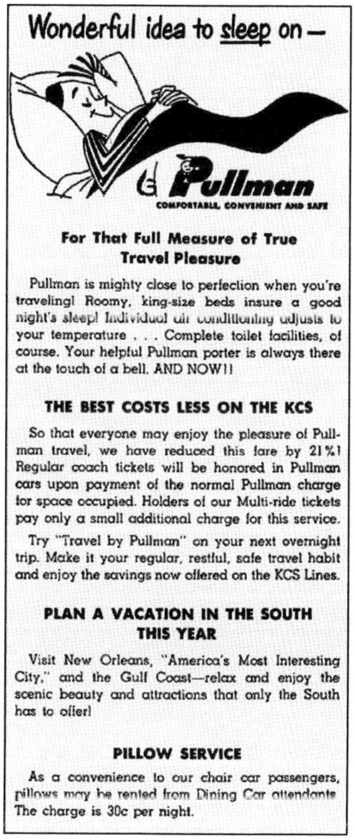

This advertisement taken from a KCS passenger train schedule advertises the benefits of traveling first class. Until shortly before the passenger trains were discontinued, Pullman car service was a part of train travel on the *Southern Belle*. The traveler paid an extra fare to ride in the sleeping cars. (Courtesy of Philip L. Moseley.)

RAILROAD FARES

RAIL FARES in effect March 1, 1969. Subject to change without notice

BETWEEN	6 Months Coach One Way	6 Months Coach Round Trip	30 Day Multi-Ride
Kansas City and			
Pittsburg	$ 4.10	$ 7.40	$ 5.80
Joplin	4.89	8.85	6.90
Neosho	5.52	10.00	7.80
Siloam Springs	7.29	13.15	10.25
Sallisaw	9.26	16.70	13.00
Fort Smith	9.95	18.00	14.00
Mena	12.09	21.80	17.00
De Queen	13.80	24.90	19.35
Texarkana	15.57	28.05	21.85
Shreveport	17.91	32.30	25.10
Alexandria	21.82	39.35	30.60
Baton Rouge	26.03	46.90	36.50
New Orleans	28.56	51.45	40.05
Pittsburg and			
Joplin	.80	1.50	1.20
Neosho	1.43	2.60	2.05
Siloam Springs	3.19	5.80	4.55
Fort Smith	5.86	10.55	8.25
Mena	7.99	14.40	11.25
De Queen	9.70	17.50	13.60
Texarkana	11.48	20.70	16.15
Shreveport	13.82	24.90	19.40
Alexandria	17.72	31.95	24.85
Baton Rouge	21.93	39.55	30.75
New Orleans	24.47	44.05	34.30
Joplin and			
Neosho	.63	1.20	.90
Siloam Springs	2.39	4.40	3.40
Fort Smith	5.06	9.15	7.10
Mena	7.19	13.00	10.10
De Queen	8.90	16.10	12.50
Texarkana	10.68	19.30	15.00
Shreveport	13.02	23.50	18.30
Alexandria	16.93	30.50	23.75
Baton Rouge	21.14	38.10	29.65
New Orleans	23.67	42.65	33.20
Neosho and			
Siloam Springs	1.76	3.20	2.55
Fort Smith	4.43	8.00	6.25
Mena	6.56	11.85	9.20
De Queen	8.27	14.95	11.60
Texarkana	10.05	18.15	14.10
Shreveport	12.39	22.35	17.40
Alexandria	16.30	29.35	22.85
Baton Rouge	20.51	37.00	28.75
New Orleans	23.04	41.50	32.30
Siloam Springs and			
Sallisaw	1.97	3.60	2.80
Fort Smith	2.68	4.85	3.80
Mena	4.81	8.70	6.80
De Queen	6.51	11.80	9.15
Texarkana	8.28	15.00	11.60
Shreveport	10.63	19.20	14.95
Alexandria	14.54	26.20	20.40
Baton Rouge	18.74	33.80	26.25
New Orleans	21.27	38.35	29.85
Sallisaw and			
Fort Smith	.70	1.35	1.00
Mena	2.84	5.15	4.00
De Queen	4.54	8.20	6.35
Texarkana	6.31	11.40	8.90
Shreveport	8.65	15.60	12.15
Alexandria	12.57	22.65	17.65
Baton Rouge	16.78	30.25	23.55
New Orleans	19.30	34.80	27.05
Fort Smith and			
Mena	3.54	6.45	5.00
De Queen	5.24	9.45	7.35
Texarkana	7.01	12.65	9.90
Shreveport	9.36	16.85	13.15
Alexandria	13.27	23.95	18.60
Baton Rouge	17.47	31.50	24.50
New Orleans	20.00	36.05	28.05
Mena and			
De Queen	1.71	3.10	2.45
Texarkana	3.49	6.30	4.90
Shreveport	5.83	10.50	8.20
Alexandria	9.73	17.55	13.65
Baton Rouge	13.94	25.10	19.55
New Orleans	16.46	29.70	23.10
Texarkana and			
Shreveport	2.34	4.25	3.35
Alexandria	6.25	11.30	8.80
Baton Rouge	10.46	18.85	14.65
New Orleans	12.99	23.45	18.25
Shreveport and			
Minden	.96	1.75	1.40
Winnfield	3.14	5.70	4.45
Alexandria	[illegible]	7.85	[illegible]
Baton Rouge	8.12	14.65	11.40
New Orleans	10.65	19.25	14.95
Alexandria and			
Baton Rouge	4.21	7.65	5.95
New Orleans	6.73	12.15	9.45
Baton Rouge and			
New Orleans	2.53	4.60	3.60

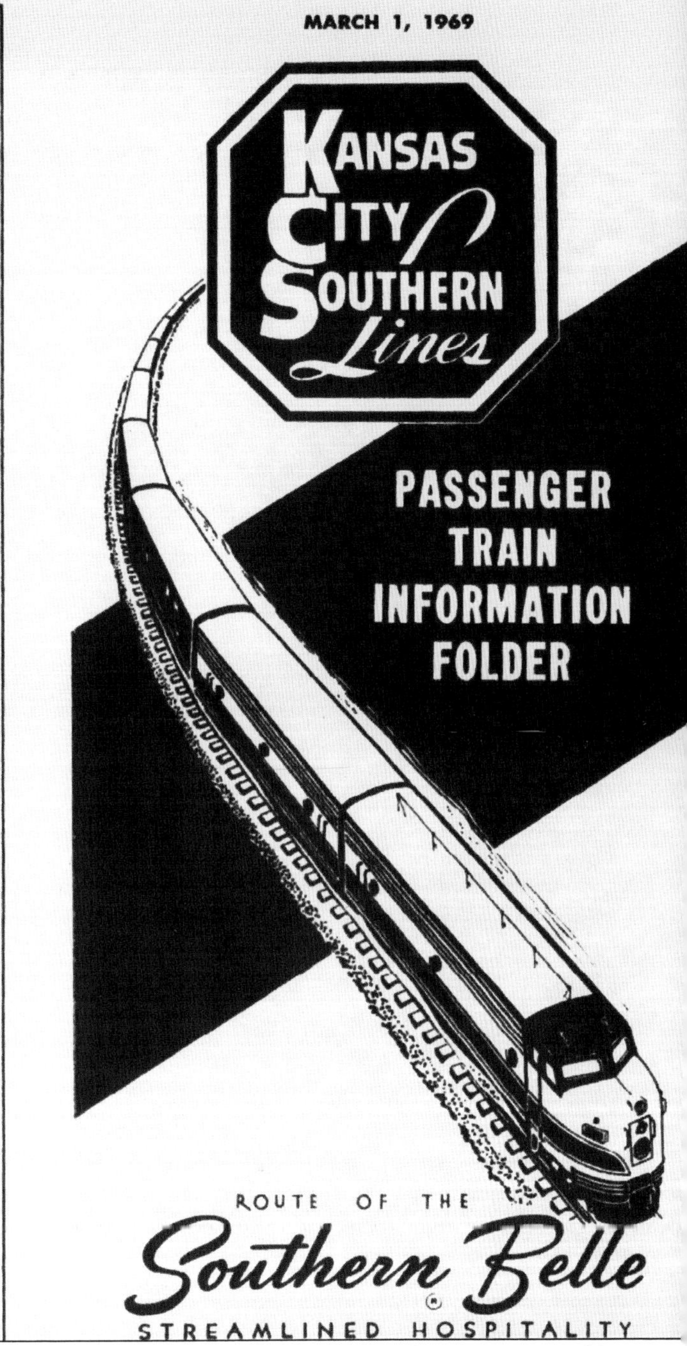

One of the last official passenger schedules issued by the KCS is this March 1, 1969, timetable. Notice the railroad is only operating one train each way daily over its route from Kansas City to New Orleans. It was discontinued the following November 2. Only coach seats were available

THROUGH SERVICE AND EQUIPMENT

All Cars Streamlined—Air Conditioned

KANSAS CITY—SHREVEPORT—NEW ORLEANS

Southern Belle

Trains 1 and 2

Chair Cars between Kansas City-New Orleans.

Cafe—Lounge—Observation Car between Kansas City-New Orleans. (Bar service in Missouri and Louisiana.)

Read Down — **KANSAS CITY—NEW ORLEANS** — Read Up

Train 1	Miles From K. C.	STATIONS	Miles From N. O.	Train 2
10 30	0.0	Lv....... Kansas City, Mo. ★ .... Ar	893.0	7 10
f 11 00	23.5	.... Grandview, Mo.	869.5	f 6 35
12 40	129.2	Ar....... Pittsburg, Kan. Lv	763.8	4 50
12 50	129.2	Lv....... Pittsburg, Kan. .... Ar	763.8	4 35
1 30	154.3	.... Joplin, Mo. ★	738.7	3 55
		Gateway to Ozarks		
2 01	174.1	.... Neosho, Mo.	718.9	3 25
2 45	200.7	.... Noel, Mo.	692.3	2 45
3 25	229.3	.... Siloam Springs, Ark. (Boston Mts.)	663.7	2 00
b 3 46	244.4	.... Westville, Okla. .... ↑	648.6	b 1 35
f 4 02	258.2	.... Stilwell, Okla. .... ↓	634.8	h 1 19
4 40	291.1	Ar....... Sallisaw, Okla. .... (Boston Mts.) Lv	601.9	12 40
		K. C. S. Bus Service		
5 25	312.1	Ar....... Fort Smith, Ark. ★ Lv	622.9	11 40
3 45	312.1	Lv....... Fort Smith, Ark. .... Ar	622.9	1 40
		Fort Chaffee, See Note 2		
4 40	291.1	Lv....... Sallisaw, Okla. .... Ar	601.9	12 40
		Cross the Arkansas River		
b 5 03	311.7	.... Spiro, Okla.	581.3	b 12 15
5 25	326.4	.... Poteau, Okla. .... (Quachita Mts.)	566.6	11 55
b 5 35	333.0	.... Howe, Okla. .... ↑	560.0	b 11 46
5 45	338.0	.... Heavener, Okla	555.0	11 40
6 45	379.8	.... Mena, Ark. .... ↓	513.2	10 40
7 55	433.3	.... DeQueen, Ark. .... (Quachita Mts.)	459.7	9 30
c 8 07	442.8	Ar....... Neal Springs, Ark. Lv	450.2	c 9 15
		Bus Service		
c 8 20	443.5	Ar....... Horatio, Ark. Lv	450.9	c 8 55
c 7 45	443.5	Lv....... Horatio, Ark .... Ar	450.9	c 9 35
c 8 07	442.8	Lv....... Neal Springs, Ark. .... Ar	450.2	c 9 15
f 8 34	467.9	.... Ashdown, Ark.	425.1	f 8 46
		Cross the Red River		
9 00	487.3	Ar....... Texarkana, Ark.-Tex. ★ Lv	405.7	8 20
9 25	487.3	Lv....... Texarkana, Ark.-Tex. .... Ar	405.7	8 05
f 10 12	526.8	.... Vivian, La.	366.2	f 7 15
11 05	561.0	Ar....... Shreveport, La., U. S. ★ Lv	332.0	6 30
11 30	561.0	Lv....... Shreveport, La., U. S. .... Ar	332.0	6 05
		Cross the Red River		
		Pass Barksdale A.F.B., See Note 1		
12 30	589.8	.... Minden, La.	303.2	5 00
f 1 03	615.6	.... Castor, La.	277.4	f 4 27
1 50	658.3	.... Winnfield, La.	234.7	3 35
		Cross the Red River		
2 45	704.6	Ar....... Alexandria, La. ★ Lv	188.4	2 25
3 05	704.6	Lv....... Alexandria, La. .... Ar	188.4	2 05
		Fort Polk, See Note 3		
3 45	734.5	.... Mansura, La.	158.6	1 25
		Cross the Atchafalaya River		
		Cross the Mississippi River		
5 25	812.7	Ar....... Baton Rouge, La. ★ .... Lv..	80.0	11 45
5 40	812.7	Lv....... Baton Rouge, La. .... Ar	80.0	11 30
f 6 06	833.2	.... Gonzales, La.	59.8	f 11 02
d 7 13	880.2	.... Kenner, La.	12.8	d 10 00
7 40	890.4	.... Carrollton Ave., La.	2.6	9 38
8 00	893.0	Ar....... New Orleans, La. ★ Lv	0.0	9 30
		Union Passenger Terminal		

Southern Belle **NO CHECKED BAGGAGE OR REMAINS HANDLED ON KCS LINES** *Southern Belle*

INFORMATION FOR PASSENGERS

TIME—Central standard time is used throughout this folder. **A. M.** time is shown in light faced figures and **P. M.** time in dark faced figures.

This folder is for public information. The utmost care is taken to keep it revised to date of issue, but the Company cannot guarantee perfect accuracy nor hold itself responsible for any existing errors. The Company also reserves the right to deviate from or change the figures herein given without public notice.

While the Company uses every reasonable effort to run its trains according to schedule time, it does not guarantee that its trains will run according to schedule, nor that they will make connections at junction points with the trains of any particular line. All tickets are sold subject to such delays as might be caused by the elements or other unforeseen circumstances.

TRAINS WILL MAKE STOPS only at stations where time is given or as indicated by special or conditional stops as shown in notes in this folder. Agents of this Railroad or connecting line agents have no authority to change or vary from these conditions.

PERSONS DESIRING COUPON TICKETS at stations where they are not regularly on sale can obtain them by giving Ticket Agent sufficient notice to enable him to procure them.

CHILDREN under five years of age free, when accompanied by parent or guardian; five years of age and under twelve, one-half fare; twelve years of age or over, full fare. When a child under five (5) years of age accompanied by parent or guardian occupies exclusively a berth or seat in sleeping car, in section other than that occupied by parent or guardian, half-fare rail ticket will be collected in addition to the Pullman rate.

ADJUSTMENT OF FARES—In cases of misunderstanding with conductors or agents pay the fare required, take receipt and communicate with Passenger Traffic Manager, Shreveport, La.

TICKETS MUST BE USED WITHIN LIMIT—Tickets will be honored for passage to reach destination prior to midnight of date indicated thereon, except when otherwise specified on tickets. Passengers not making continuous trip should arrange to board trains scheduled to reach their final destination prior to midnight of limit indicated on ticket.

REDEMPTION OF TICKETS—Tickets unused, or partly used, will be redeemed, under tariff regulations at proper value.

STOPPING TRAINS ON SIGNAL—Where trains are scheduled to stop only on signal, advance notice should be given in all cases, so that necessary arrangements may be perfected.

STOPOVERS—Stopovers are permitted on practically all regular one-way and round trip tickets, provided destination is reached prior to expiration of the ticket. Detailed information as to stopovers may be had from any ticket agent or from any representative.

S. A. WATSON
Passenger Traffic Manager
KCS LINES
4601 Blanchard Road
Shreveport, Louisiana

ONLY ONE COUPON NEEDED
FOR TRAVEL VIA KCS-L&A LINES

Explanation of Signs and Notes

CENTRAL STANDARD TIME USED
All train service is daily.
A.M.—Light Face Type. P.M.—Dark Face Type.
b—Trains will stop on flag to pick up or discharge revenue passengers to or from stations where trains regularly stop.
c—Trains will stop on flag to pick up or discharge revenue passengers to or from Sallisaw or beyond and to or from Texarkana or beyond with tickets from or to Horatio, Ark.
d—Trains will stop on flag to pick up or discharge revenue passengers to or from Baton Rouge or beyond.
f—Flag stop to pick up or discharge revenue passengers.
★—Rent-A-Car available at these stations.
Note 1—Reached by bus from Shreveport.
Note 2—Reached by bus from Fort Smith.
Note 3—Reached by bus from Alexandria.

on the *Belle* from Kansas City to New Orleans by the time this table was issued. (Courtesy Philip L. Moseley.)

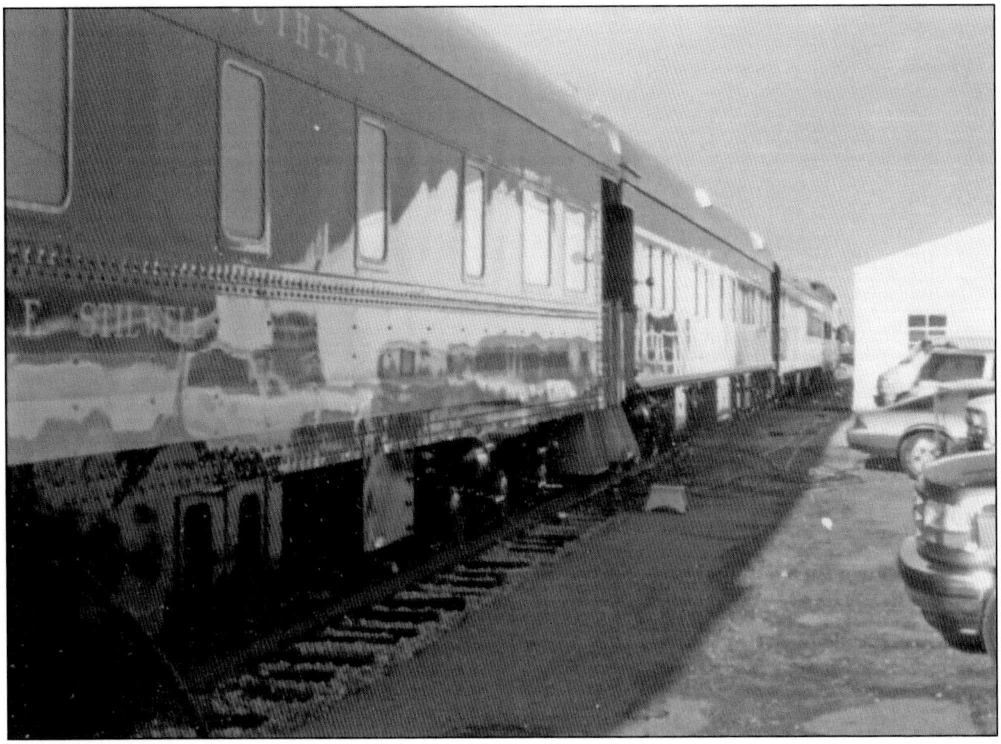

A KCS business train is in Shreveport, Louisiana, getting ready to go out on another trip. (Author's collection.)

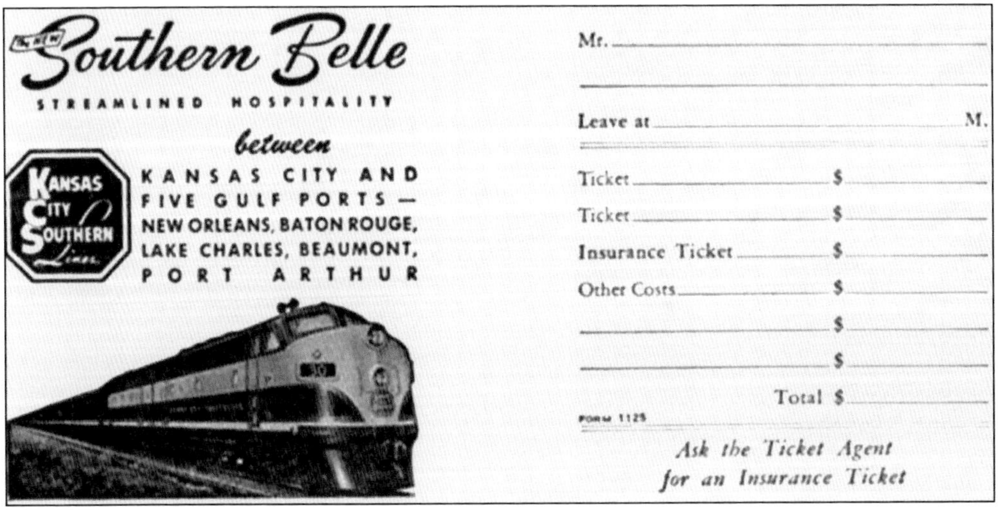

Upon purchase of a ticket from a KCS agent, the travel voucher was placed in the envelope seen above. (Author's collection.)

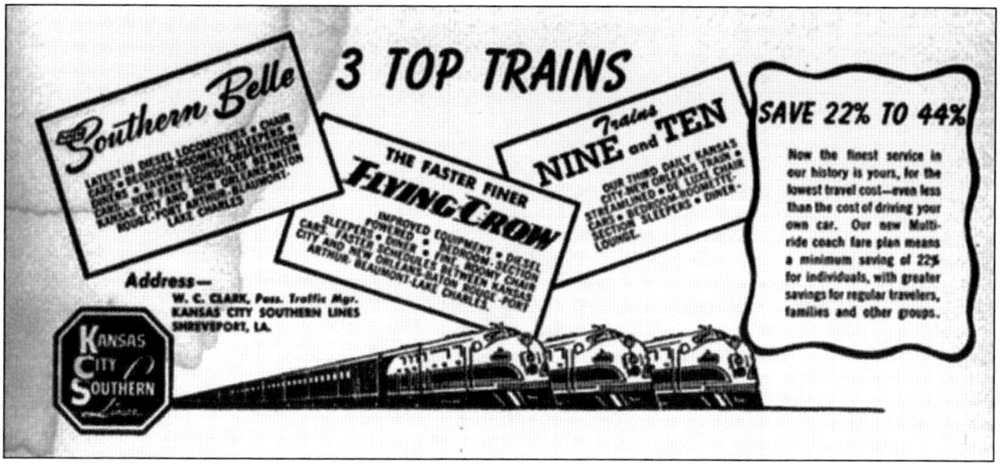

This KCS printout seems crude by today's advertising standards. It was used to promote passenger service on the line. (Author's collection.)

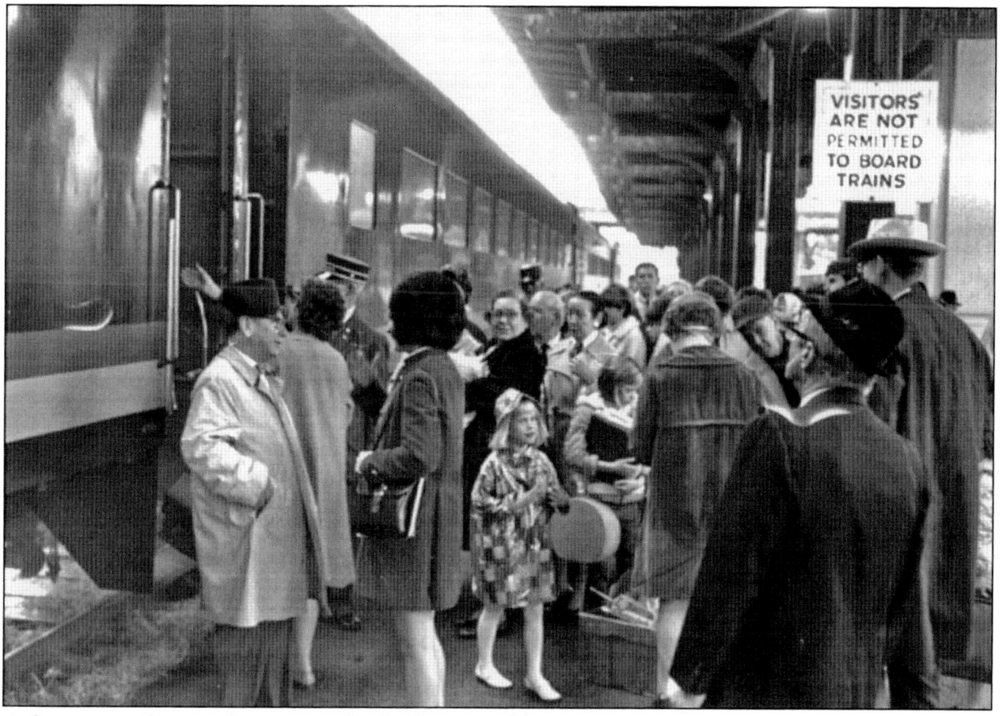

A large crowd turned out to ride the last northbound *Southern Belle* from Joplin, Missouri, to Kansas City. Bringing up the rear was a KCS office car ridden by vice president R. J. Blair. (Courtesy Joplin Public Library.)

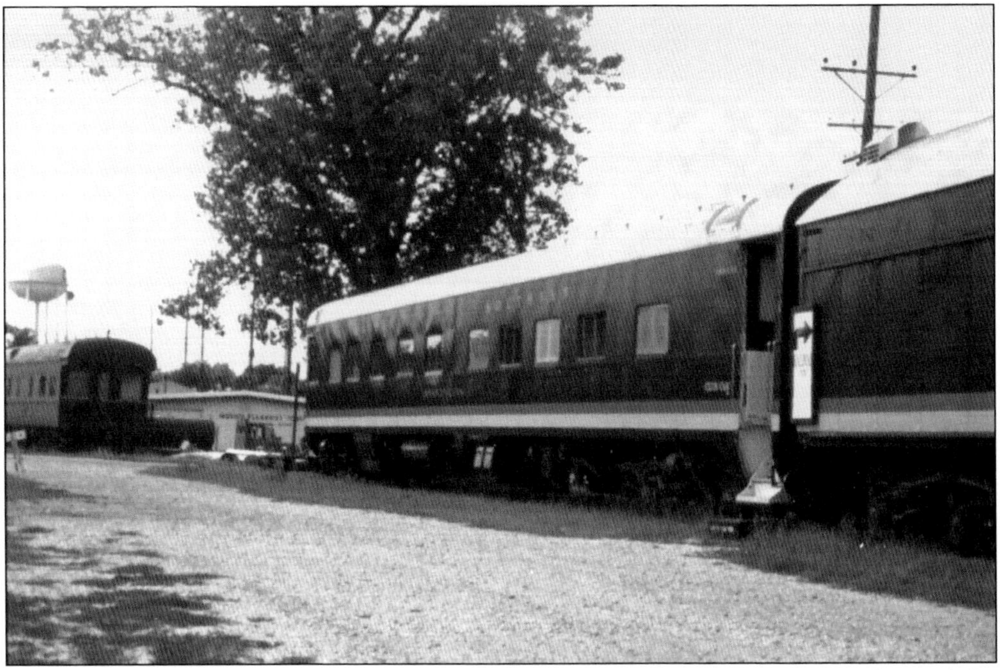

An ex–*Southern Belle* observation car is parked at Belton, Missouri, on the trackage of the Belton, Grandview and Kansas City Railroad. (Courtesy Glen Roark.)

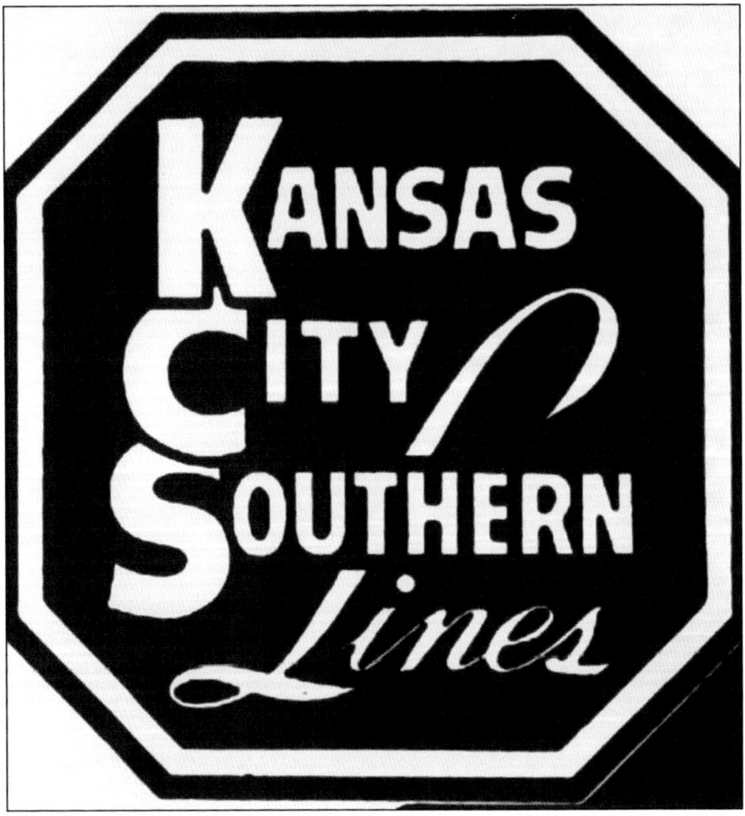

The symbol shown is the official railroad trademark for the KCS. All major railroads had an identifying icon. This symbol appeared on the nose of KCS passenger diesels that operated the *Southern Belle* and other passenger trains on the line. (Author's collection.)

Five

The End of Passenger Train Service

New scheduling for postwar operations included an additional set of New Orleans-to-Kansas City trains on the schedule of the old *Southern Belle*. The *Belle* now had a 19-hour running time leaving both terminals at 4:00 in the afternoon. The *Southern Belle* name was now being used on a Port Arthur, Texas, connection that took 17 hours to go from Kansas City to Port Arthur. The *Flying Crow* had its schedule trimmed by 45 minutes. The Kansas City-to-New Orleans schedule was cut by two and a half hours.

The original *Southern Belle* coaches were rebuilt and renumbered. They were also given names of towns along the line. The Osgood Bradley coaches, nicknamed American Flyer cars, also continued to operate and were among the cars given new names.

Despite the railroad's good intentions, a series of events would prove to be the undoing of KCS passenger service.

The October 1966 timetable contained a statement of hope for KCS passenger service. William N. Deramus III, KCS president, had stated the railroad's intention of remaining in the passenger business. Less than two years later, circumstances caused the issuance of a very different statement.

The cessation of passenger service was felt along the KCS line in places like Alexandria, Louisiana, and Neosho, Missouri. Philip L. Moseley was an agent at DeQueen, Arkansas, and recorded his sentiments on the passing of the *Belle*.

Last Days of The Southern Belle
By Philip Moseley

When I first started railroading in the mid-1960s as an agent telegrapher, the age of luxury passenger trains in the U.S. had already started to end. I have always considered myself very lucky to have gotten in on the end of the Golden Age with passenger trains, small town depots, express mail business, and telegraph.

It indeed was the glorious and romantic age of railroading. The only thing I missed was steam.

But this is the story of the last years of operation and then the sudden death of the "Sweetheart of American Trains, "the Kansas City Southern's "Southern Belle," which made its daily cruise from Kansas City to New Orleans passing through what I believe is the most scenic country east of the Rockies, the mountains of eastern Oklahoma and western Arkansas.

In 1968 when I came over to the KCS from Uncle John's Santa Fe, the Southern Belle was still in operation and was still one of the nicest, cleanest trains in the U.S. It had just lost its RPO car due to the government's scrapping of mail contracts because official Washington said it was too expensive to haul mail by rail.

By the way, in 1968 you could mail a first class letter for 6 cents. Today it is 37 so that should tell you something.

Due to declining passenger revenues and the killing cut the loss of the mails the KCS found itself in the same position all railroads found themselves in the 1960s. Passenger deficits rose and ridership dropped. Most railroads, in an attempt to discourage patrons, let their trains go, delaying them intentionally, using dirty equipment and such tricks as that, but not the KCS. Even in the mid and late 60's, management on the KCS tried to keep their trains in A-1 condition. They even remodeled and refurbished passenger equipment in 1966.

In March 1968 the KCS dropped trains 15 and 16 between KC and Shreveport and Port Arthur. These trains ran through Green Country in eastern Oklahoma at night, but they still kept the old Southern Belle, which gave a spectacular tour of the mountains of Missouri, Oklahoma and Arkansas in daylight hours.

The Southern Belle in all the time I knew her was very seldom late on her schedule. Usually 30 minutes or so into DeQueen going south and about that going north.

The KCS managed to make good connections in KC with other railroads. Example, No. 2's arrival at KCUS connected with less than a two-hour layover with UP No. 9's train the City of Saint Louis to San Francisco, LA and the Pacific Northwest. Also the train made good connections to Chicago on the ATSF and St. Louis on the MOP.

But in 1968 the KCS had to come to the realization that the trains were

This article originally appeared in the *Dispatcher*, the newsletter of the Central Oklahoma Chapter of the National Railway Historical Society. (Courtesy Arkansas Railroader.)

costing too much and had to go. As I mentioned the old Flying Crow number 15 and 16 went first in the spring of 1968. But the Southern Belle held on until November 1969.

In May 1969 the Pullmans came off, but were returned to service in September and pulled off for the last time in October 1969. The observation diner however remained until the end. The KCS had one of the nicest dining cars with the most reasonably priced and tasty meals of any railroad its size in the U.S. Also there was always a most courteous crew and dining car staff.

Unlike the Katy and Frisco which allowed their passenger trains to go down terribly in the last days, the KCS kept the Southern Belle's equipment clean and in top notch shape until the very last run.

I was working that night, November 3, 1969, when the last southbound run of the Southern Belle made its way into DeQueen. I remember it very well No. 1 the Southern Belle left Heavener with engine 23 thirty minutes off the advertised and didn't make up any time.

So it was called at DeQueen 30 minutes late. I sold more tickets that night than I had sold in any night in the more than a year I had worked second trick at DeQueen. People came from everywhere to ride it and watch her pullout for the last time.

The engine crew who changed at DeQueen was called. Note the regular old head crew had laid off, I guess they didn't want to take her out to pasture. The last engine crew to take her out of DeQueen was engineer W.J. Thomas and fireman A.J. Henry.

Right on the 30 minute late call No.1 pulled into DeQueen with engine 23, a B unit, one baggage car, two chair cars, and business cars Kaysee and Tolmak on the rear occupied by then vice president R.J. Blair. The Belle eased to a stop and carmen iced the engine. Rail fans and others boarded her and the platform full of people watched in a rather somber mood as

She whistled off and pulled out of town for the last time. I watched the red marker light on the rear of the Tolmak as it faded in the darkness and around the curve south of town.

Somewhere in the darkness down around Alexandria, La. it would meet the last No.2 the northbound Southern Belle and fade into history.

Before I closed the books out I sold myself the last ticket issued at DeQueen a round trip coach ticket to Neal Springs, Ark., nine miles south of DeQueen. It cost 35 cents.

I still have that ticket and the last set of train orders given No. 1 that night.

The story also appeared in the May 1986 issue of the *Arkansas Railroader* and is reprinted here with permission. (Courtesy Arkansas Railroader.)

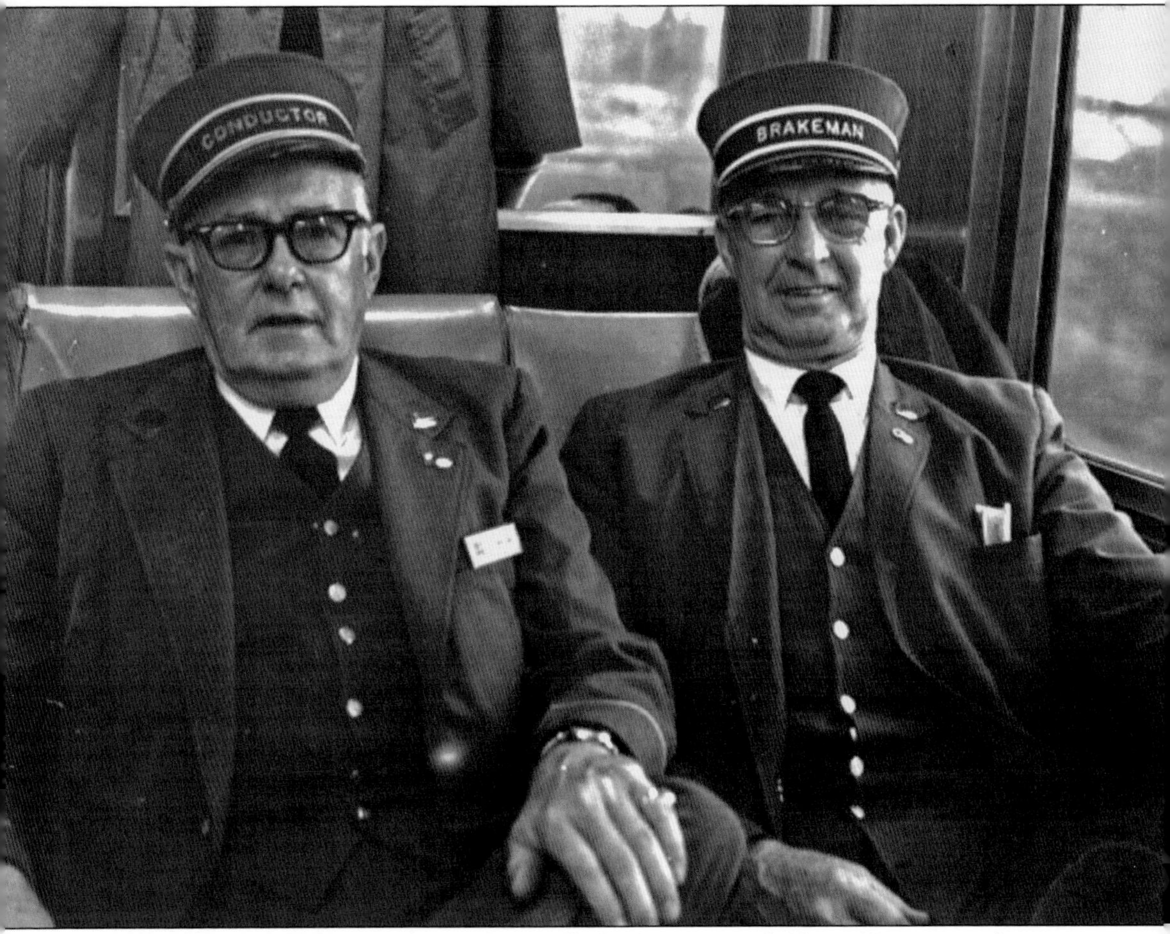

Jack Moberg, brakeman on the *Southern Belle* for 39 years, and Glenn Watson, conductor, are seated on the last train. Said Watson, "I saw people born and people die on this train, happy reunions and sad ones. I worked through three wars. I've taken young men to war and brought them home in the baggage car with a military escort." (Courtesy Joplin Public Library.)

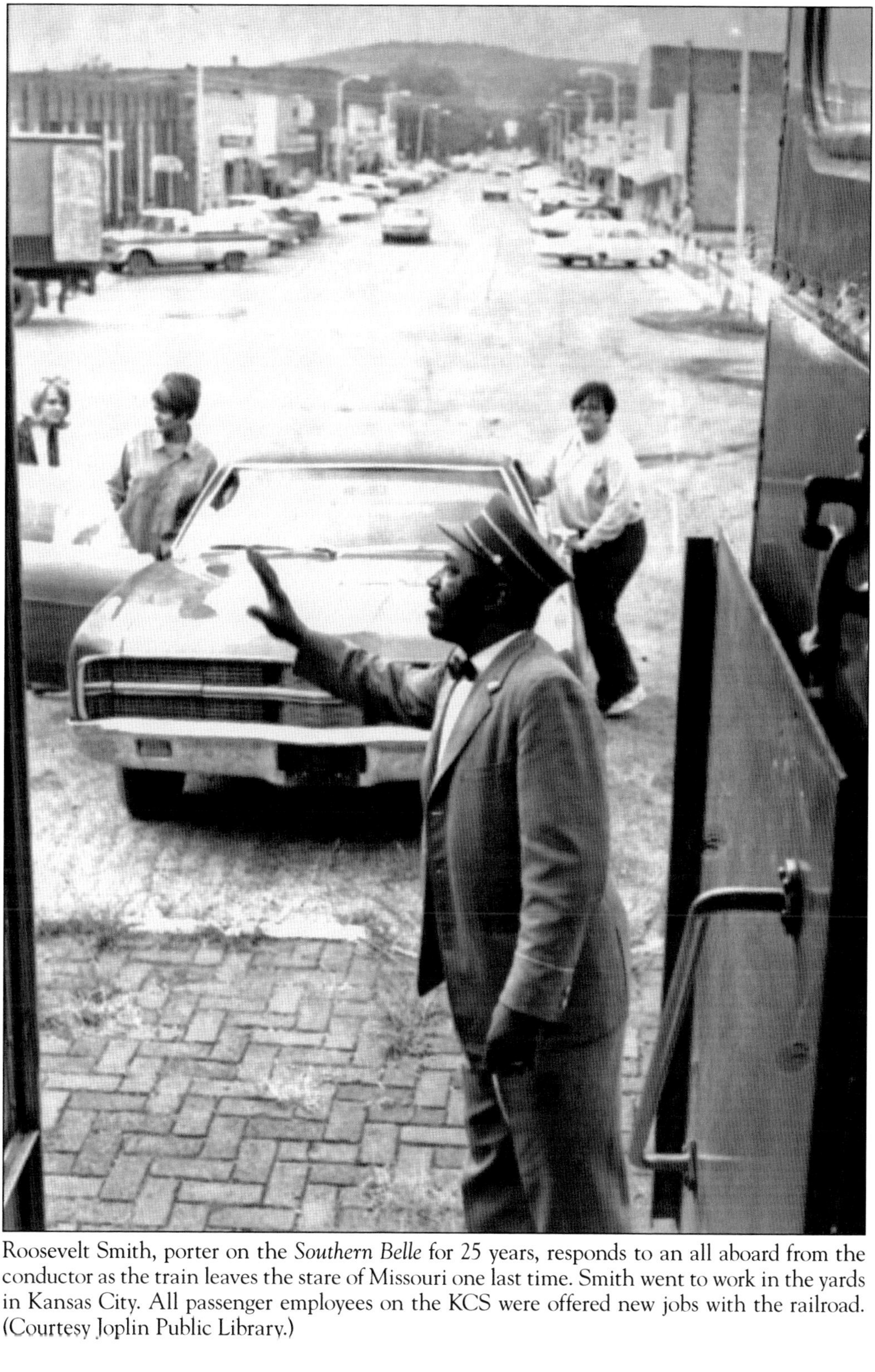

Roosevelt Smith, porter on the *Southern Belle* for 25 years, responds to an all aboard from the conductor as the train leaves the stare of Missouri one last time. Smith went to work in the yards in Kansas City. All passenger employees on the KCS were offered new jobs with the railroad. (Courtesy Joplin Public Library.)

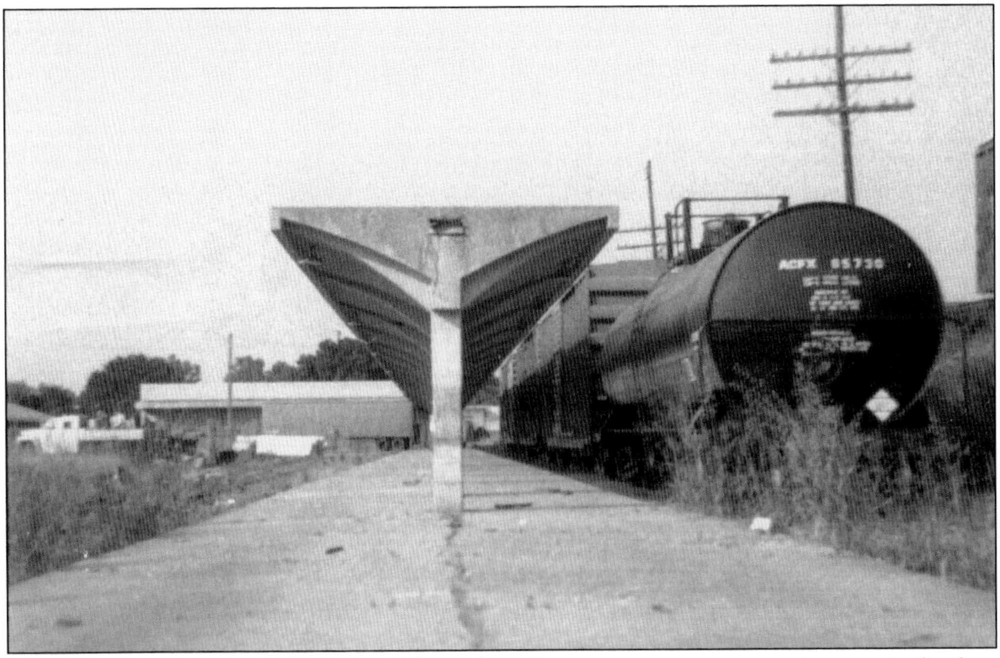

Here is all that remained of the Alexandria, Louisiana, passenger train terminal when photographed in the early 1980s. These shelters were once used by passengers who boarded the *Southern Belle* on their way to New Orleans or Kansas City. The tracks are being used to store freight cars in the absence of passenger service. (Courtesy Belinda S. Carter.)

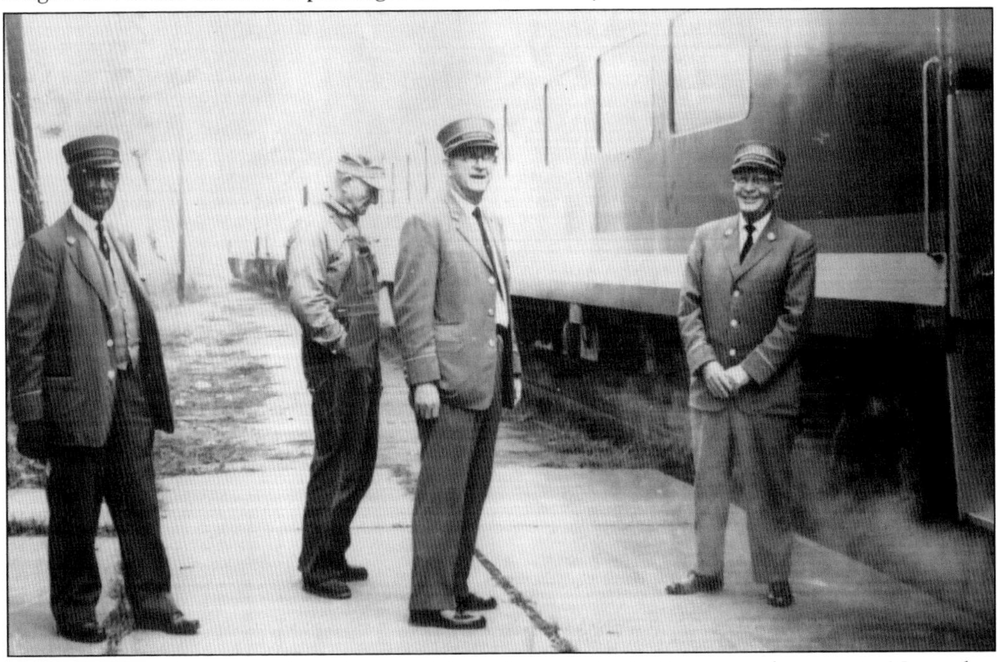

Shown here is the crew of the last northbound No. 2 in DeQueen, Arkansas, in November 1969. From left to right are porter Lucien Stewart, carman Peck Brooks, conductor R. E. Poco Meredith, and brakeman Jim Bales. Telegrapher John Graig was on hand to capture the crew's expressions as an era comes to an end. (Courtesy Philip L. Moseley.)

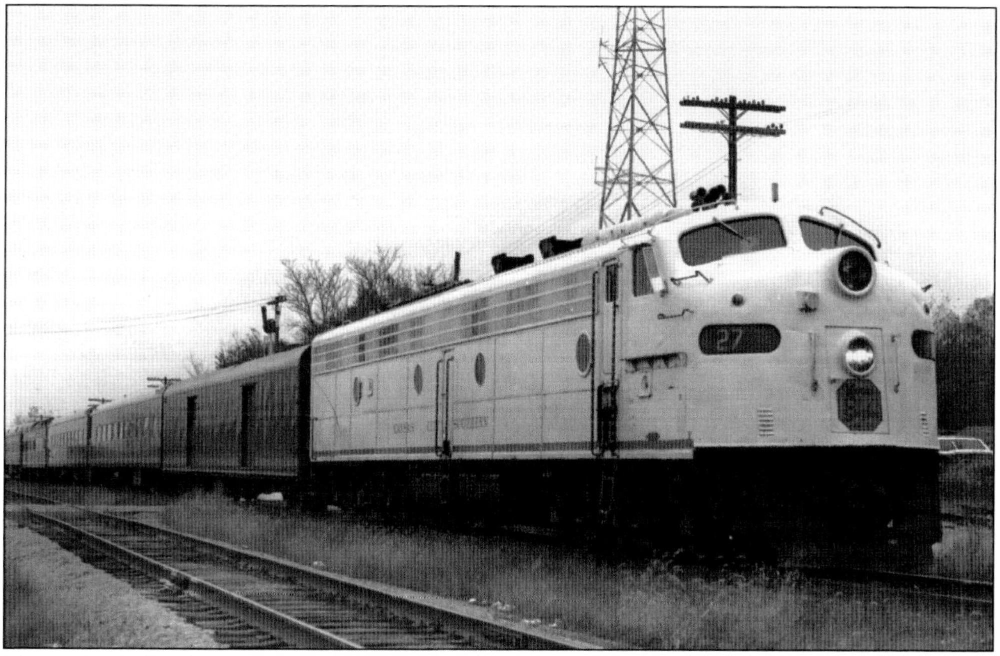

Train No. 1, the *Southern Belle*, passes Grandview, Missouri, for the last time on November 2, 1969, as passenger service on the KCS comes to a close. The last car is an official car occupied by R. J. Blair, an officer of the line. (Courtesy Harold K. Vollrath.)

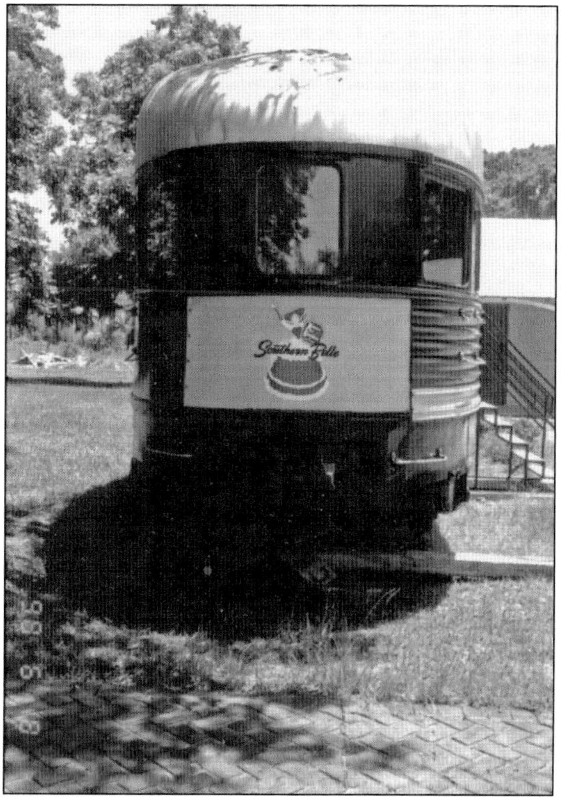

This symbol of the end of an era, a former KCS passenger car, is now a restaurant in Jackson, Louisiana. (Courtesy John Reed.)

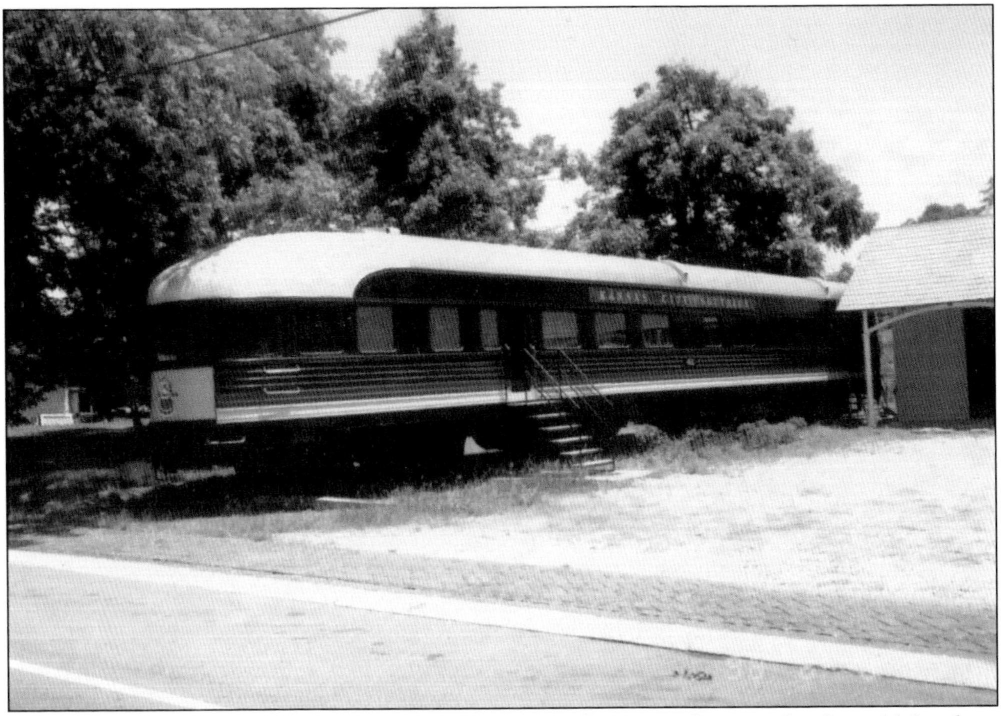

Ready for business, but only as a stationary restaurant, here is a photograph of an old *Southern Belle* observation car. (Courtesy John Reed.)

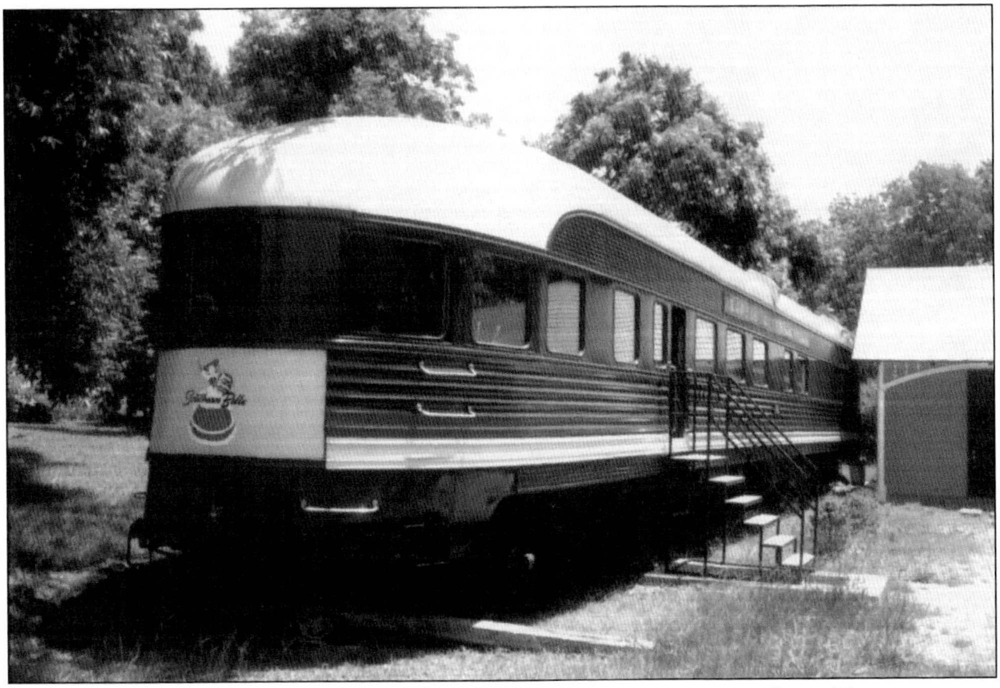

Notice the door open for business even though the train is not going anywhere. Hungry patrons will soon be arriving for dinner at this snack car-turned-restaurant in Jackson, Louisiana. (Courtesy John Reed.)

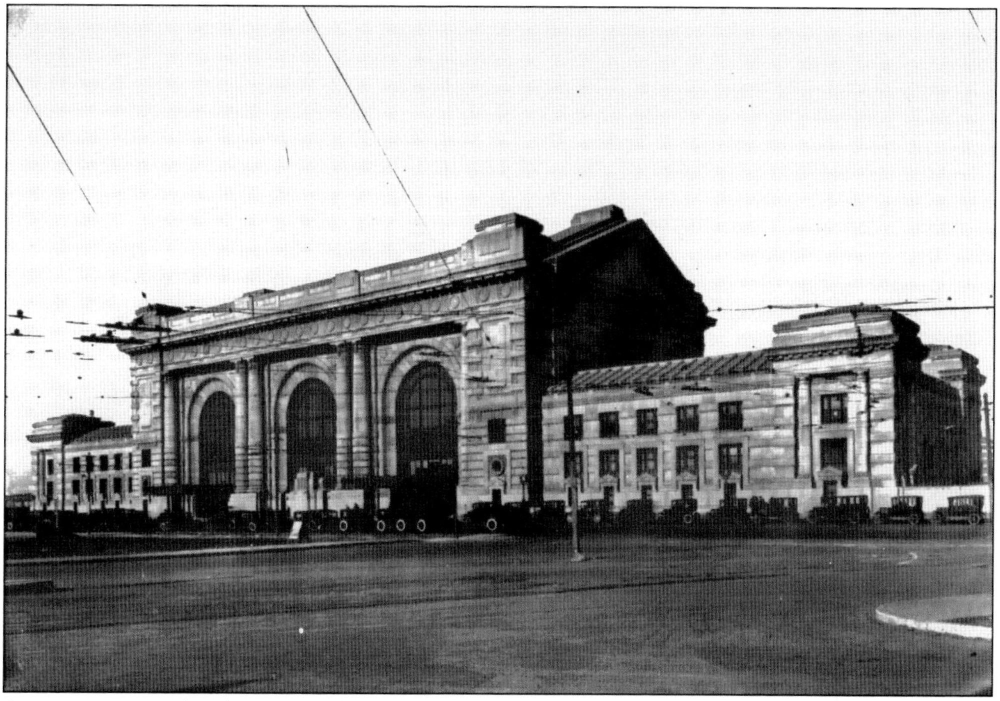

A masterpiece of architectural design, Kansas City Union Station in Missouri once serviced hundreds of daily trains from limiteds to doodlebugs. When Amtrak began operating in 1971, the station was down to a handful of trains each day. Today the station is renovated and Amtrak has a ticket office inside the building. The Fred Harvey House has even been reopened. (Courtesy Harold K. Vollrath.)

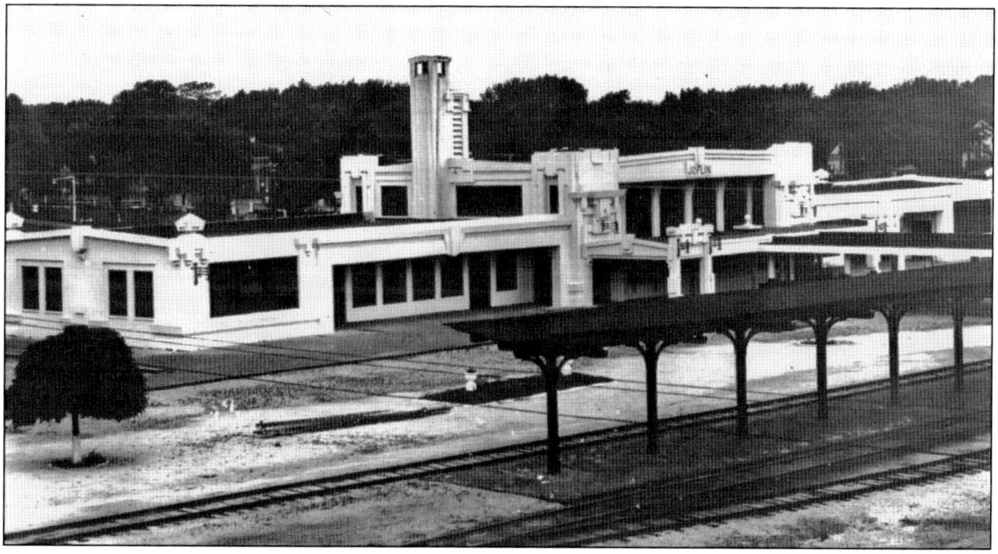

Joplin, Missouri, once boasted three passenger terminals: the Missouri Pacific Railroad terminal, the St. Louis and San Francisco Railroad (Frisco) stub-ended terminal, and this palace through which passengers of the KCS, the Katy, and the lesser Missouri and Arkansas Railroad booked passage. The year is 1917 as the stately structure stands awaiting its next arrival. (Courtesy Harold K. Vollrath.)

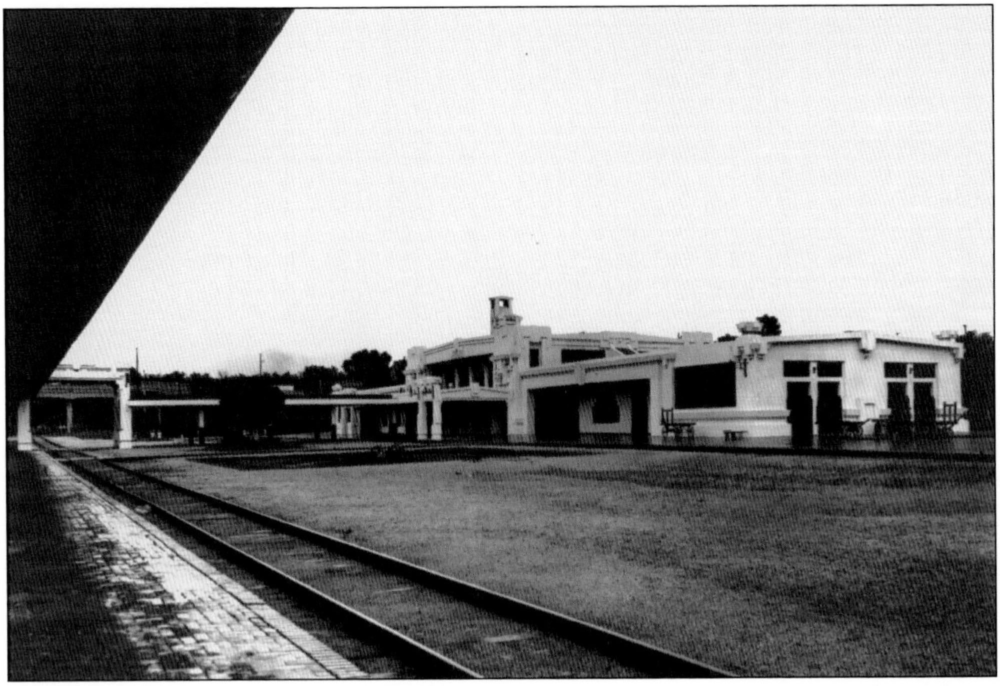

Every decent-size town was once accessible by passenger train. This impressive structure welcomed arriving and departing passengers at Joplin, Missouri. The union station awaits its next arrival in 1917. (Courtesy Harold K. Vollrath.)

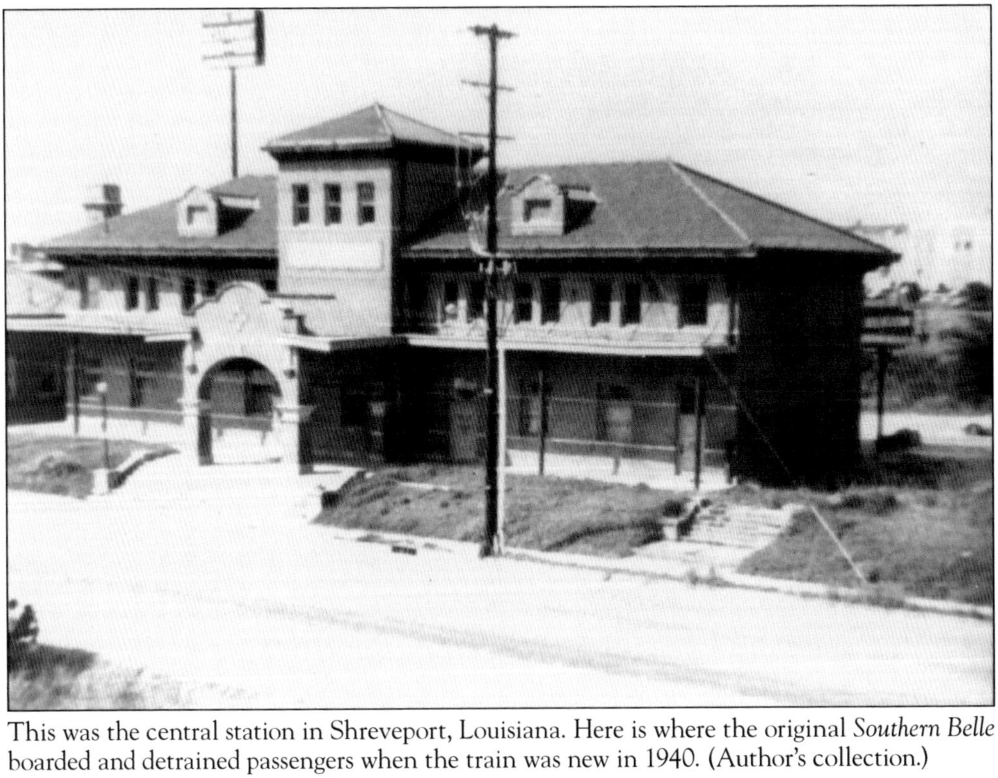

This was the central station in Shreveport, Louisiana. Here is where the original *Southern Belle* boarded and detrained passengers when the train was new in 1940. (Author's collection.)

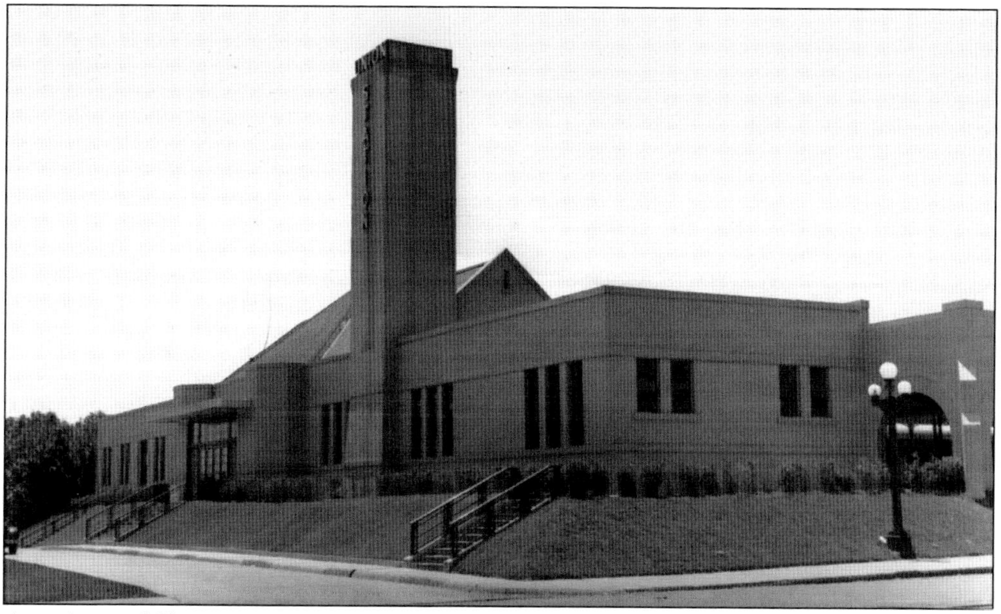

A modernized Shreveport Union Station was once home to the KCS, the L&A, and the Illinois Central Railroad. This photograph was taken in 1940, the year the streamlined *Southern Belle* debuted on the run from Kansas City to New Orleans. Service ended here in November 1969 with the last run of the *Southern Belle*. By coincidence, the building was destroyed by fire a few days later. (Courtesy Harold K. Vollrath.)

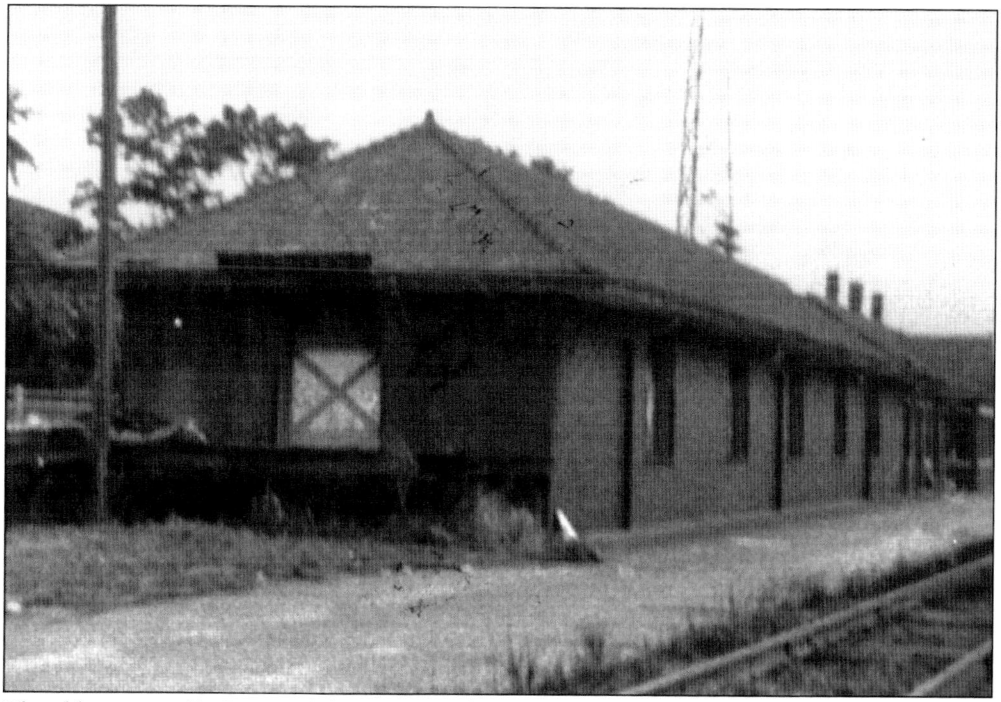

The old station at DeQueen, Arkansas, was photographed years after the last passenger train had gone through. The building was demolished not long after this photograph was taken. (Courtesy Belinda S. Carter.)

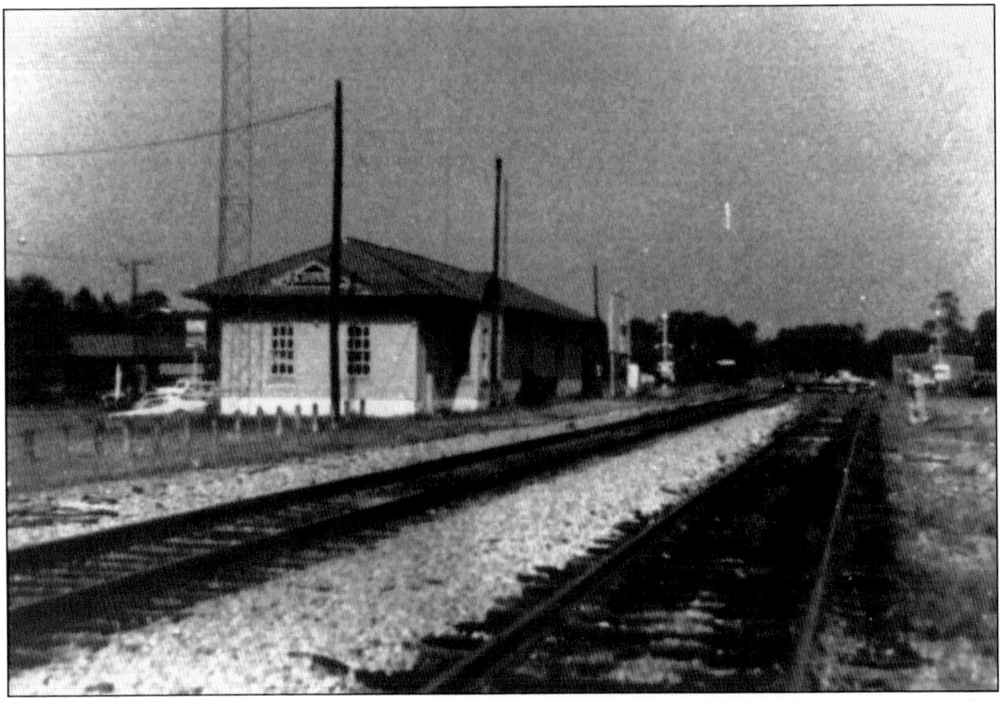

Once a stop for the *Shreveporter* on its trip to Port Arthur, Texas, here is the depot at Zwolle, Louisiana, shown sometime in the 1980s. (Courtesy Belinda S. Carter.)

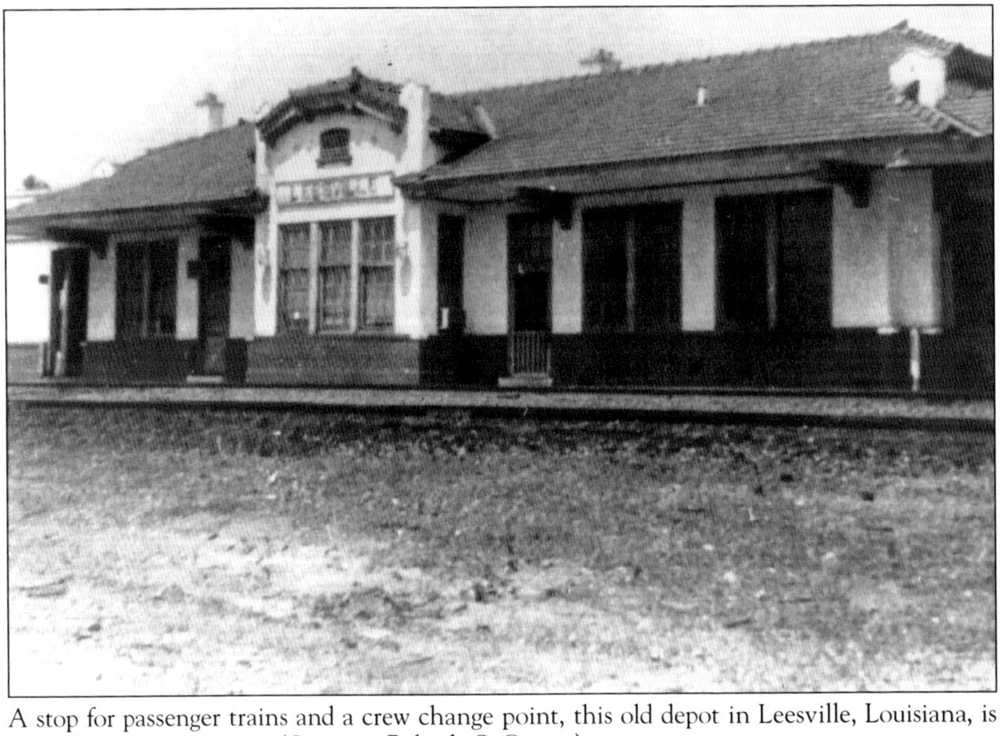

A stop for passenger trains and a crew change point, this old depot in Leesville, Louisiana, is today home to a museum. (Courtesy Belinda S. Carter.)

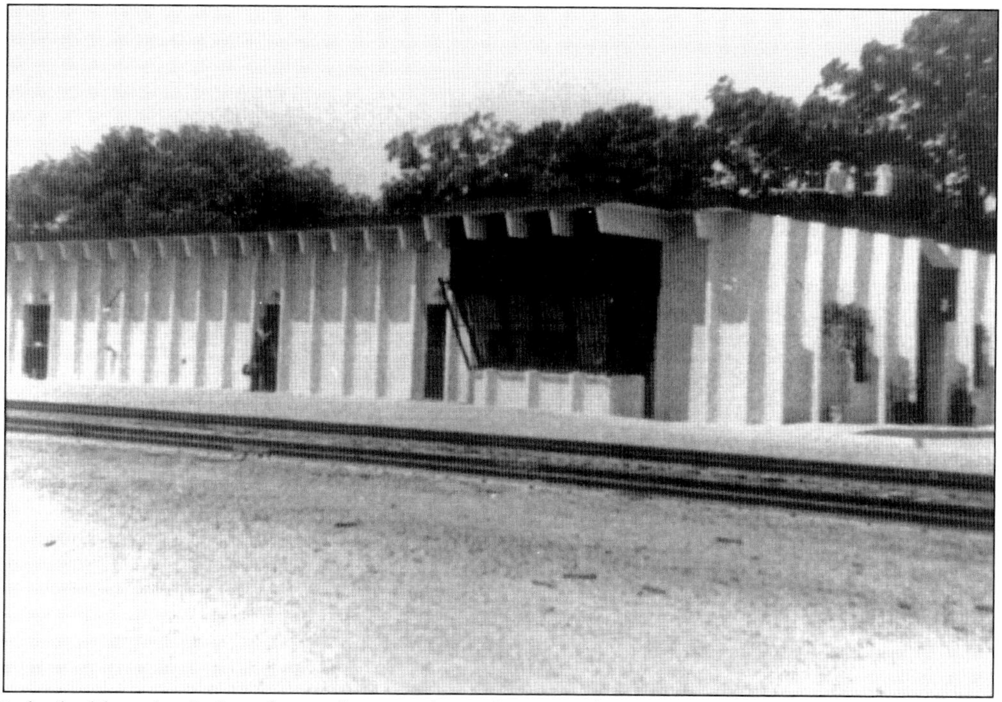

It looks like a bank, but this is the new depot for crew change at Leesville, Louisiana. The old depot houses a museum. (Courtesy Belinda S. Carter.)

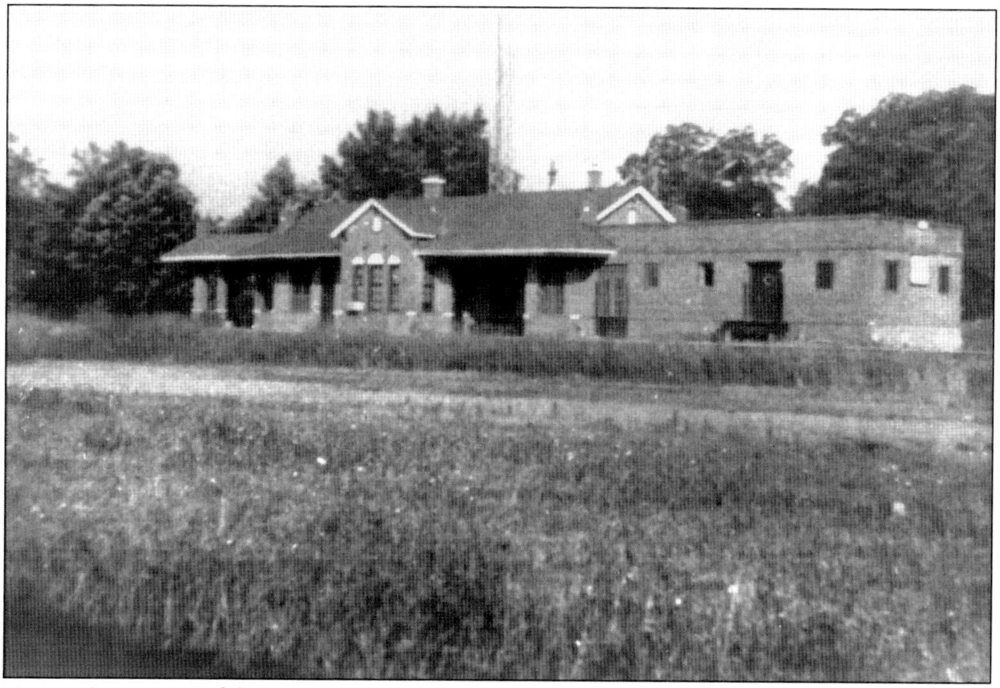

Here is the station at Mansfield, Louisiana, after passenger train service ended. The depot served for some years as a senior center. (Courtesy Belinda S. Carter.)

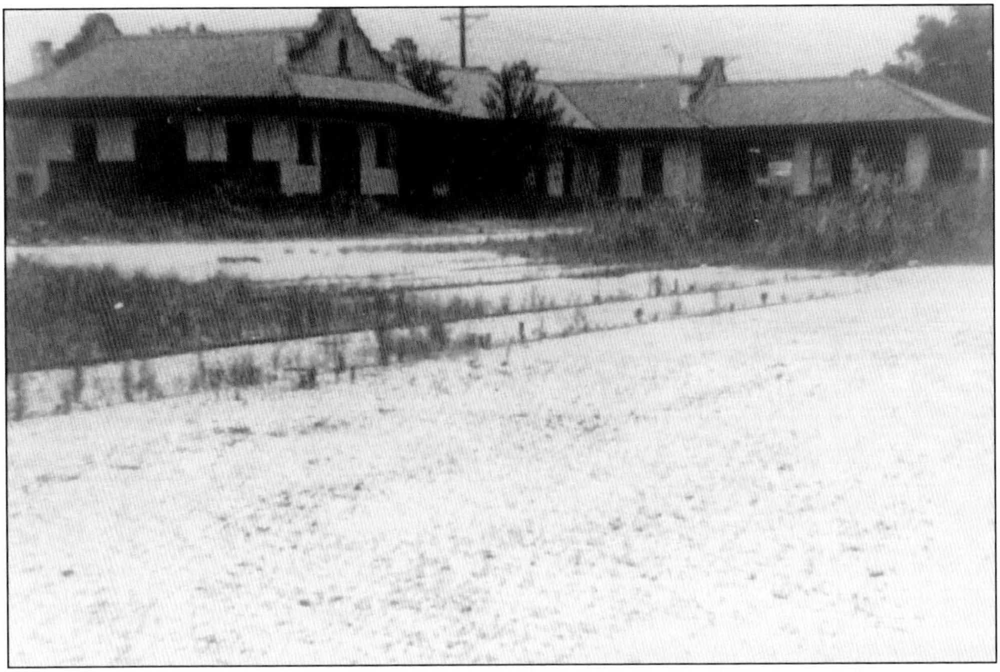

The KCS depot in Lake Charles, Louisiana, is seen here. During the 1940s, branch line passenger train service was provided to DeQuincy, Louisiana, where a connection could be made for travel to Kansas City. After the train was discontinued, buses provided daily service to DeQuincy. (Author's collection.)

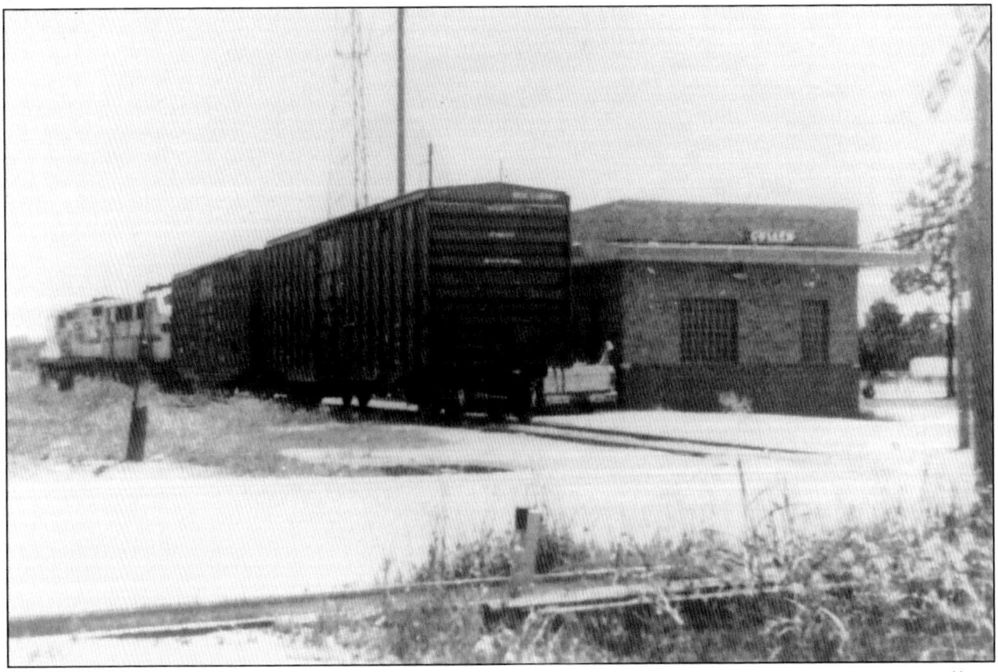

Here the local freight train provides less-than-carload lot freight service to patrons at Cullen, Louisiana. The author observed appliances being unloaded from the boxcar on the day of this photograph in 1982. (Courtesy Belinda S. Carter.)

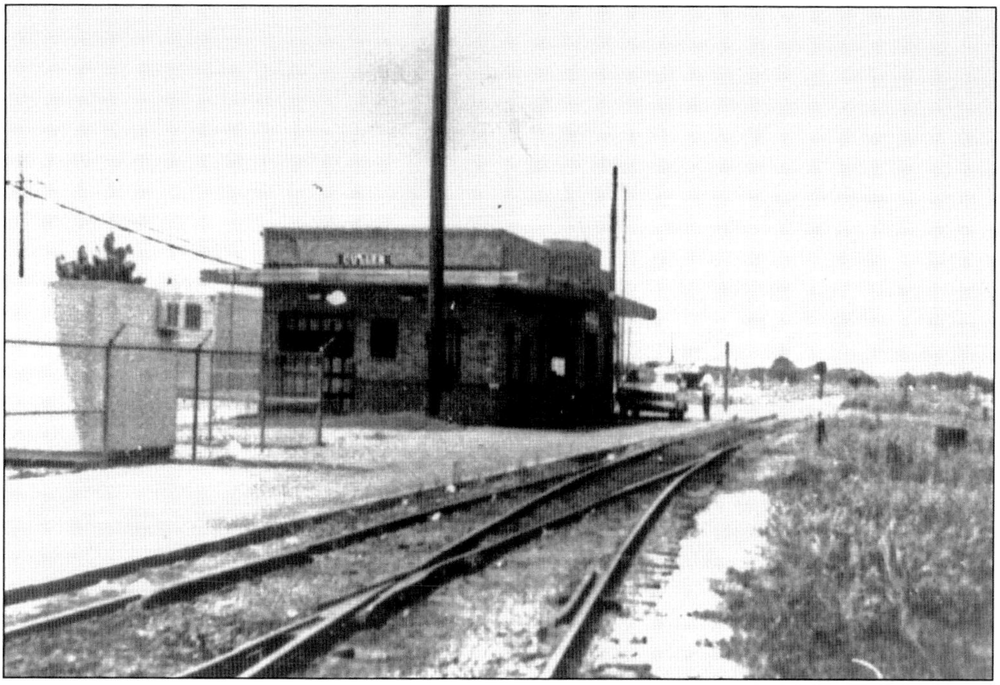

Here is another look at the Cullen station in 1982. Obviously not the original depot, this one had been constructed when the line was busier than today. (Courtesy Belinda S. Carter.)

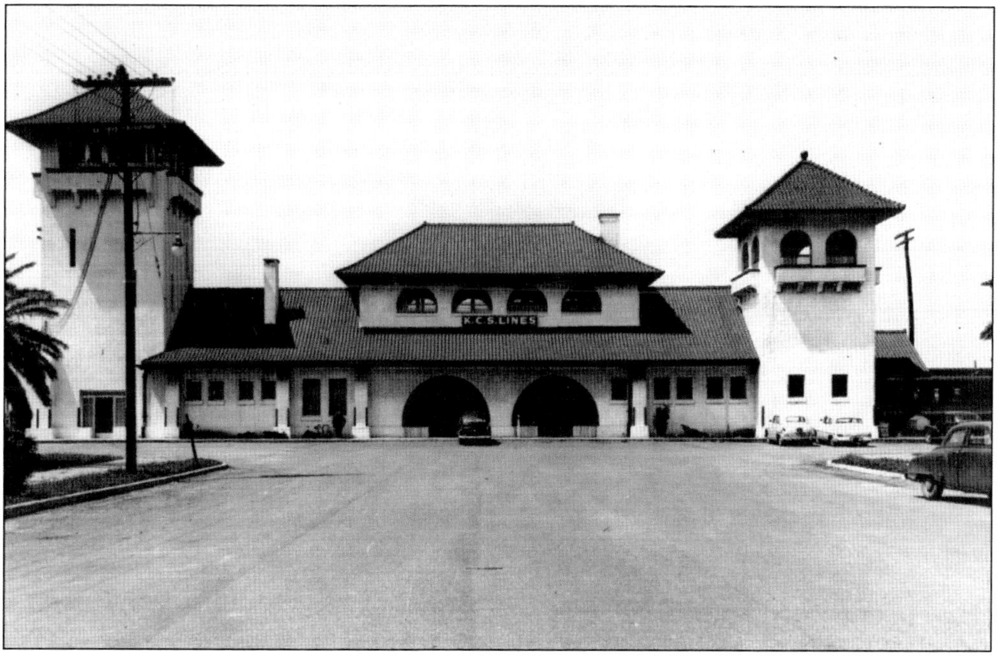

Once the southernmost arrival point of the KCS, this impressive structure at Port Arthur, Texas, saw multiple daily runs toward Kansas City. The town named after Arthur Stilwell was chosen as a destination point over Galveston, Texas, after Stilwell claimed he had a dream advising him not to build the railroad to Galveston. A short time later, Galveston was destroyed by a hurricane. (Courtesy Harold K. Vollrath.)

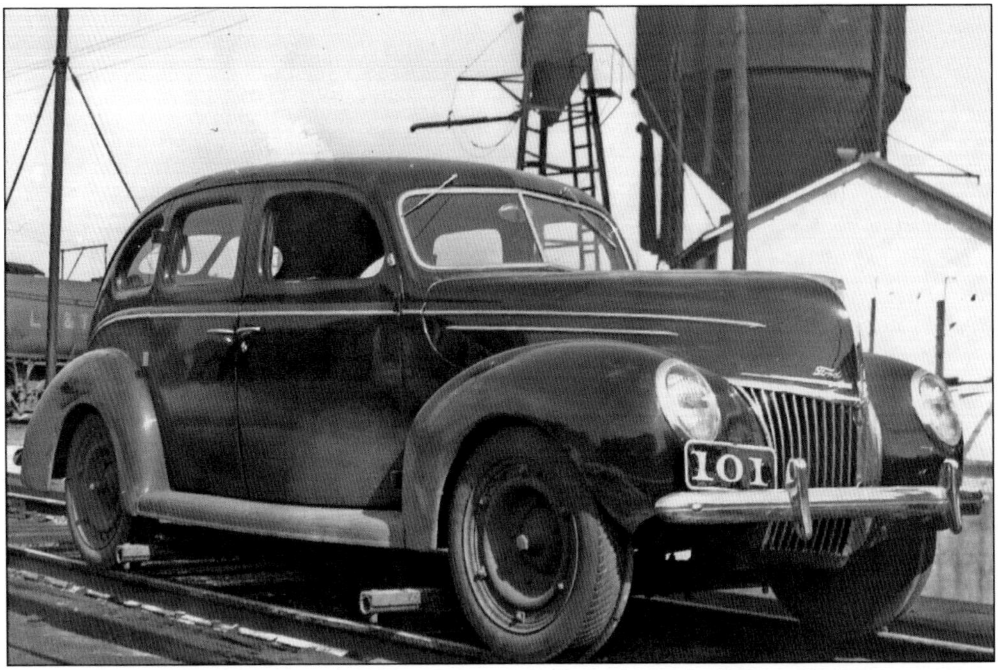

Once upon a time, inspecting the high iron was done from the end of brass-rail observation cars. Every superintendent was afforded such a conveyance. Also used for inspecting roadbed was an automobile attached to flanged wheels. An example, in the form of a 1939 Ford, is seen resting between assignments at Shreveport, Louisiana. (Courtesy Harold K. Vollrath.)

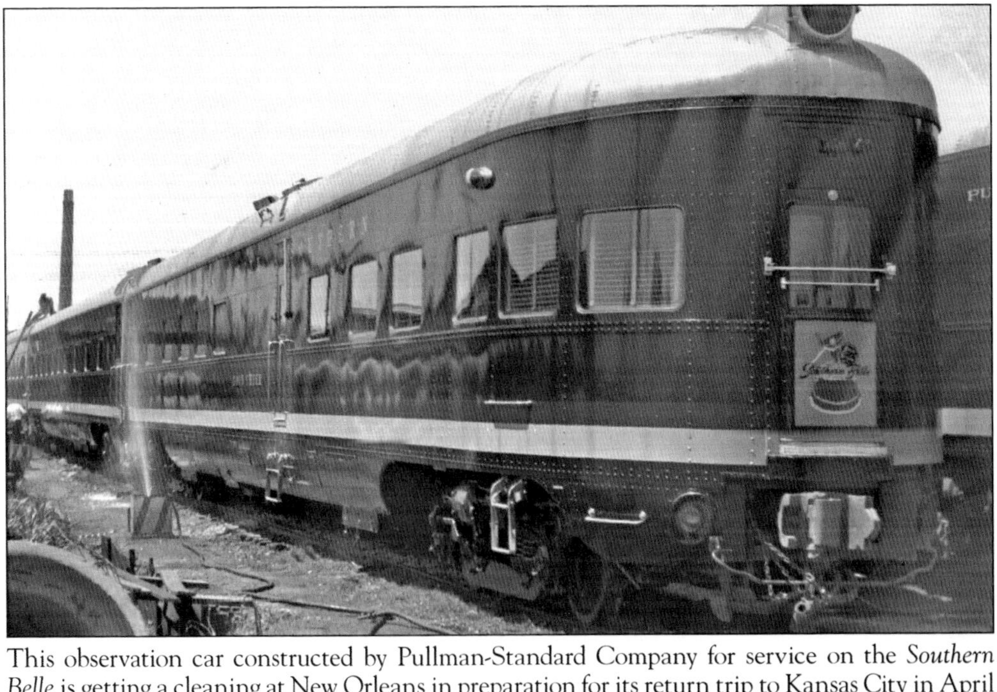

This observation car constructed by Pullman-Standard Company for service on the *Southern Belle* is getting a cleaning at New Orleans in preparation for its return trip to Kansas City in April 1949. By the time the author was riding the *Good Cheer* in 1964, it was operating on the tail end of the local from Shreveport, Louisiana, to Port Arthur, Texas. (Courtesy Harold K. Vollrath.)

Two veterans of the KCS say farewell to DeQueen, Arkansas, in 1969 as the *Southern Belle* leaves town for the last time. Philip L. Moseley was a station agent and recorded the story of the train's last run. Note car No. 270 was one of the recently purchased coaches the KCS bought shortly before deciding to get out of the passenger business. (Courtesy Philip L. Moseley.)

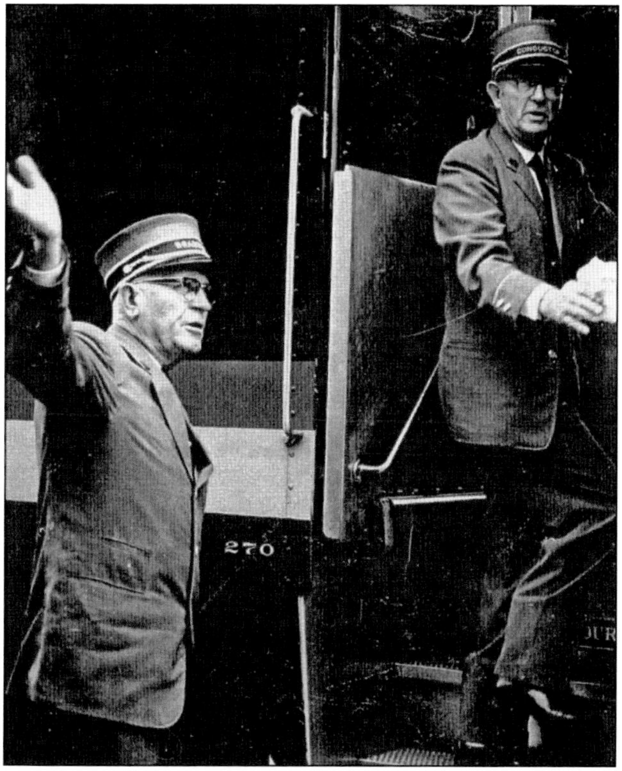

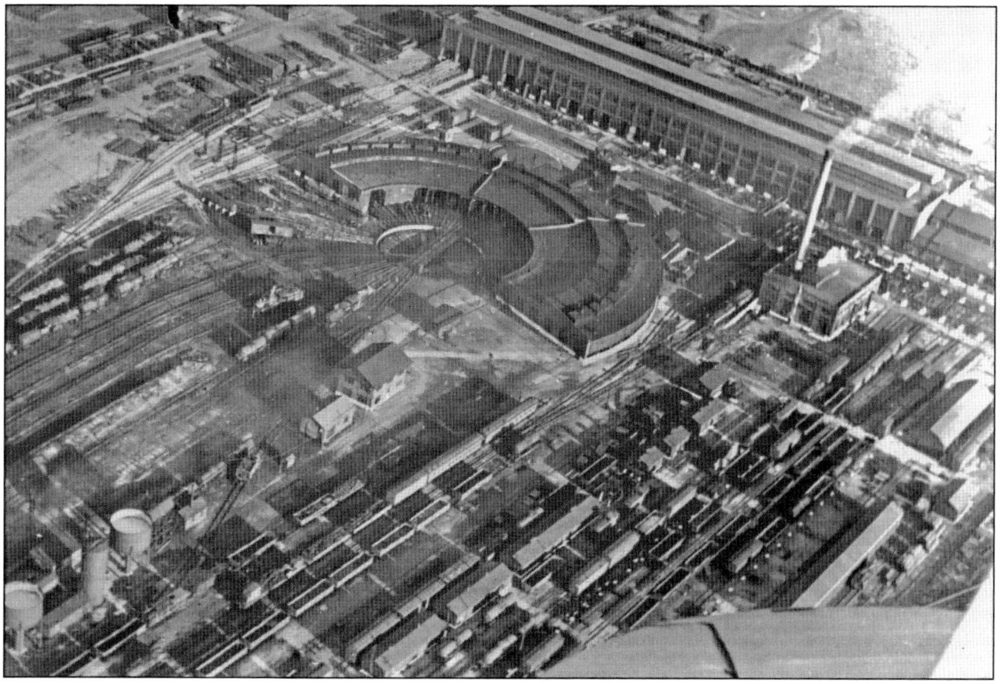

At one time, Pittsburg, Kansas, was a major stopping point on the KCS. Facilities included shops, a roundhouse, and a freight yard. This scene, taken at the close of World War II, shows the railroad hard at work. (Courtesy Harold K. Vollrath.)

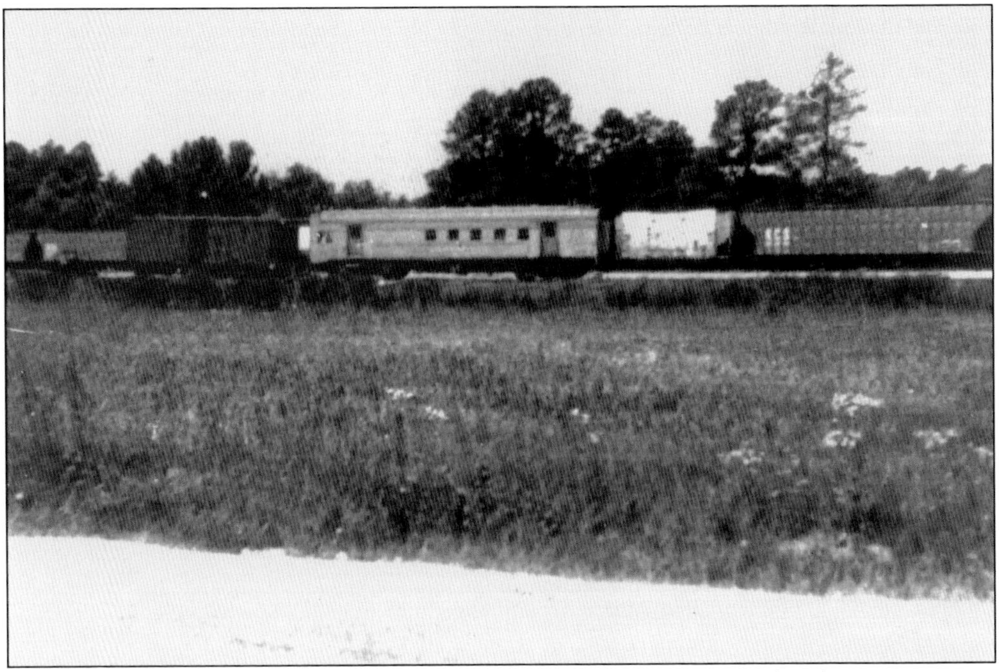

This former RPO car is shown in the yard at Leesville, Louisiana. It has been years since the RPO saw service as a mail carrier. It may be used in work train service now. (Courtesy Belinda S. Carter.)

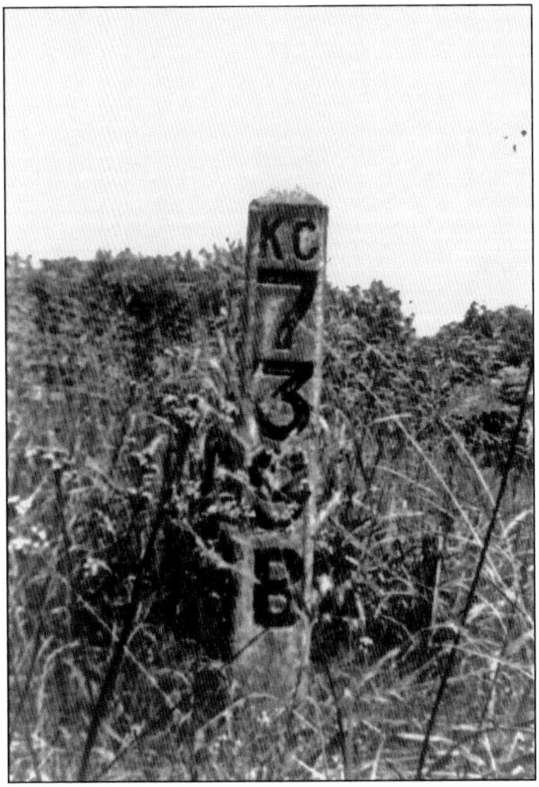

This milepost at West Lake, Louisiana, is one of many markers that showed the mileage to Kansas City. Track had been abandoned at West Lake with the KCS using Southern Pacific Railroad right-of-way into Lake Charles, Louisiana. (Courtesy Belinda S. Carter.)

Passenger Train Service Ends Here With Last Run of "Belle"

By RON BONGUE,
Joplin, Globe Reporter

The Southern Belle made its final run Monday.

For many persons who made the trip on the Kansas City Southern Lines passenger train, it was a nostalgic event, bringing back memories of days gone by.

For others, it was an exciting trip that will provide memories in later years. The retirement of the Southern Belle left most cities on its route between Kansas City and New Orleans without passenger train service.

For those in this area, the Southern Belle's final run marked the end of an era. Elderly men who remembered the birth of passenger train service in this area and young children who had never been on a train before, were among the passengers riding the memory rails Monday.

The sound of the train's warning bell at the grade crossings faded quickly as passengers on one of the cars recalled the early days of the railroad. The Kansas City Southern had its beginning in 1887 when a wealthy Indian, Mathias Split-log - living in McDonald county just west of Goodman – conceived the idea of building a railway from North Arkansas to Kansas City.

The line was first built from the Cowskin River in McDonald county to Joplin and formally opened on January 1, 1889. The name of the road was changed later to Pittsburg and Gulf. The line was completed in 1897 and the Kansas City and the Pittsburg and Gulf lines merged to form the Kansas City Southern.

But the Kansas City Southern was not the first railroad to serve the Joplin area. The first was the Joplin and Girard Railway, started in December, 1865, by Moffett and Sergeant who organized the Joplin Railway Company.

Joplin's era as a rail center began on November 2, 1876, when the Frisco bought a portion of the Atlantic and Pacific Railroad Company known then as the Missouri division.

Three years later, Frisco purchased the Joplin and Girard Railroad Company. By 1908 there were five daily passenger trains in and out of Joplin on the east-west run.

The Frisco discontinued its last passenger train through Neosho and Southwest Missouri in May, 1967. In May, 1968, two other Kansas City Southern trains, numbers 15-9 and 10-6 – The Flying Crow-were

This article originally appeared in the *Joplin Globe* and is reprinted here with permission. (Courtesy Joplin Globe.)

discontinued. The trains operated through between Kansas City and Shreveport, La.

Ding, ding, ding, the sound of the warning bell hadn't changed much in the years the trains had been plying the tracks.

A 79-year-old Oklahoma man who rode the first Kansas City Southern passenger train in eastern Oklahoma, drove 20 miles from his home in Marble City to Sallisaw Monday to ride the last passenger train on the line.

Watie Davault, a retired merchant, rode the train as far as Stilwell, Okla., a trip of 31miles. "When I was five years old, I made the first trip which was from Gans to Redland in Indian Territory. My mother dressed me for the occasion," he said of the childhood ride. "A friend picked me up at the Redland station and kept me all day. Then he sent me back when the train returned that night."

A native of Sequoyah county, Davault said he has never lived more than 700 feet from the railroad tracks. "I haven't ridden a train in 25 years," Davault said while waiting for the Southern Belle at the Sallisaw depot. "But I rode the first one and I want to ride the last one."

Also boarding the train at the Sallisaw depot and departing at Stilwell were Mrs. Darrell Martin and her 19-month-old son, Darren, both of Sallisaw. It was the first train ride for young Darren who didn't seem too excited about the historical event.

"We never rode the train very much," Mrs. Martin said. "Now I think we will regret not riding the train more when we had the opportunity."

Back in the lounge car, Mrs. Frances Tewell of Girard, Kan., was enjoying a hamburger with her grandson, Timmy Joe Tewell, 2, who was making his first train trip. Mrs. Tewell, who has made six round trips to Shreveport, La., within the last year, said she packed until midnight last Tuesday after hearing about the Southern Belle being discontinued.

I grew up riding this train and I hate to see it go," she said. "I wanted to make one last trip.

Mrs. Tewell took the Southern Belle to Shreveport Wednesday where she visited with relatives until catching the train Monday morning to return to her home. Her grandson made the trip with her.

W. H. Johnson of Kansas City, waiter in charge of the lounge car, wiped a smear of mustard off the counter of the snack bar, as the train passed through Westville, Okla.

An employee of Kansas City Southern since 1944, Johnson said he would be working in some capacity for the company but he didn't know what. "This is my job," he said, swinging his arm in an arc around the lounge car. "But now I will have to learn something new.

"I don't think this is the end. I think they will bring the passenger

The first *Southern Belle* left the Kansas City Union Station on a publicity tour on August 23, 1940. (Courtesy Joplin Globe.)

trains back some day. I still think there is a place in our economy for the railroad.

"When you get rid of the competition of low train fares, the price of bus fares in the area is going to go up."

The door to the vestibule swung open admitting the roar of the train and the muffled sound of the big diesel engine's whistle singing its goodbye warning at every grade crossing. The train crossed the state line into Arkansas and began to slow down for a scheduled stop at Siloam Springs.

Jack Moberg, Riverton, Kan., brakeman on the Belle for 40 years, sat down and ordered a cup of coffee. "I hate to see them go," he sighed. "Not for me, but for everyone else concerned. The area we served has inadequate bus service and it's going to be hard on a lot of people."

Moberg said he would go back to being brakeman on the freight trains after Monday's final run. The trip ended at Pittsburg for Moberg.

"Ya-hoo!" The shrill scream, must have startled the group of by-standers at the Gentry station who came down to wave goodbye to the Southern Belle.

"Ya-hoo!" Roosevelt Smith, porter, leaned out the window of the vestibule and cut loose with another loud war hoop as Decatur, Ark., flashed by the open window.

Smith, who lives in Kansas City, has been a porter on the Southern Belle for the past 25 years. Now he will go to work in the switching yards in Kansas City.

But Monday he was whooping it up. "I know someone at every station along the line," he said, rubbing his mustache. The train slowed down at Gravette and he leaned out the window again.

"Ya-hoo,,," Hise Green, 77, 2102, Pennsylvania Ave., was one of 157 persons who boarded the Southern Belle at Joplin Sunday for one last ride. He rode as far as Noel before getting off to return to Joplin.

"That was the biggest crowd I've seen since Christmas," MoBerg said. "They were standing in the aisles when we left Joplin."

But Green changed his mind and drove to Neosho Monday and rode the train back to Joplin. "I just had to ride it one more time." he explained.

Green, who obtained the autographs of all of the train crew members and some of the passengers, said he recalled his first train ride. "My father worked for the Missouri-Pacific, and we rode the train from St. Louis to Little Rock. Ark., over Iron mountain." Green said he was six years old at the time.

The tiny vestibule between the cars was filled with the grinding and groaning of metal wheels on the tracks, and the unending squeaks and squeals that have become as familiar to the railroad traveler as the conductors' cry of "ail board."

An event at the Neosho depot Monday brought tears to the eyes of

The final run of the *Southern Belle* came in 1969. (Courtesy Joplin Globe.)

Conductor Glenn Watson of Pittsburg.

A woman waiting on the platform called out his name, handed him a letter and a box containing a cake. The letter was from the woman's daughter, Nancy Jones, 112 North High street in Neosho.

In her letter, 13-year-old Nancy explained that she and a friend rode the train to Kansas City last summer and. that she remembered how nice the conductor had been to them. "My parents used to bring me down to the station and the engineer would wave at me," the letter read. "I just want to wish you happiness and thank you for the trips."

A conductor since 1941 and an employee of Kansas City Southern for 45 years, Watson said he would go back to conducting on Freight trains after Monday's final run.

The diesel motors on the big engine hummed their song of power and the Southern Belle crept slowly away from Joplin's Union station Monday afternoon.

The train picked up speed, bucked and dipped, swayed and rolled - seemingly straining to free itself from the iron rails that held it to the ground. The iron rails that were leading it back to Kansas City and retirement.

As this article shows, the *Southern Belle* left countless people with wonderful memories. (Courtesy Joplin Globe.)

Six

The Kansas City Southern after Passenger Service

With the last run of the *Southern Belle* in November 1969, the KCS found itself in the ranks of freight-only carriers like the Frisco. With Thomas S. Carter assuming the job of KCS president in 1973, the line began a massive program of rebuilding the right-of-way. Some $75 million was allocated for new ballast, ties, and ribbon rail. This would make it possible for the railroad to begin operating unit coal trains starting in 1976.

The unit coal trains proved to be a financial success for the railroad with revenue figures of $22.2 million generated by 1978.

Acting on the North American Free Trade Agreement (NAFTA) in 1995, the KCS decided to become a major carrier of north–south traffic. Forty-nine percent of Mexrail, the parent company of Texas Mexican Railway from Laredo to Corpus Christi in Texas, was purchased. In 1995, the KCS partnered with Transportación Marítima Mexicana to win the concession for operating rights from Mexico City to Laredo. When the concession was awarded in 1997, it was possible to run trains from Mexico City to Kansas City. In 2005, KCS acquired Transportación Marítima Mexicana interest. KCS also acquired the remaining 51 percent of Mexrail that same year. The Mexican subsidiary is now called Kansas City Southern de Mexico.

In 1996, Gateway Western Railway was purchased to provide access to East St. Louis, Illinois, and northeastern cities via Conrail. I&M Rail Link and the KCS entered into a marketing agreement, giving the railroad entry into Chicago and Minneapolis, an alliance that has persisted through several mergers affecting KSC's northern connection.

What was a regional railroad a quarter century ago is now a rail network. The railway hauls bulk commodities and continues to serve the various industries along its lines. Piggyback, coal, and general merchandise trains powered by modern computerized diesel units operate over ribbon rail on schedules that accommodate shippers and their customers.

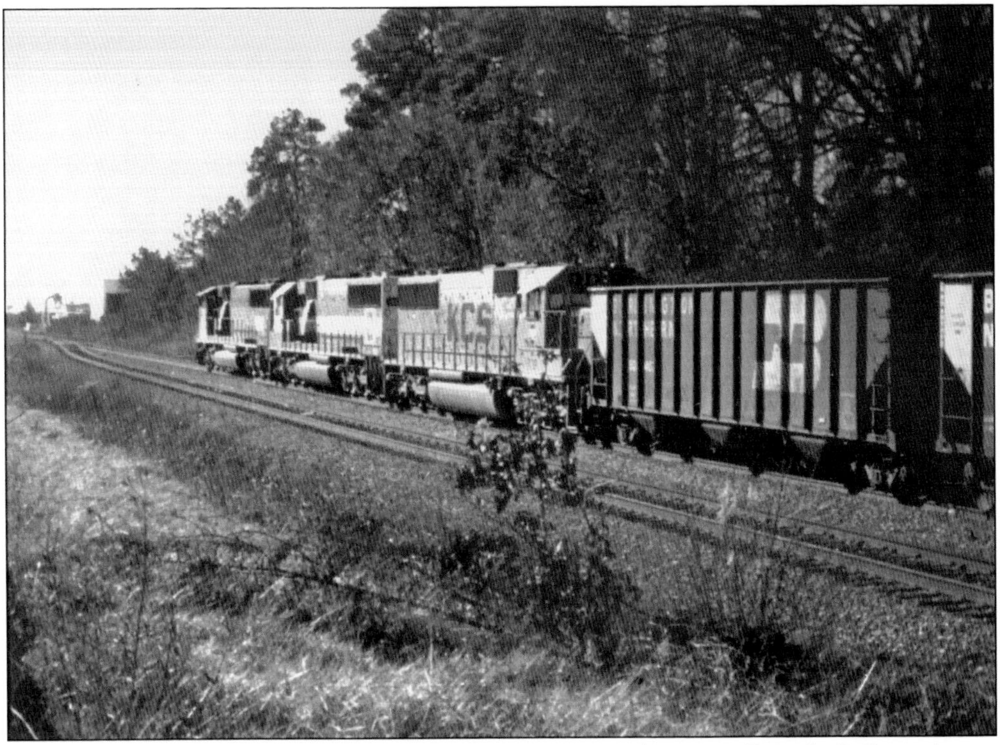

A southbound KCS coal train leaves Shreveport, Louisiana. (Courtesy Belinda S. Carter.)

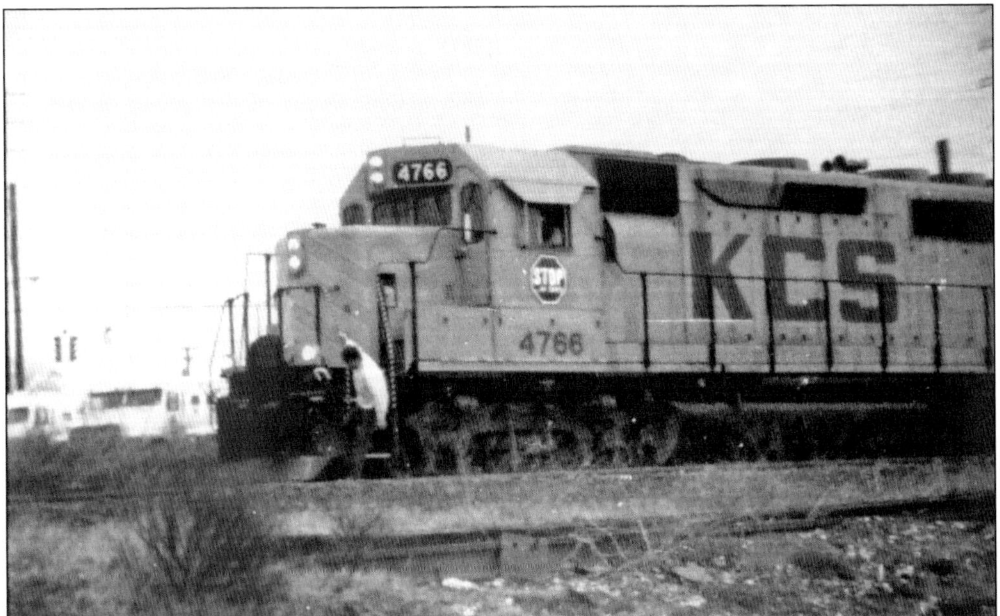

A KCS employee steps down from the lead locomotive to throw a switch at Shreveport. Notice the stop sign on the locomotive, which was an increased effort to get drivers to pay attention to passing trains. (Courtesy Belinda S. Carter.)

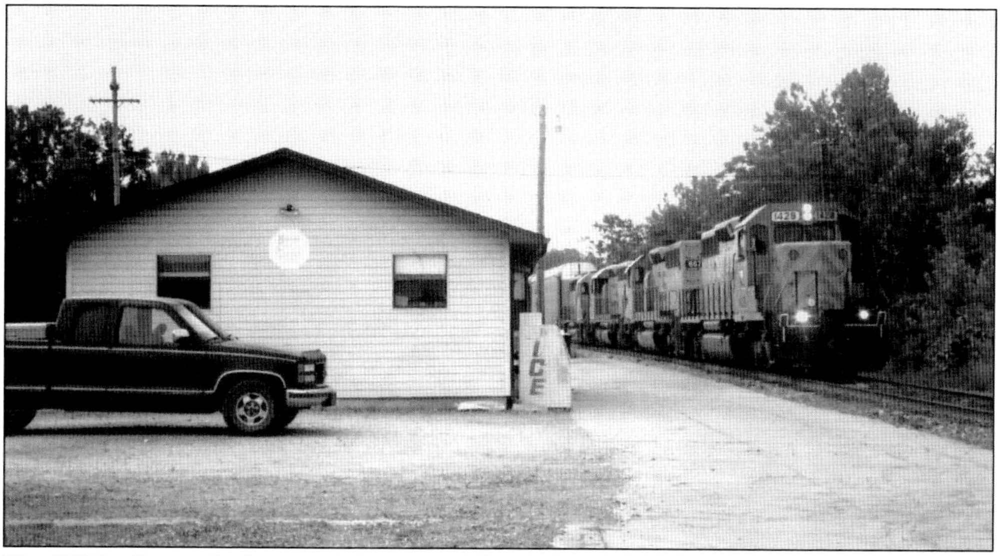

The KCS office in DeQueen, Arkansas, is adjacent to the platform that was part of the old passenger station. On a hot August afternoon, a four-unit freight powered by SD40-2 No. 1428 awaits instructions on proceeding to Shreveport. Thirty-three years prior to this photograph, DeQueen was still a regular daily stop for the *Southern Belle*. (Courtesy Belinda S. Carter.)

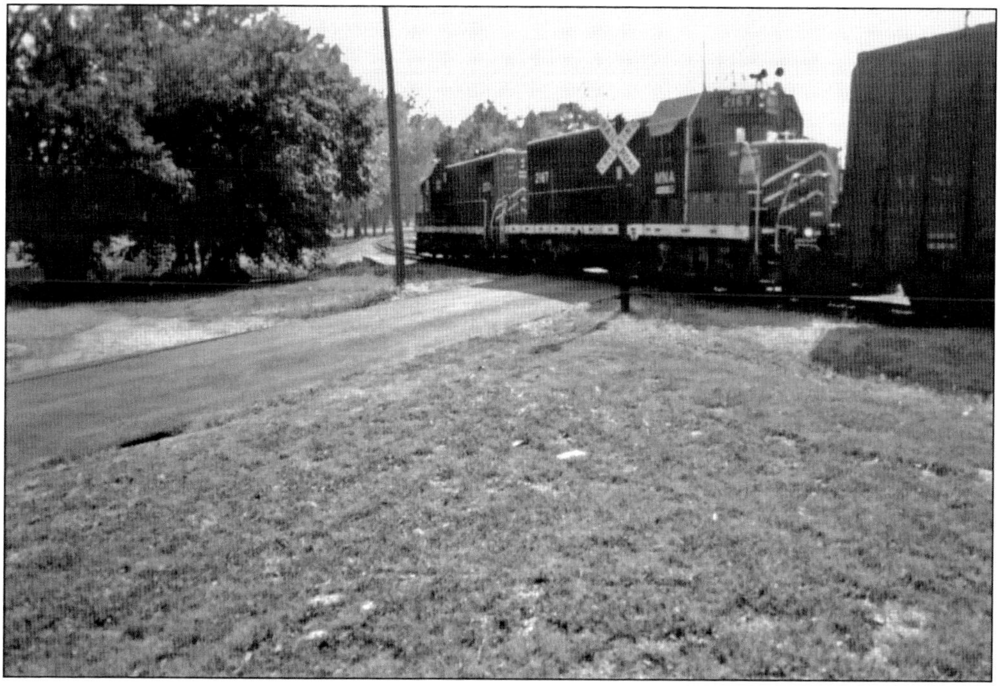

Two locomotives of the Missouri and North Arkansas Railroad (M&NA) deliver freight to Joplin, Missouri. Here the M&NA connected with the main line of the KCS. These locomotives were formerly used by the Santa Fe Railroad until being rebuilt and put into freight service. (Courtesy Belinda S. Carter.)

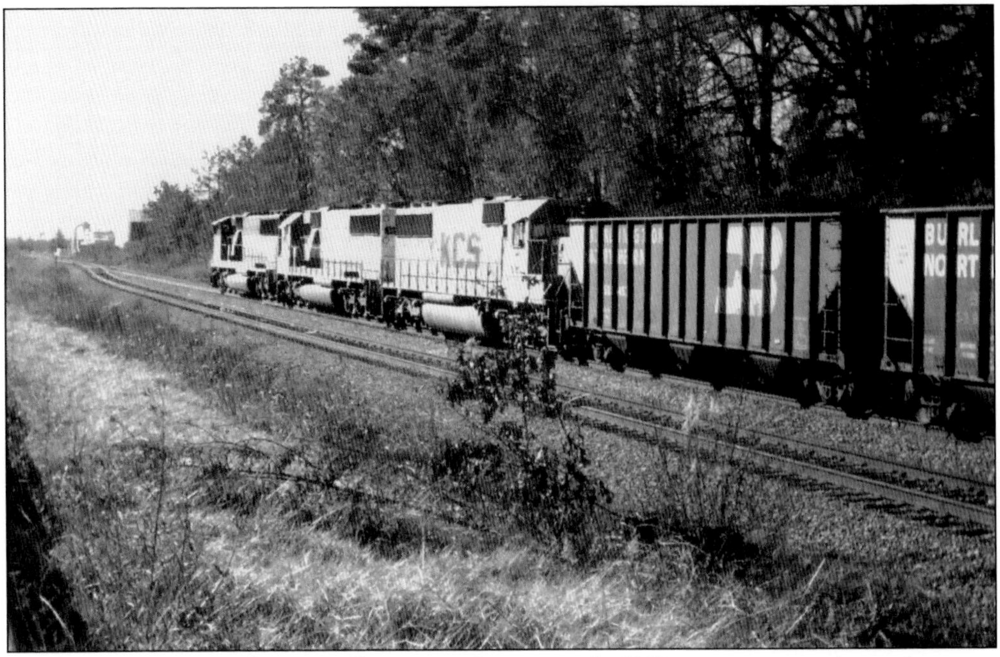

EMD units power a coal train at Shreveport, Louisiana. In 1993, an increasing share of revenue was derived from coal trains on the KCS. Newer power, such as SD60s and SD70s, was able to handle more tonnage. (Author's collection.)

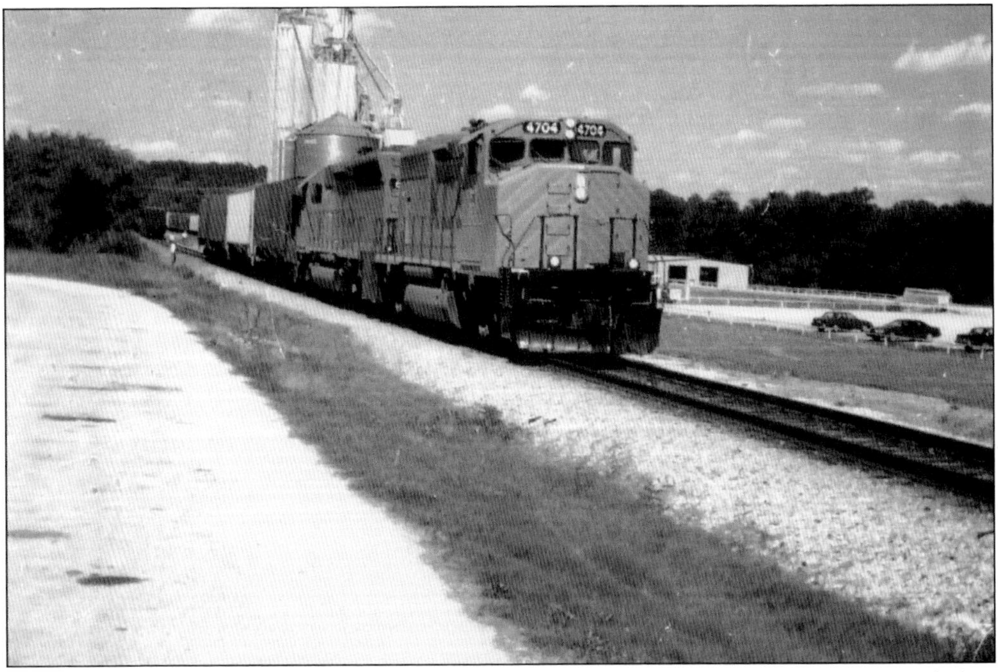

A diesel bought from the Canadian National Railway and repainted in KCS colors is coupled up with an SD45 at Anderson, Missouri, in 1998. The KCS was no stranger to secondhand power, having purchased passenger units from the Maine Central Railroad in the 1960s and GP units from the Illinois Central Railroad in the 1980s. (Author's collection.)

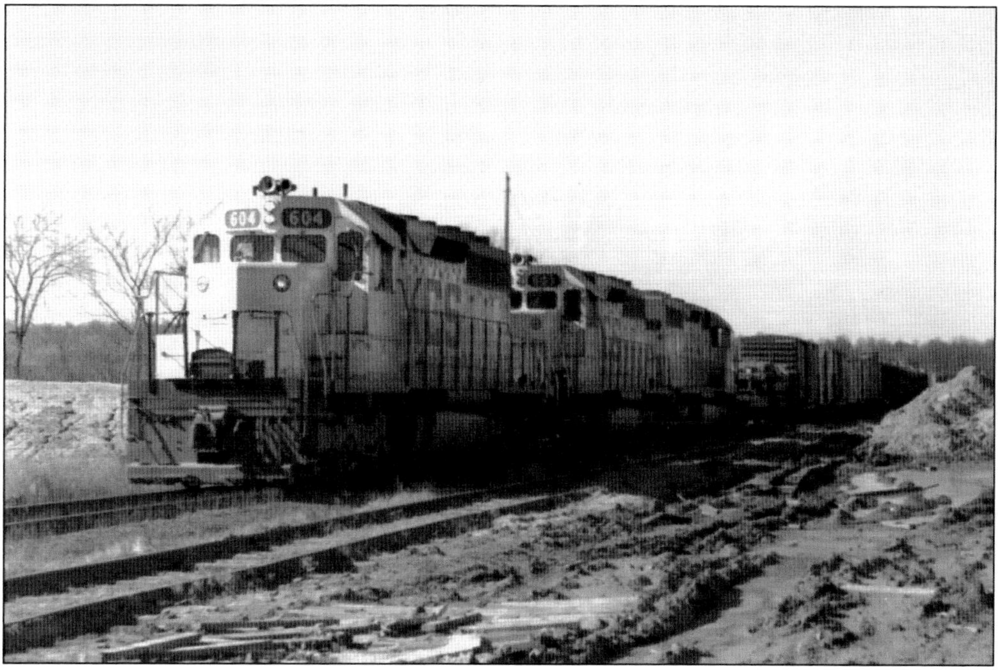

KCS SD40s in a triple lineup are pulling train No. 41 near Redlands, Oklahoma, in August 1971. These units were built in 1966 and replaced first-generation F-units. (Courtesy Harold K. Vollrath.)

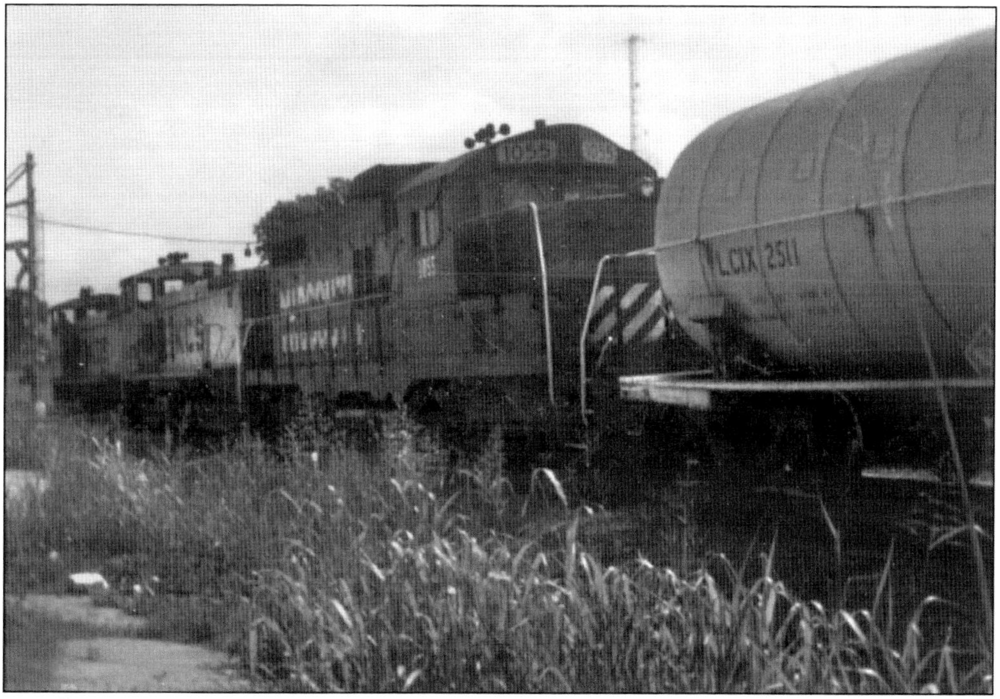

Switch engines sometimes were called on to handle road freight as is illustrated in this photograph of a KCS train wading through the weeds somewhere in Louisiana in the 1990s. (Courtesy Belinda S. Carter.)

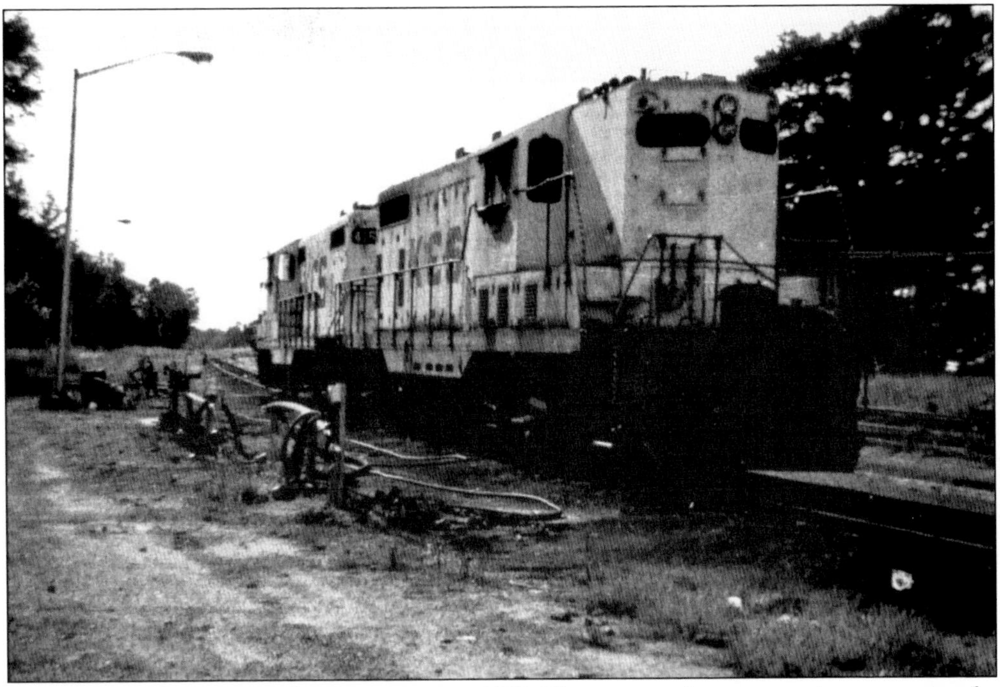

Two GP7 diesels sit at Minden, Louisiana, in 1983. These general-purpose units were active for over 40 years. Some were scrapped and some found their way to other lines such as the Louisiana and North West. (Courtesy Belinda S. Carter.)

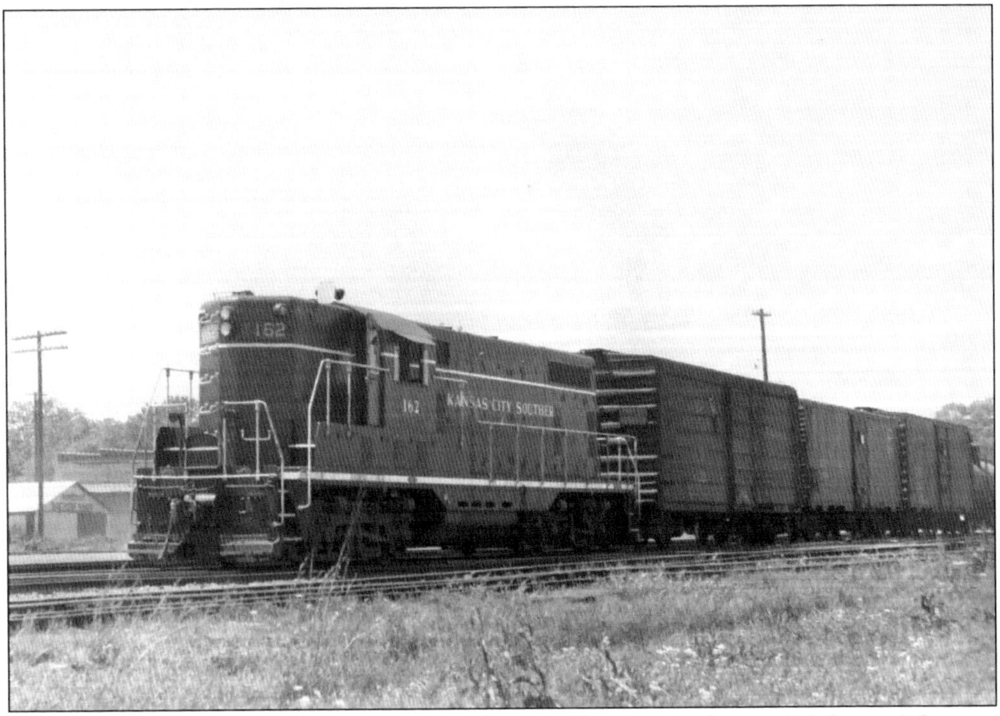

An earlier photograph of a GP7 in the original paint scheme was taken at Ashdown, Arkansas, in August 1953. (Courtesy Harold K. Vollrath.)

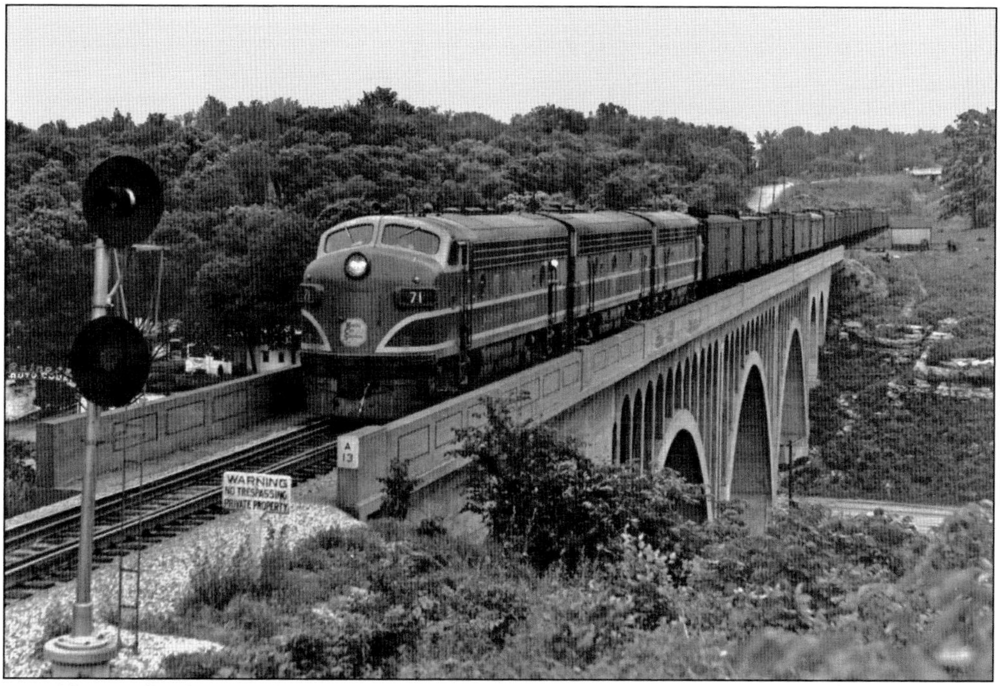

Harold K. Vollrath took this picture of KCS train No. 71, pulled by a trio of F-units including F7 No. 50. The reefer hatches are open on the wood-sided cars. The fireman seems anxious to be included in the photograph. This viaduct had been the scene of several passenger shots. (Courtesy Harold K. Vollrath.)

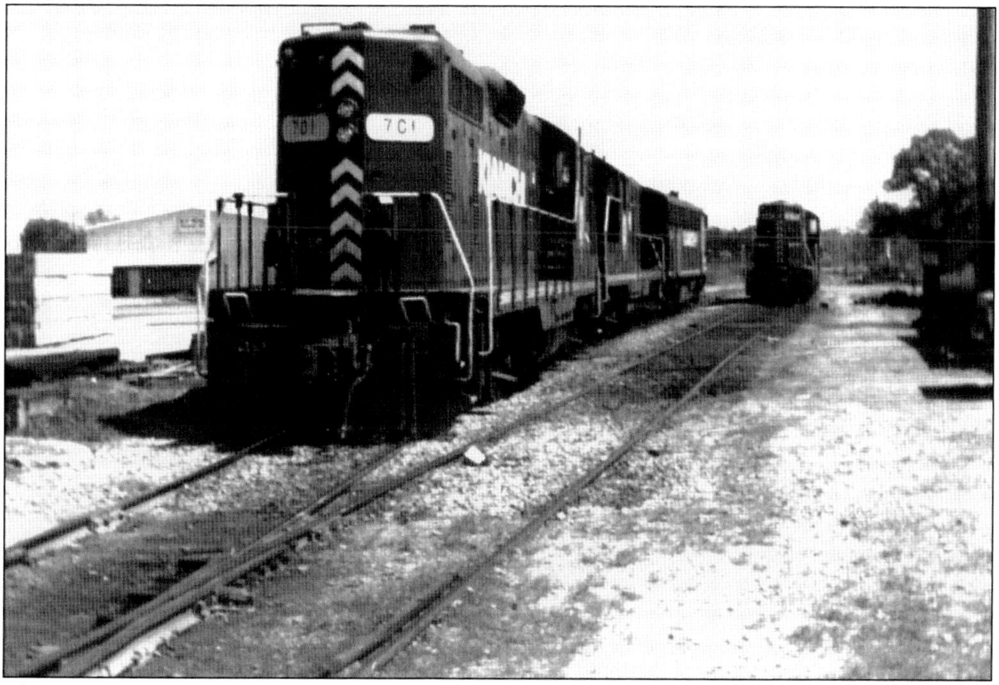

The Kiamichi Railroad connects with the KCS at Ashdown. Here are some geep units parked on the siding awaiting their next assignment. (Courtesy Belinda S. Carter.)

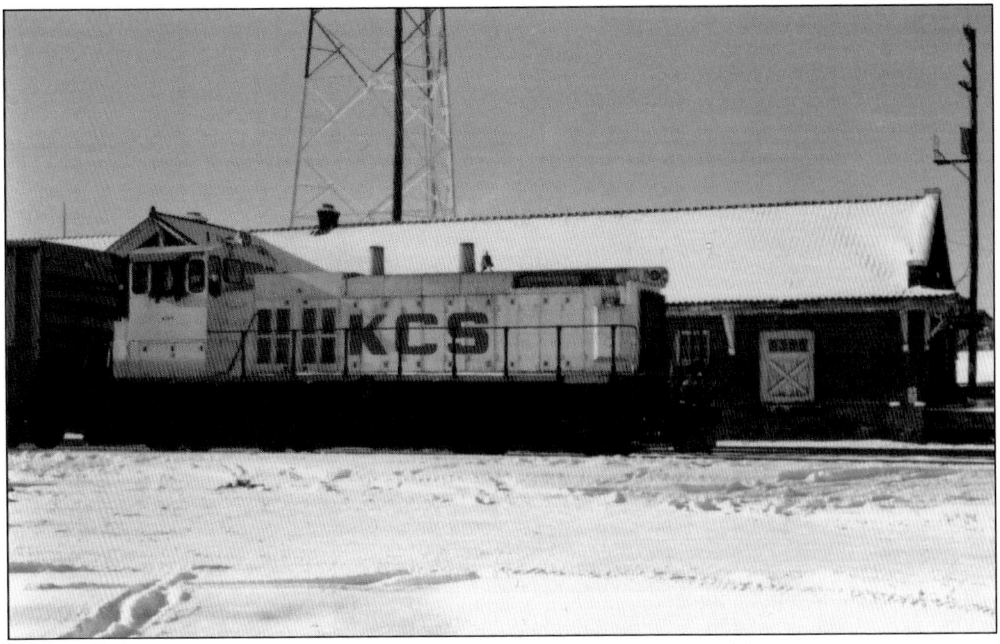

A KCS switcher is on duty at Neosho, Missouri. (Courtesy Glen Roark.)

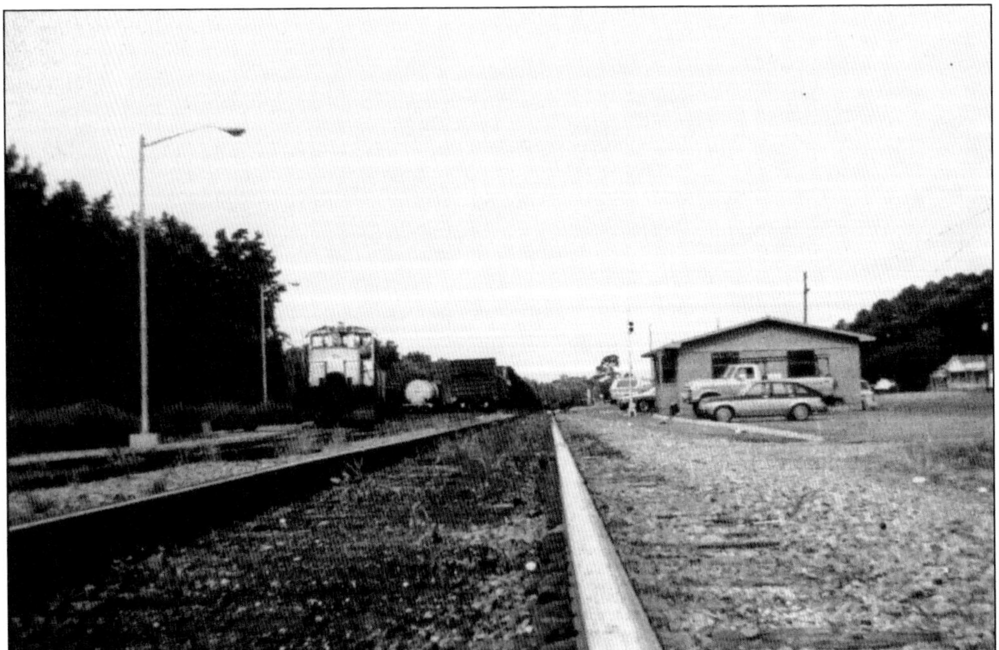
Here a switch engine rests between assignments at the KCS yard in Hughes Springs, Texas. This is part of the former L&A line the KCS operates. (Courtesy Belinda S. Carter.)

A KCS freight pulls into DeQueen, Arkansas. The bottom two lights on the freight locomotive are called ditch lights and were mandated by the government for safety purposes. (Courtesy Belinda S. Carter.)

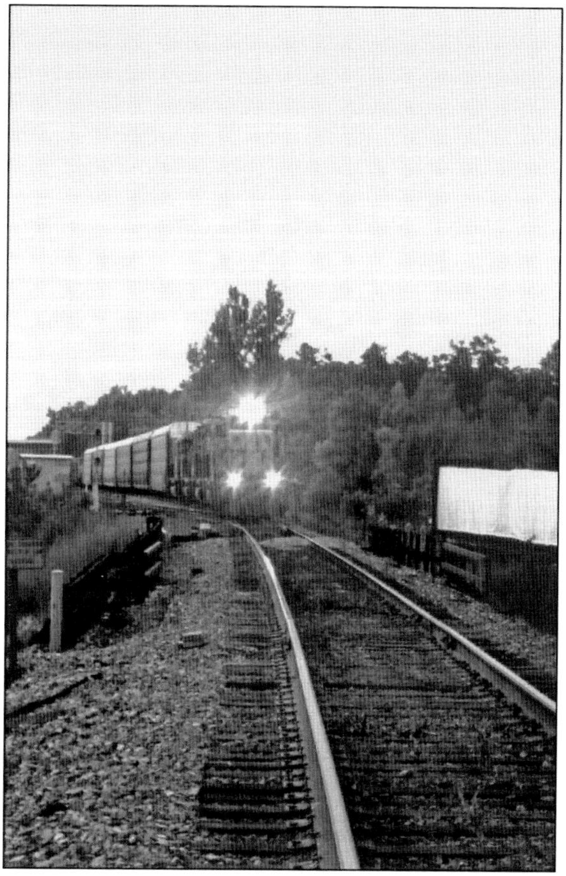

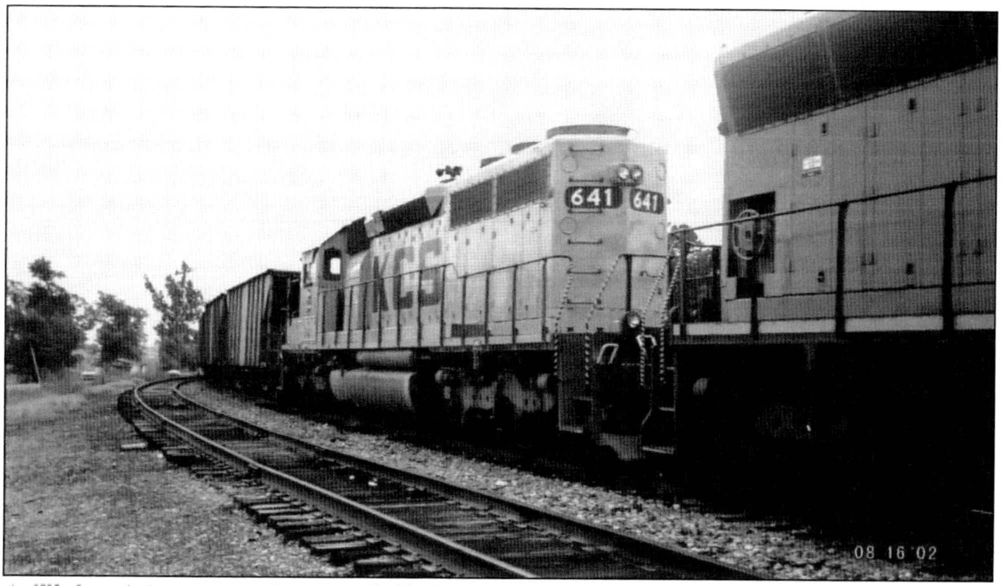

At Wickes, Arkansas, a coal train pulled by EMD diesel units rolls by the siding. The KCS continued to derive increased revenue from its coal trains in the 1990s. (Courtesy Belinda S. Carter.)

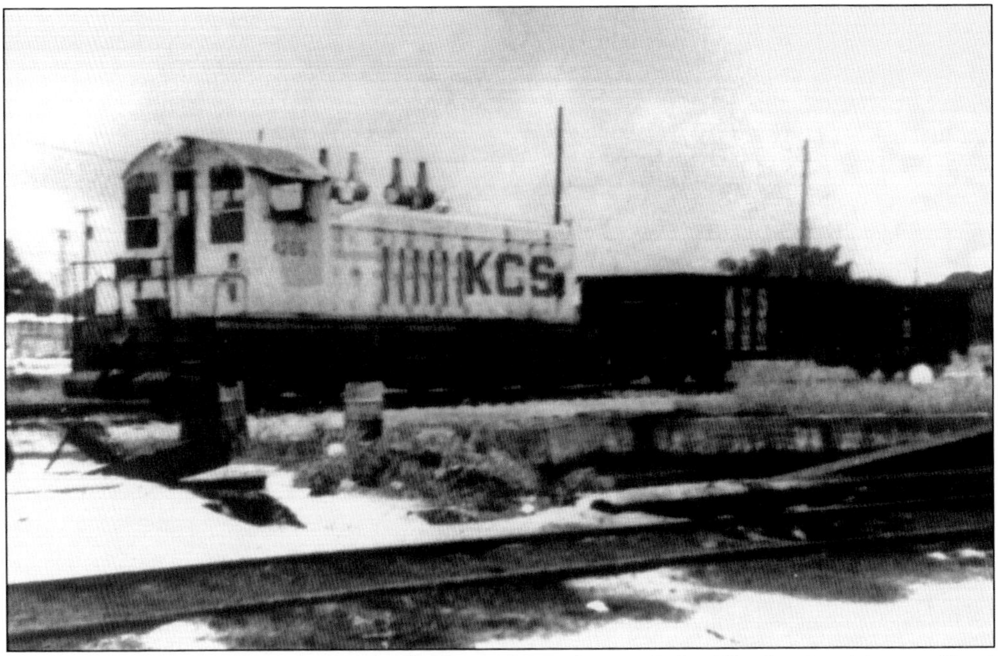

About 1953, a railroad employee who had switching duty at Lake Charles, Louisiana, offered the author and his father a ride in the cab of an SW7 switcher. They rode from the terminal track at the depot through the small yard that ran along old Highway 90. After crossing the Southern Pacific Railroad junction, they bounced along over jointed rail, took a sharp left, and headed through a swamp toward the old KCS bridge that crossed the Calcasieu River. A similar locomotive, sporting a later paint scheme, is seen here. (Author's collection.)

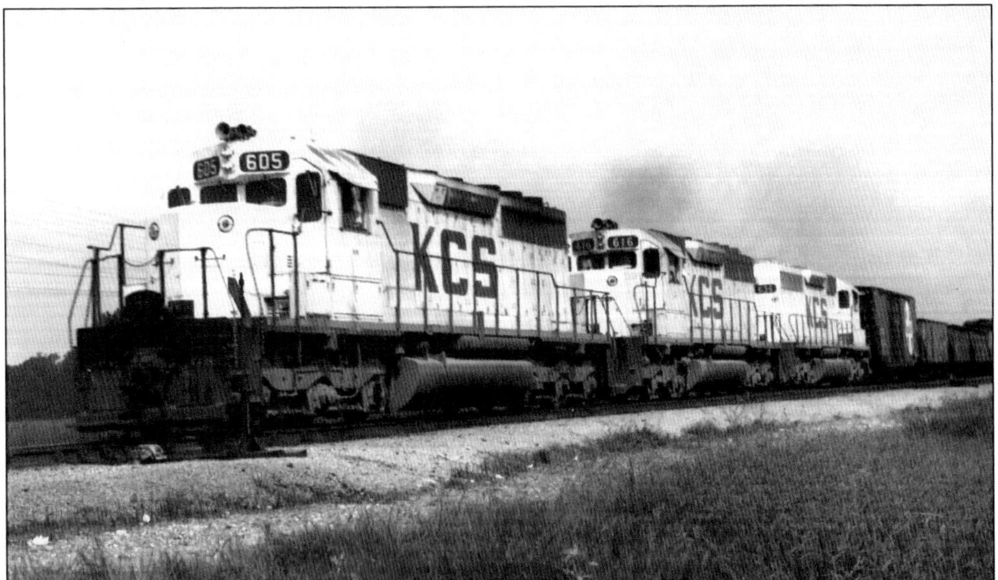

Three General Motors diesel locomotives are pulling KCS train No. 41 near Ashdown, Arkansas, in August 1971. These units were part of the second generation of diesels manufactured in the United States. (Courtesy Harold K. Vollrath.)

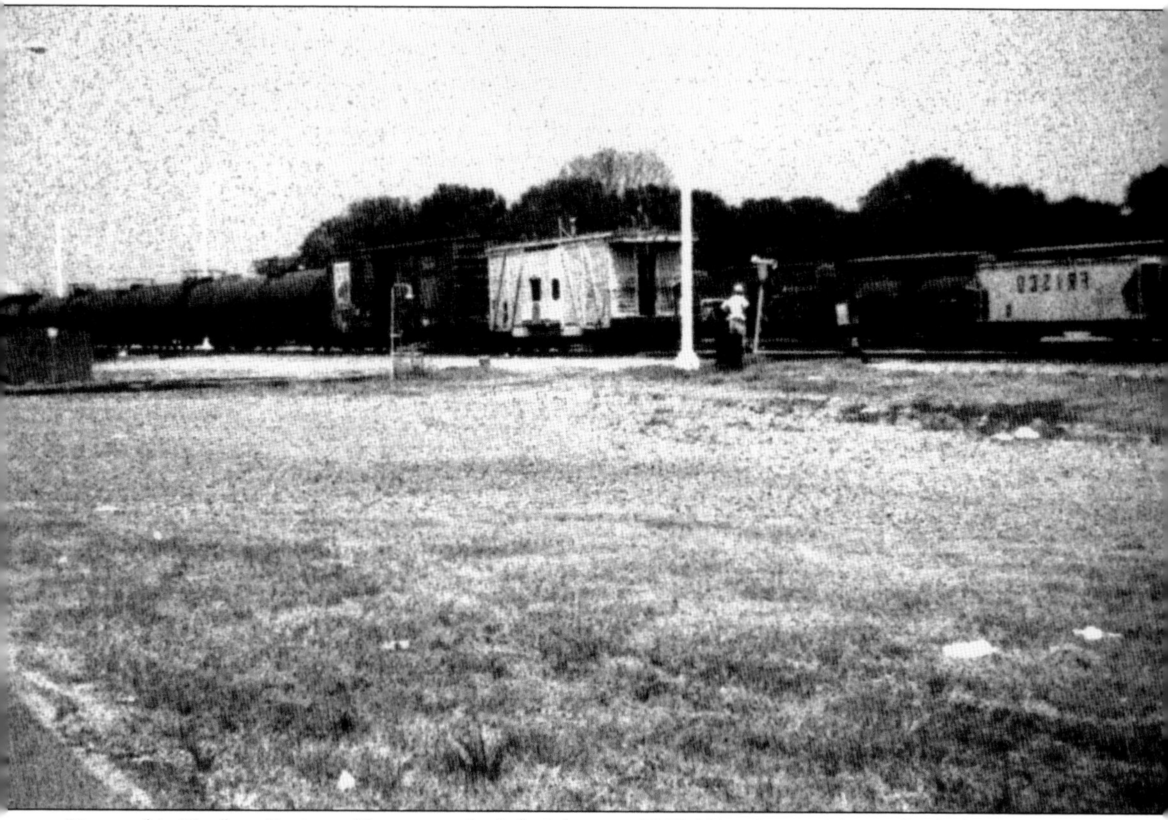

Pictured is Hughes Springs, Texas, on the L&A line in 1993. This beautiful wood-sided caboose is parked in the yard waiting for a buyer. For a time, a row of wood and steel cabooses were stored at Shreveport, Louisiana, awaiting sale or donation to city parks. (Author's collection.)

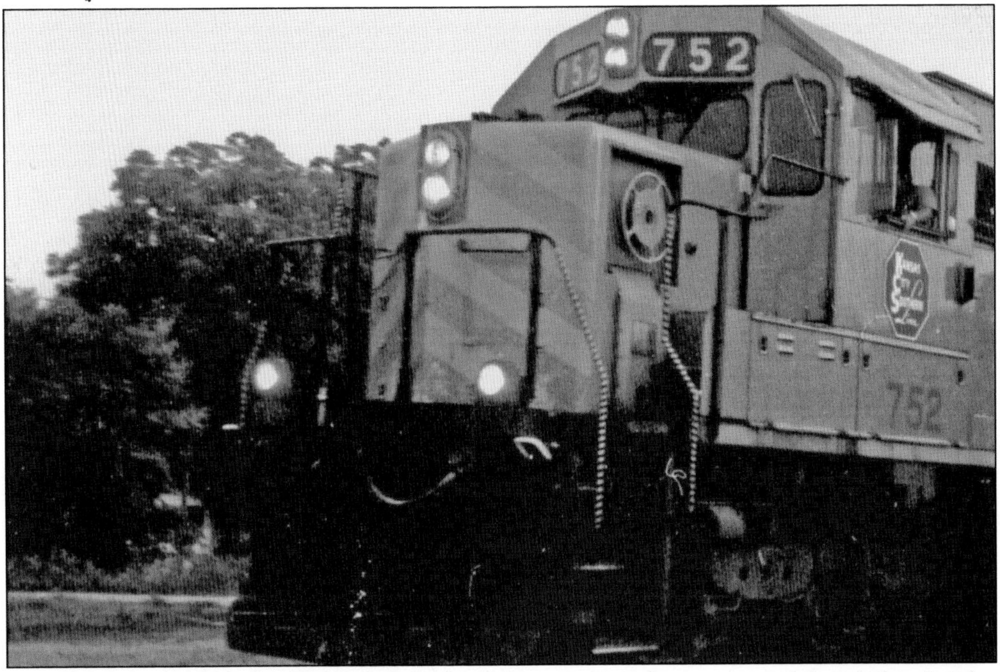

The engineer waits for a red block signal to turn green so he can proceed with his freight. Much of the life of crew members who work on freight trains is spent parked in sidings waiting the passage of other trains to which the dispatcher has given the right-of-way. (Courtesy Belinda S. Carter.)

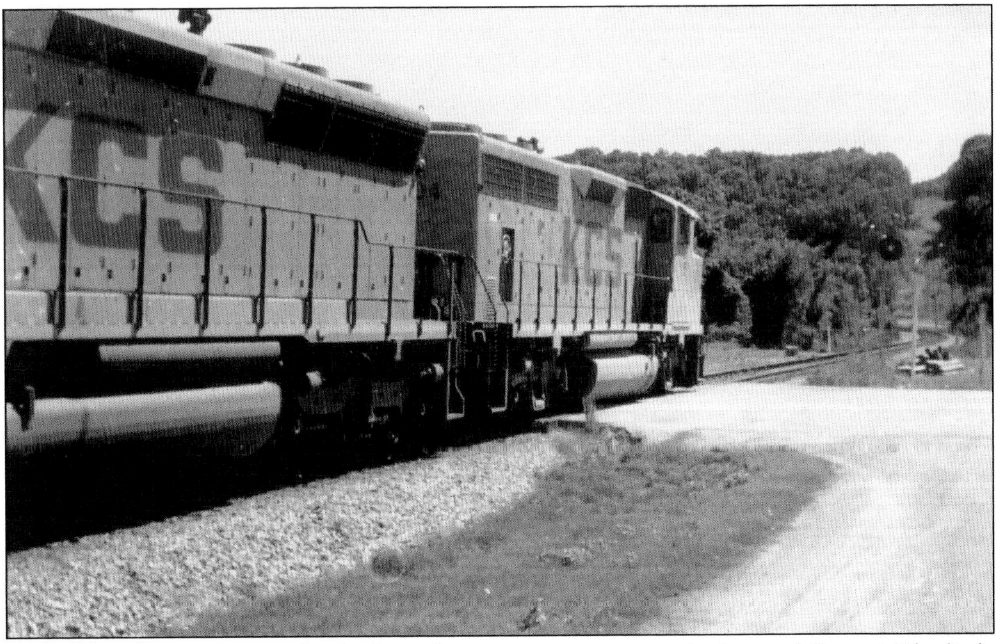

A local freight train has just finished switching some grain cars at Anderson, Missouri. The little train will head to the next town with a grain elevator where it will perform similar switching maneuvers. The head engine on this train once belonged to the Canadian National Railway. (Author's collection.)

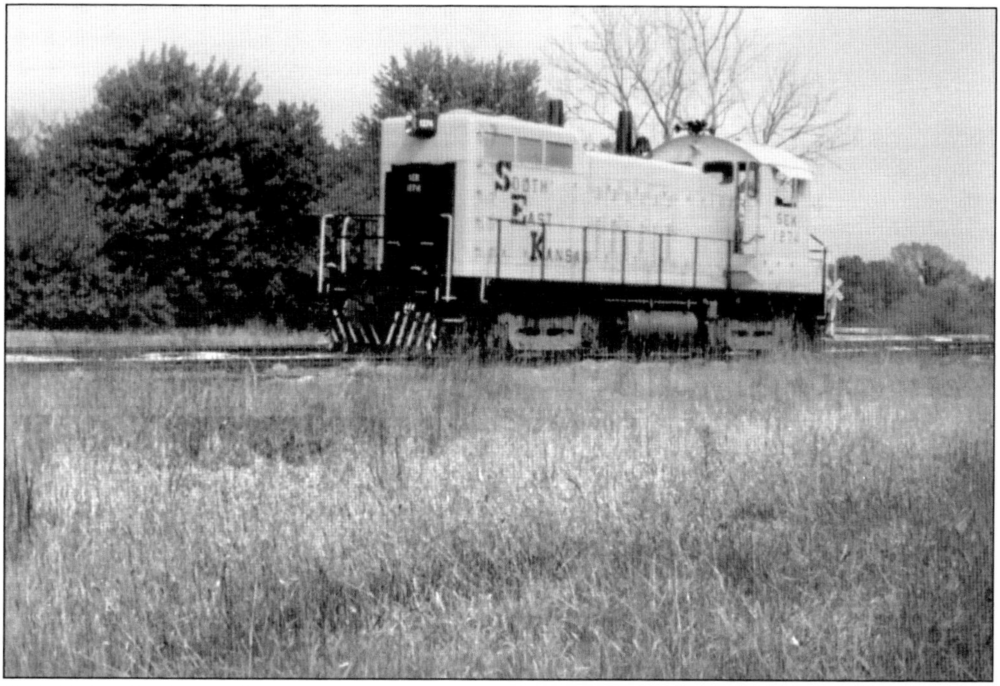

This little rebuilt switch engine is a first-generation diesel locomotive. When photographed at Pittsburg, Kansas, it was being operated by the South East Kansas Railroad, which connects with the KCS. (Courtesy Belinda S. Carter.)

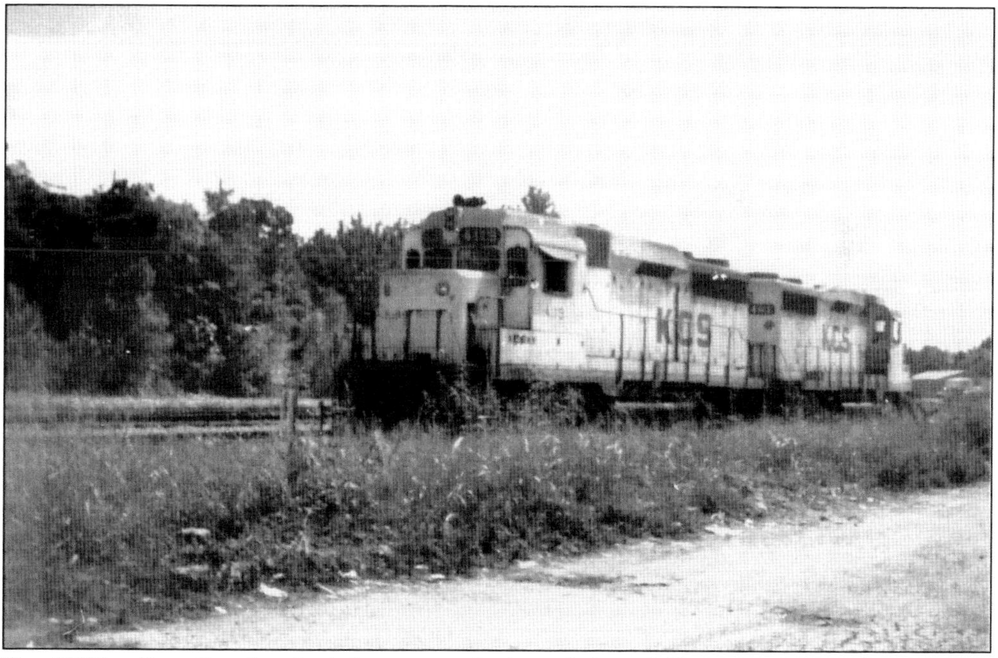

Two GP30s idle at Fort Smith, Arkansas, on the branch from Sallisaw to Fort Smith, Arkansas. Years before, passenger trains ran from the Fort Smith Union Station out to the main line at Sallisaw. In later years, a KCS bus operated. The GP30s had been operational since 1962 and were nearing trade-in time when photographed. (Courtesy Belinda S. Carter.)

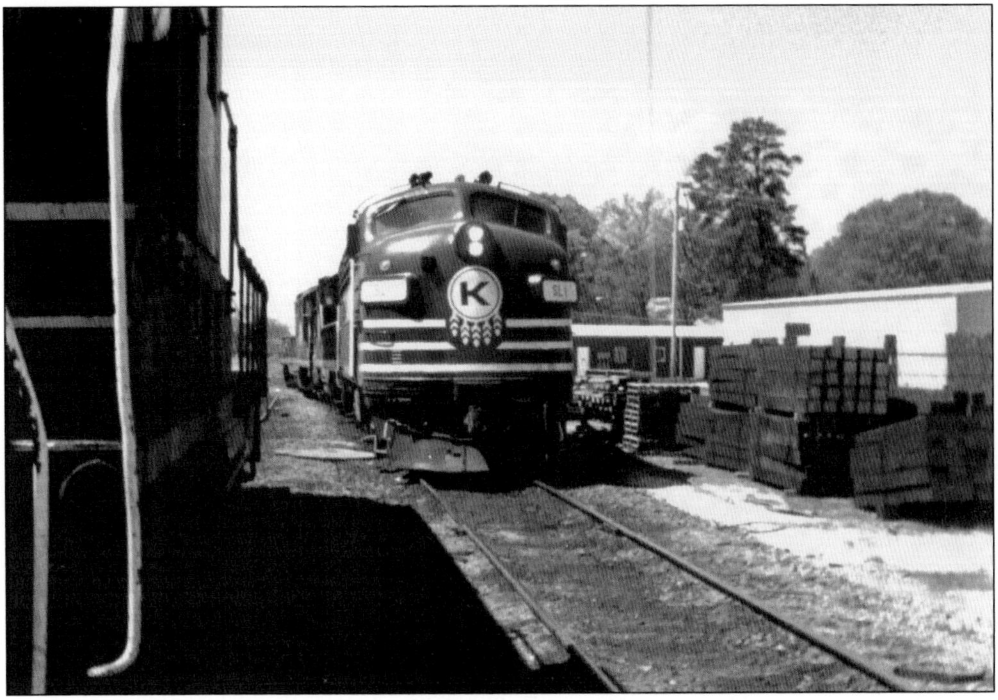

A former KCS F-unit is in service on the Kiamichi Railroad line when photographed at Ashdown, Arkansas, in the late 1980s. Some F-units ended up in slug service in coal train duty and others were traded in for newer power. (Courtesy Belinda S. Carter.)

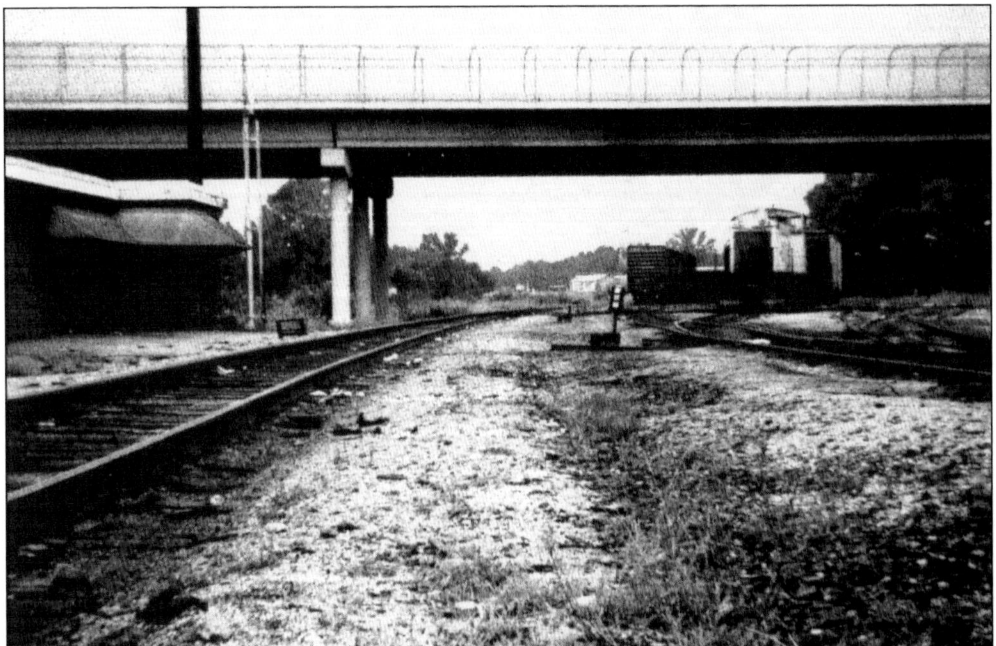

An EMD SW1500 switcher goes about daily switching chores at Texarkana, Texas, in 1983. The switchers were also used in local road service such as the route from Leesville, Louisiana, to Zwolle, Louisiana. (Courtesy Belinda S. Carter.)

No slowing down for this crossing in south Louisiana as a KCS fast freight heads south to Port Arthur, Texas. The town of Port Arthur was named after Arthur Stilwell, who was instrumental in founding the KCS. (Courtesy Belinda S. Carter.)

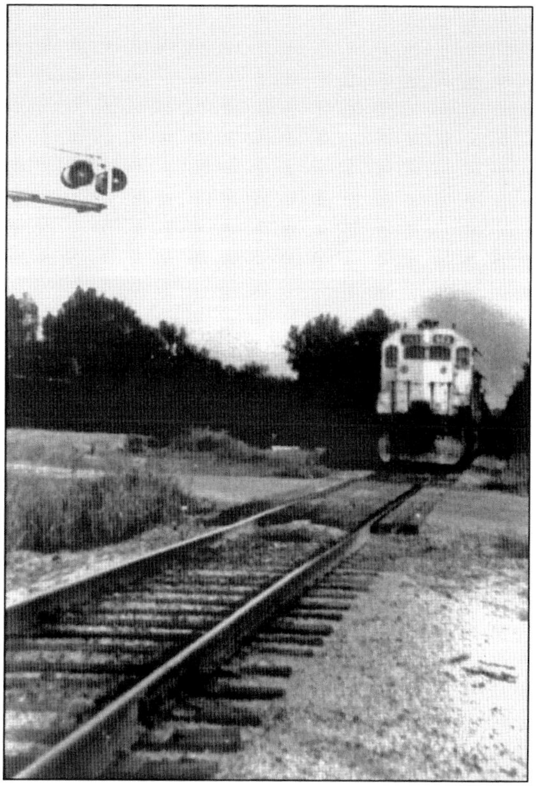

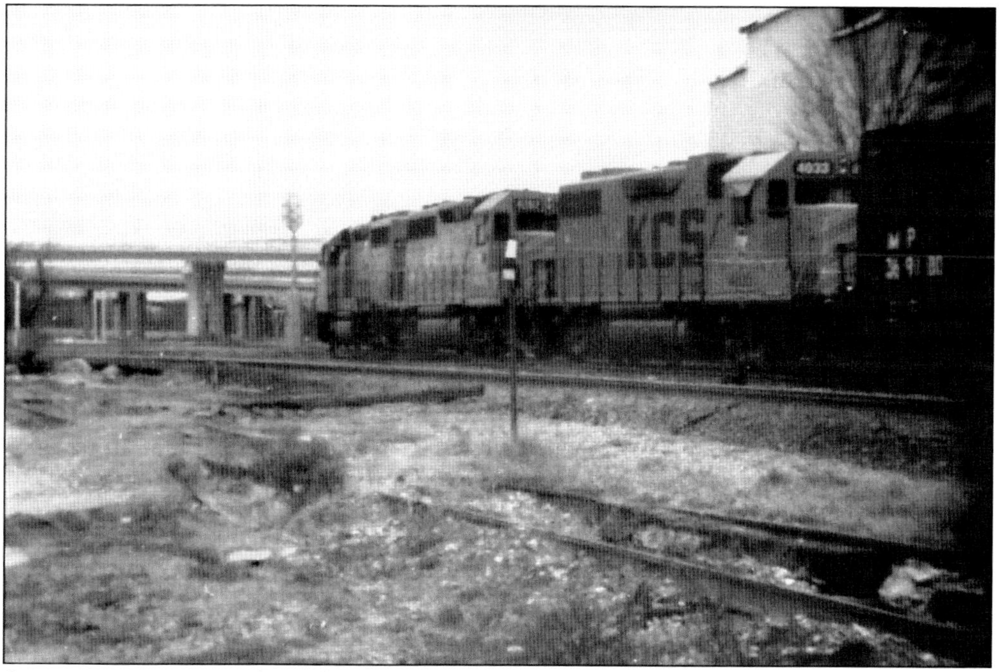

On a misty morning in the early 1990s, a KCS freight train glides through the maze of trackage south of the old station site in Shreveport, Louisiana. The interstate highways evident in the photograph have removed the need for passenger train service. (Courtesy Belinda S. Carter.)

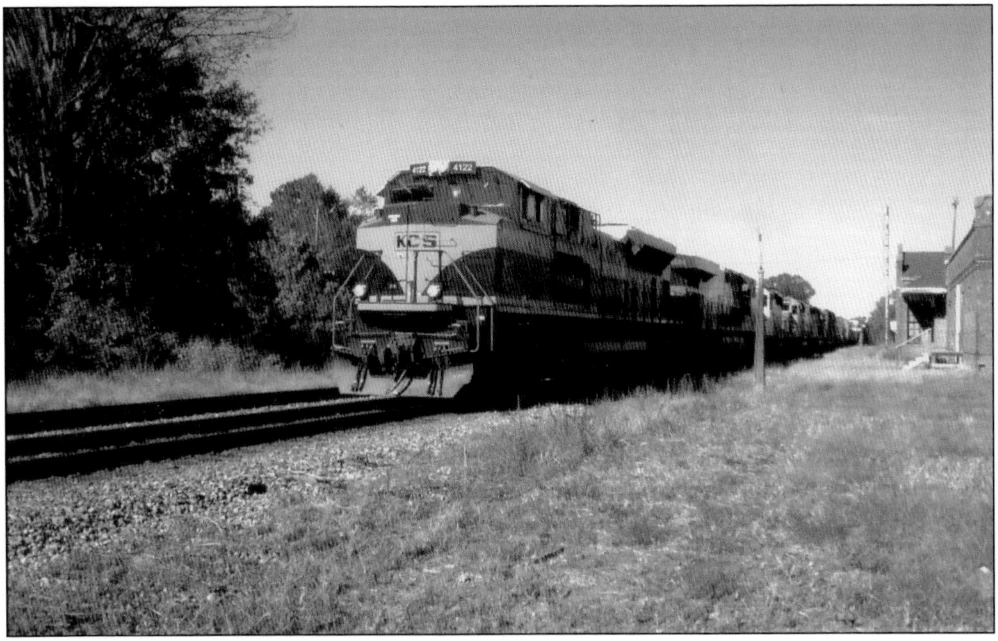

In 2008, these new freight units painted in the *Southern Belle* scheme are pulling a lengthy merchandise train through Mansfield, Louisiana, south on the KCS line. The paint scheme used on these units is similar to the one used on the passenger engines years before. (Author's collection.)

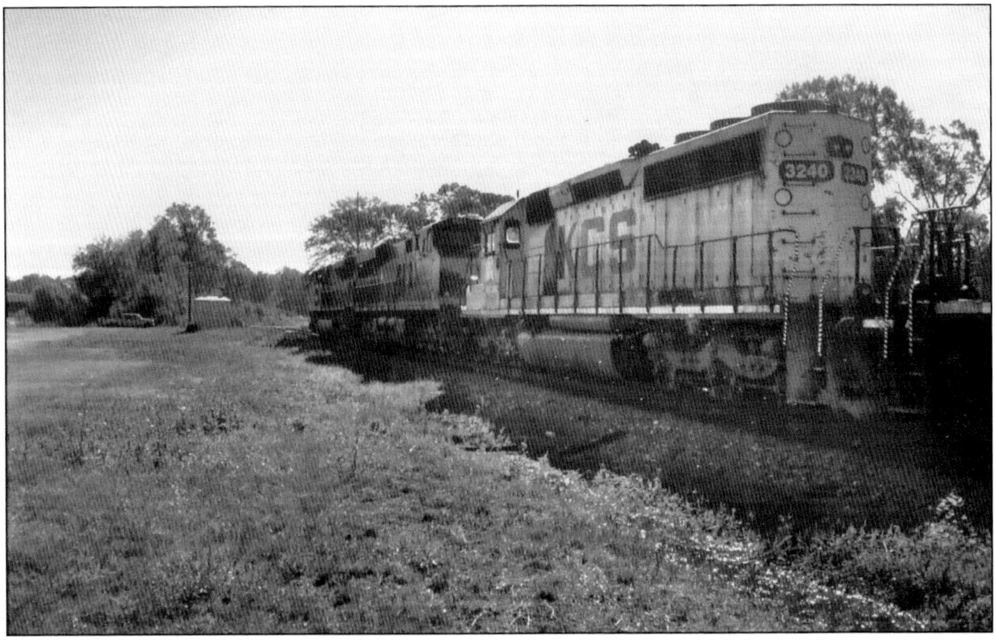

Trailing behind the new KCS freight engines is a slightly older model in the gray paint scheme. This train is at Mansfield, Louisiana. (Author's collection.)

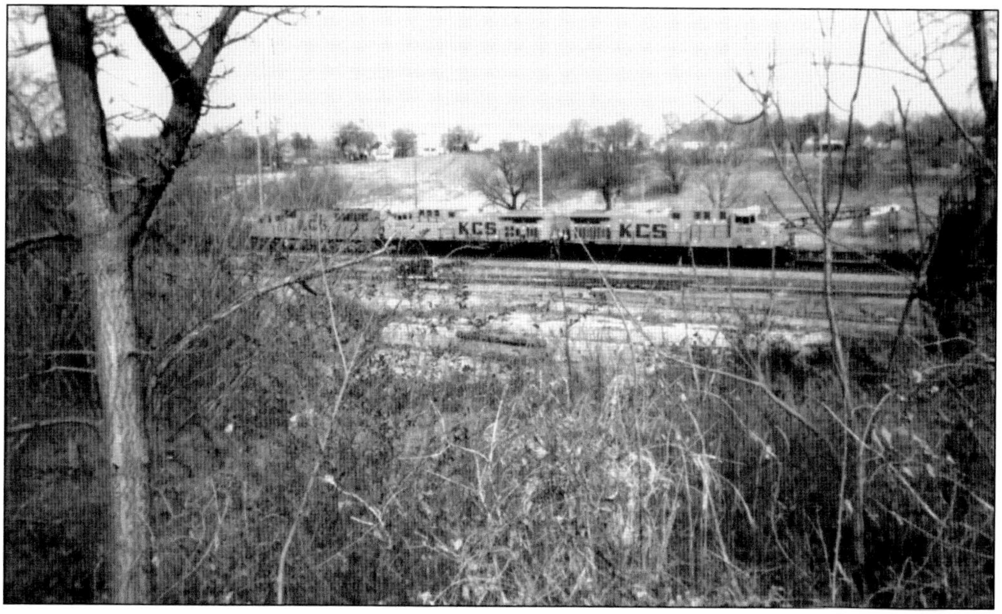

Sitting near the site of the Joplin Union Station, this KCS freight awaits another train that will be northbound for Kansas City. By the time this photograph was taken, tracks into the old station had been pulled up and the station's future was uncertain. (Author's collection.)

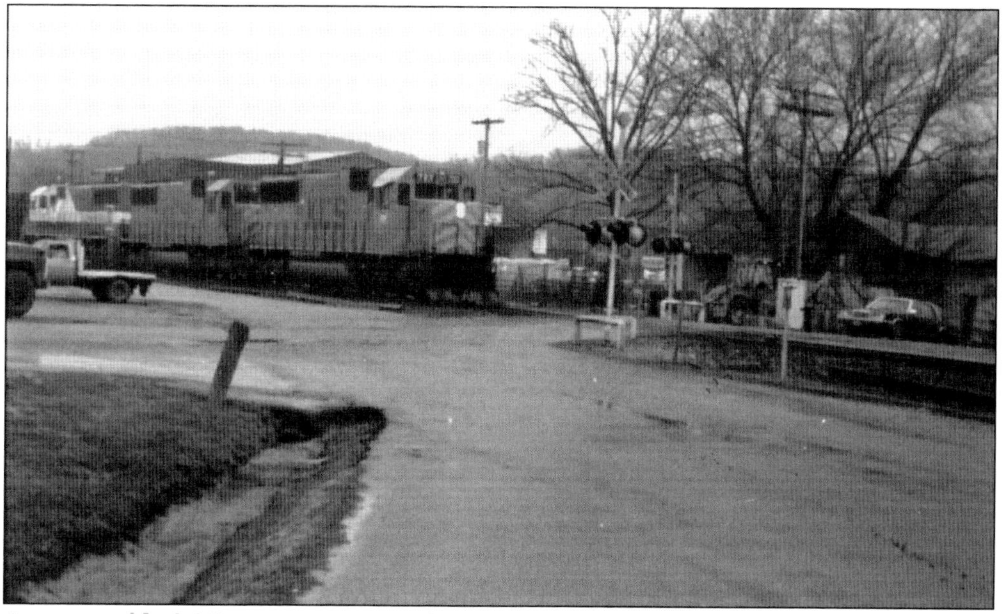
Arriving at Noel, Missouri, on a rainy afternoon, this trio of engines includes one leased from the EMD. The train is northbound for Kansas City. (Author's collection.)

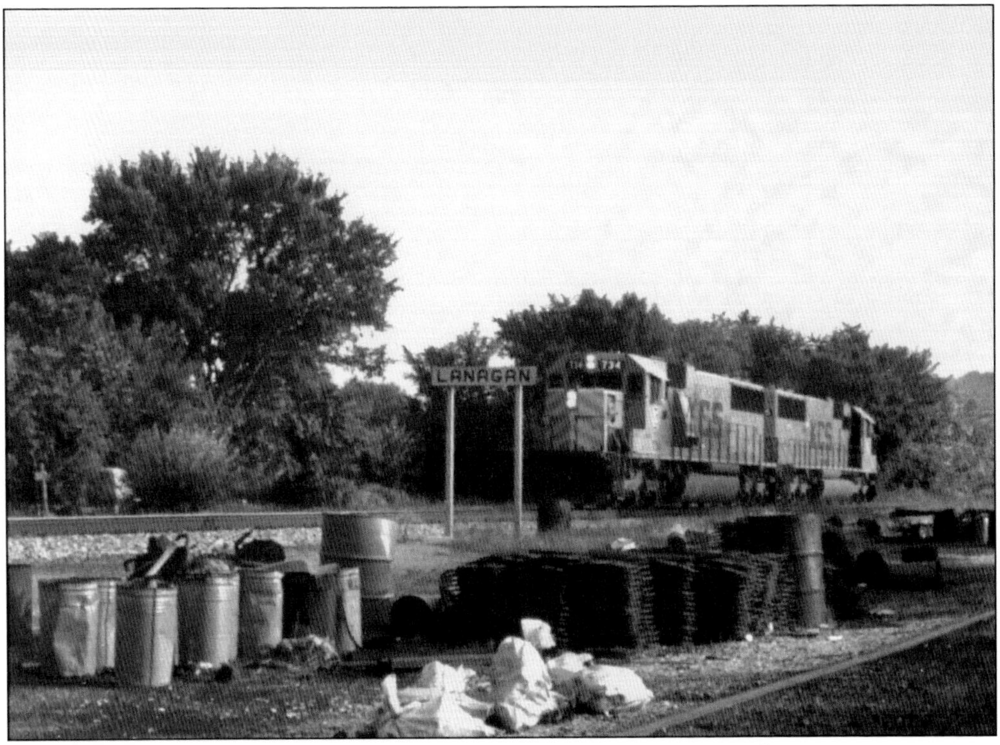

Two KCS helper units are parked on the siding at Lanagan, Missouri. Once a passenger stop, Lanagan now witnesses dozens of freight trains each day. (Author's collection.)

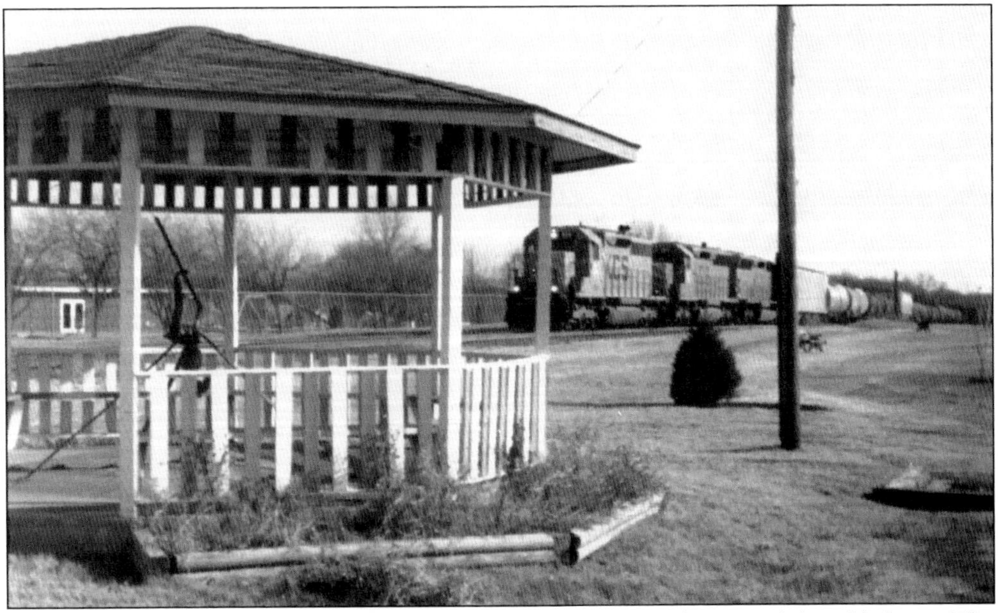

Highballing through Goodman, Missouri, this freight is near the site of the old depot. The gazebo is a resting spot for old-timers to reflect on the days when Goodman was a thriving community complete with passenger service. (Author's collection.)

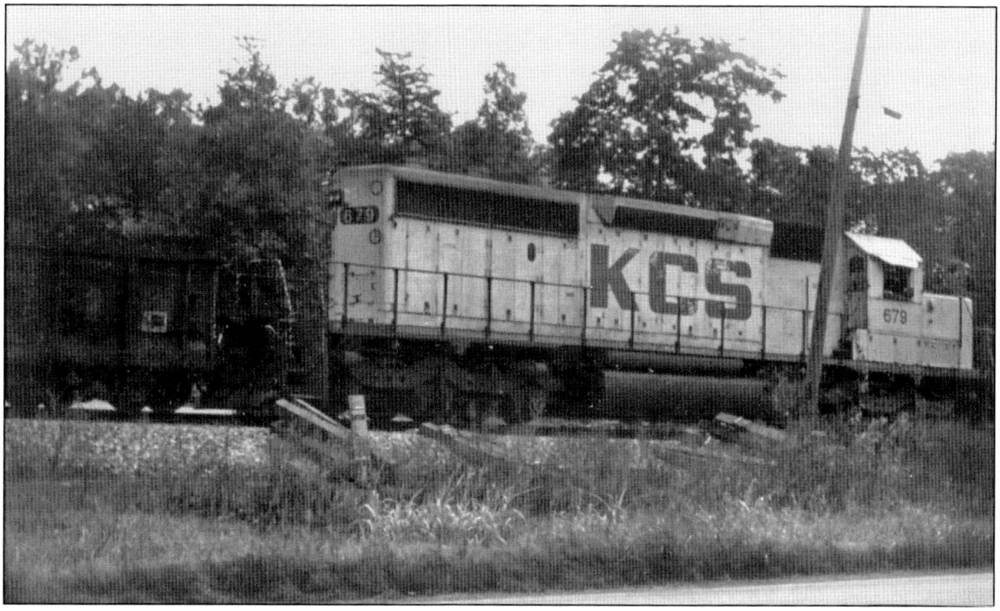

A single KCS unit has a work train in tow as it leaves Anderson, Missouri, to perform trackage maintenance duties. The train will have to pull into the siding soon as the main line sees over 20 trains daily. (Author's collection.)

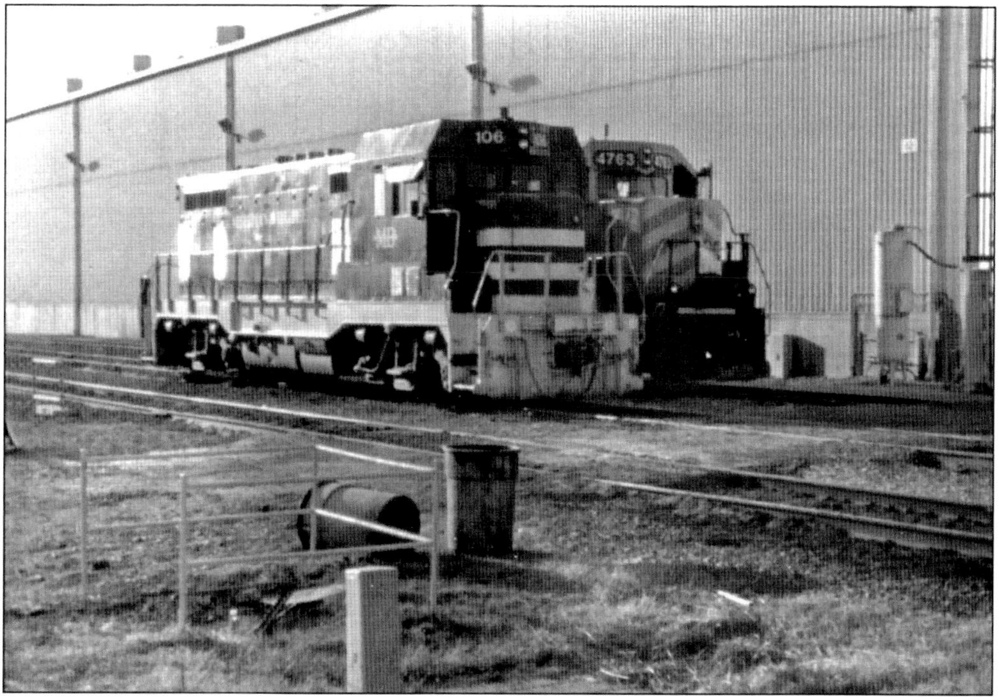

This Gateway Western Railway unit is a CF7, formerly an F7 passenger engine on the Santa Fe Railroad. The KCS inherited the engine when it acquired the Gateway Western line. (Author's collection.)

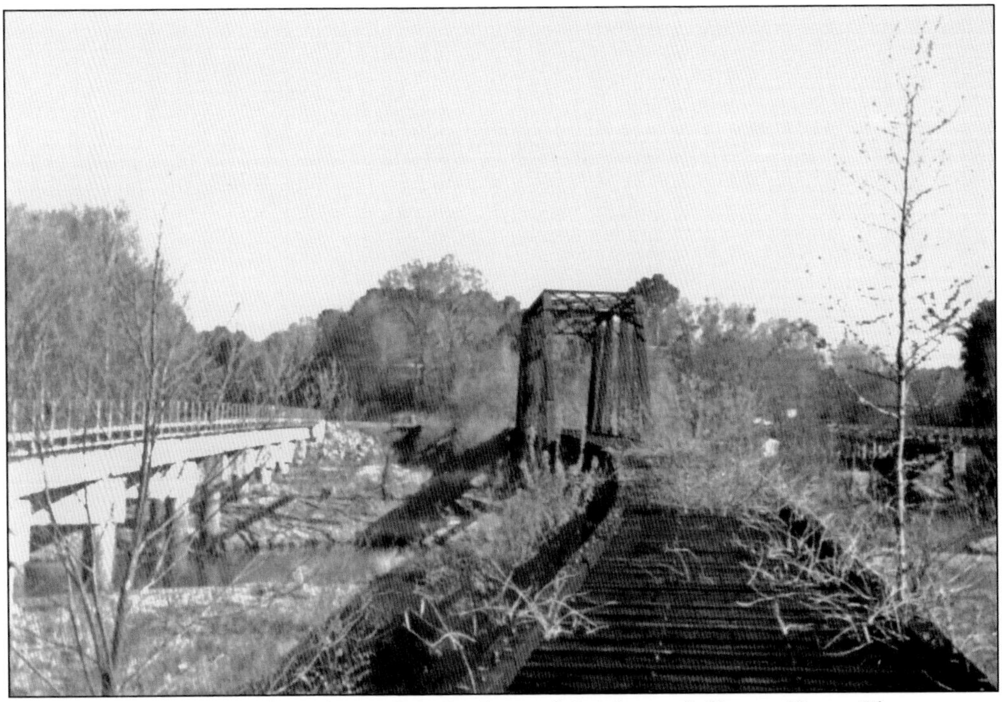

This abandoned truss bridge is located on the former L&A line at Jefferson, Texas. The span was taken out of service after construction of a more modern bridge. (Author's collection.)

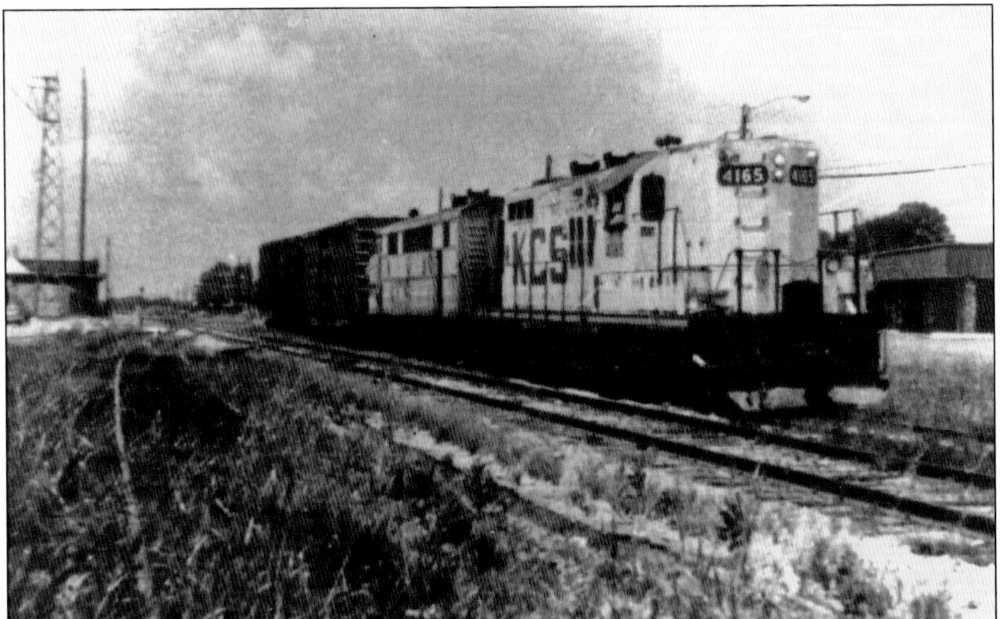

A geep locomotive sits with a first-generation F-unit on a short freight train at Cullen, Louisiana, in 1981. This train was performing less-than-carload duties the day it was photographed. (Courtesy Belinda S. Carter.)

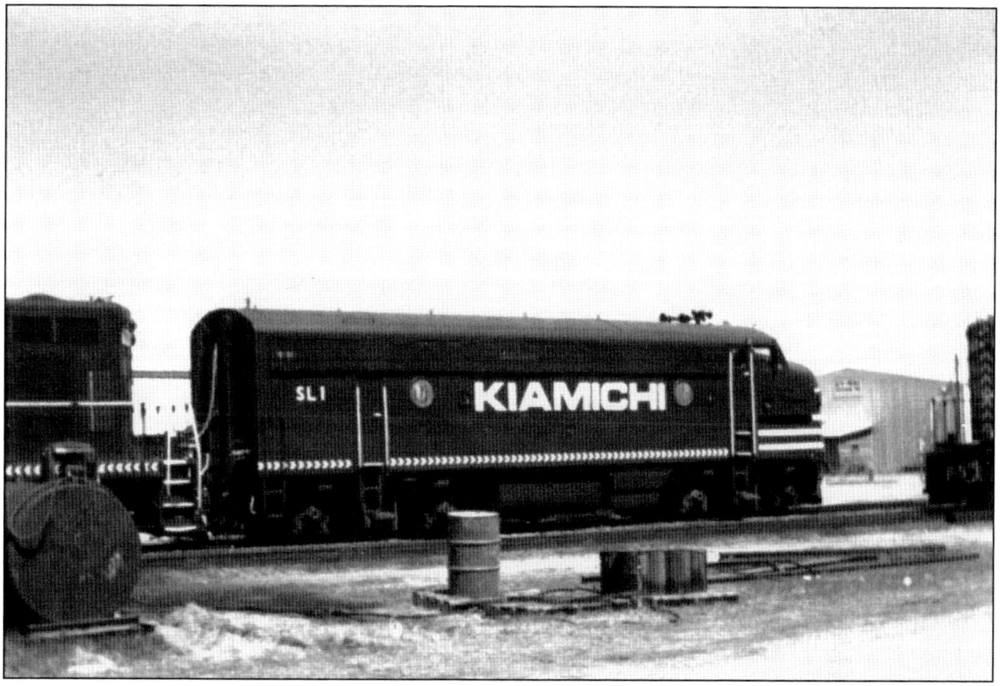

This Kiamichi Railroad diesel sits at the station in Ashdown, Arkansas, on the former Burlington Northern line. The Kiamichi Railroad intersects at Ashdown with the KCS. (Courtesy Belinda S. Carter.)

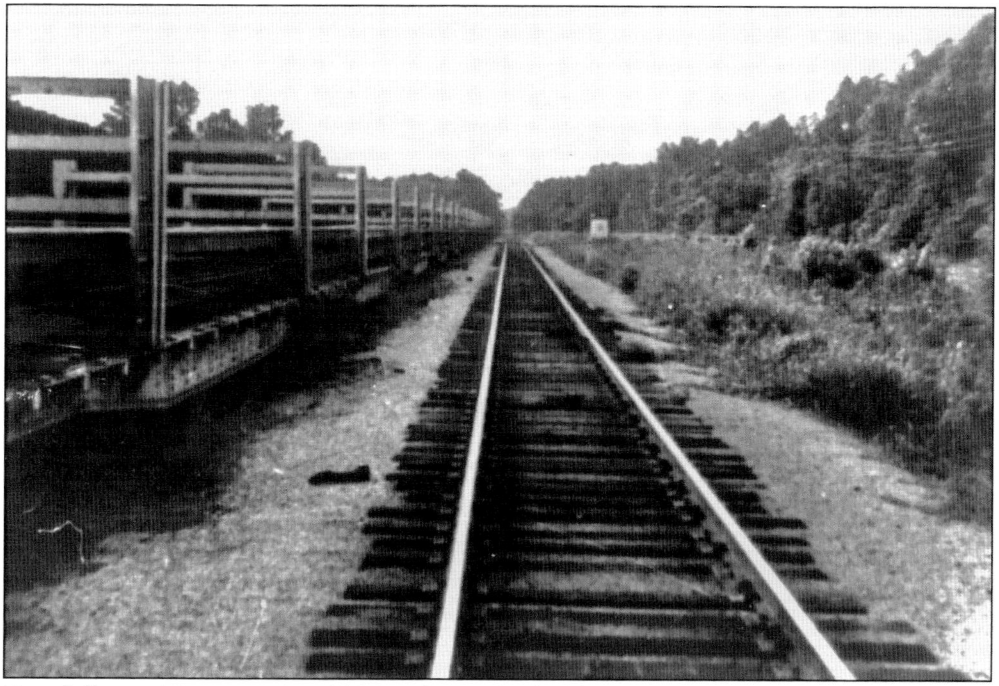

Near Jefferson, Texas, on the old L&A line, a load of flatcars containing ribbon rail is parked and awaiting installation on the line. (Courtesy Belinda S. Carter.)

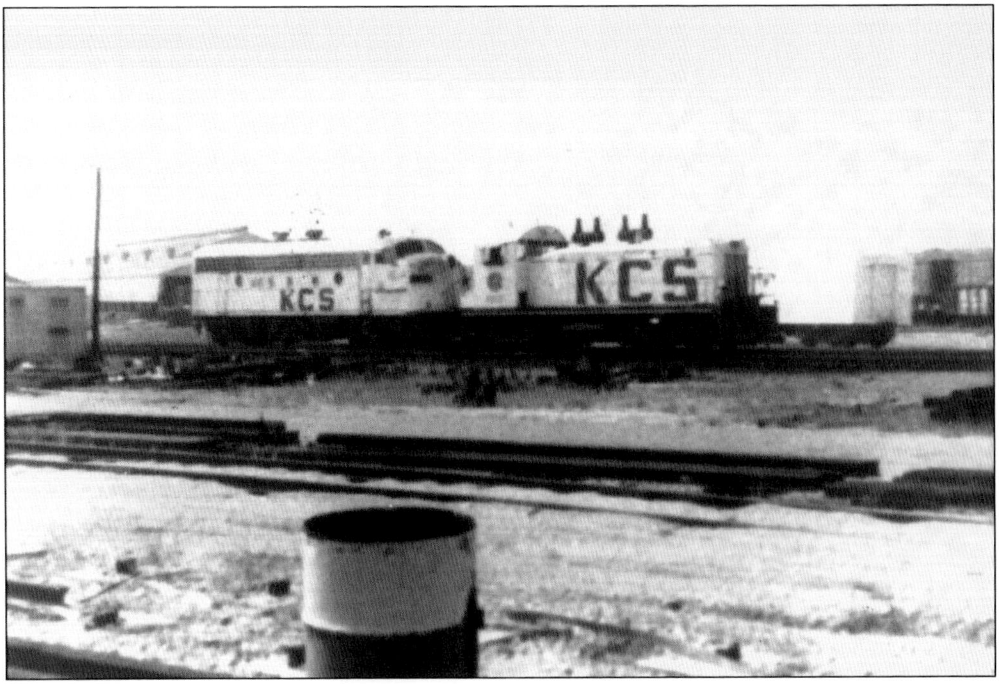

Two first-generation diesels are parked in the yard at Shreveport, Louisiana, in the early 1980s. The F-unit once saw main line passenger service. Notice the baggage car that has been repainted for work train service. (Courtesy Belinda S. Carter.)

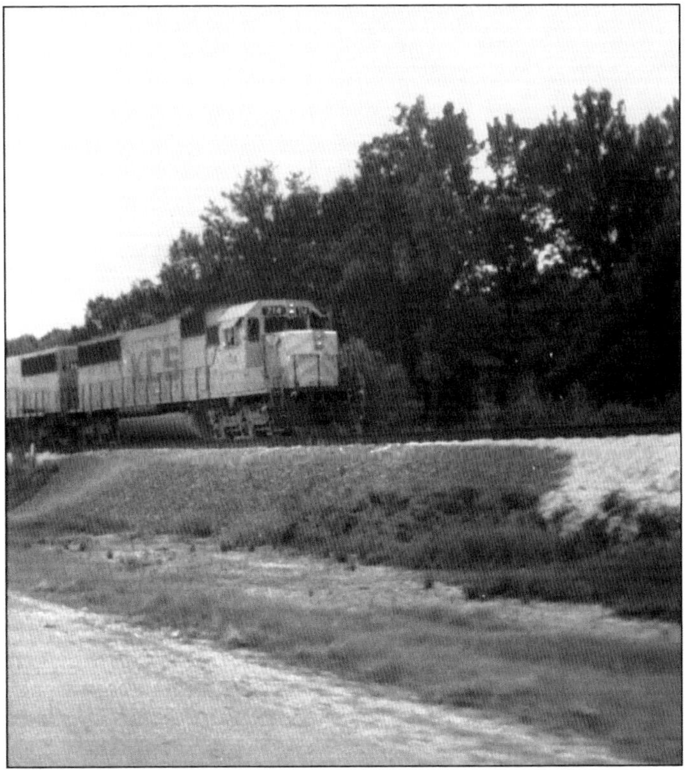

Headed north just past Ashdown, Arkansas, these EMD units are pulling a coal train. Unit trains like this one are responsible for the line's increase in profit. (Courtesy Belinda S. Carter.)

Seven

THE *BELLE* IS BACK

The original *Southern Belle* no longer runs from New Orleans to Kansas City, but the *Southern Belle* is still around in the form of an executive train, the brainchild of Michael Haverty, chief executive officer at KCS. The current *Southern Belle* fleet has nearly two dozen cars, which were originally built between 1925 and 1959 and have been significantly rebuilt for their current assignments. All equipment has been completely rebuilt at a cost of several million dollars. Power for the *Belle* came from F-units that were originally from Canadian National Railways VIA Rail Canada.

One of the *Belle* dining cars, KCS No. 56, has survived to be a part of today's train. Constructed by American Car and Foundry after World War II, it provided dining car service into the mid-1960s. Rebuilt by Pullman-Standard Company in 1965, the car was placed in storage at the Deramus yard after the cessation of passenger service. Thirty years went by and the car was rebuilt into a business car-diner lounge and renamed the *Jackson*. In addition to a lounge and dining area, the car features audiovisual equipment including satellite television and Dolby sound.

The office car *Tolmak* is also part of the new *Southern Belle*. Built in 1966 by Darby Railway Cars, the *Tolmak* had the first letter from each state the KCS served in its name. The *Tolmak* was refurbished and renamed the *New Orleans* in 1995.

Whenever an inspection trip or shipper's special goes out over the line, employees are only given brief advance notice. In addition, the train is used for civic events, private meetings, and excursions. No stops are made to pick up passengers holding tickets, but at least one can still see a passenger train in the grand manner of the original *Belle* rolling over KCS lines.

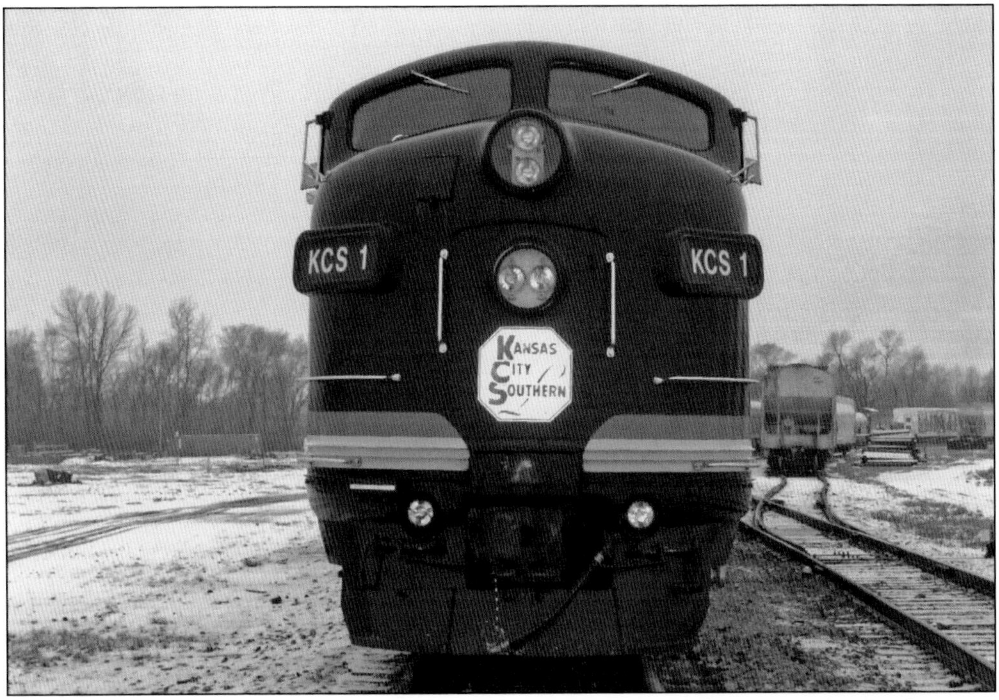

The KCS executive train is playing Santa Claus at Roodhouse, Illinois, in 2005. The paint scheme on the engines matches the cars but was changed in 2008 to the original *Belle* colors. (Courtesy Gary Coates.)

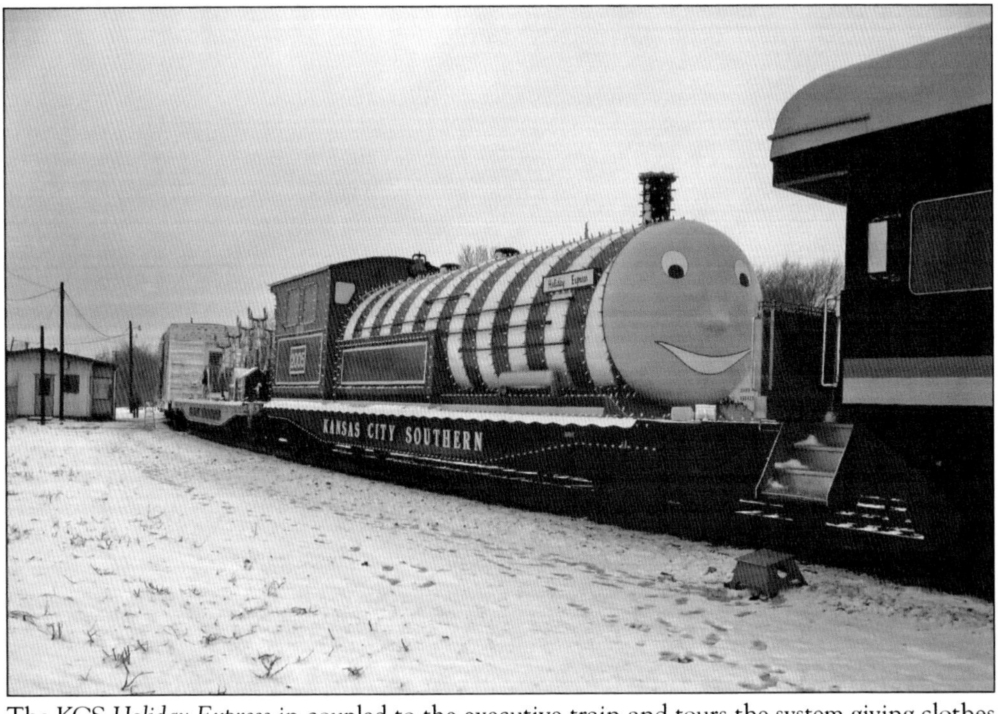

The KCS *Holiday Express* in coupled to the executive train and tours the system giving clothes and toys to children along the line of the KCS. (Courtesy Gary Coates.)

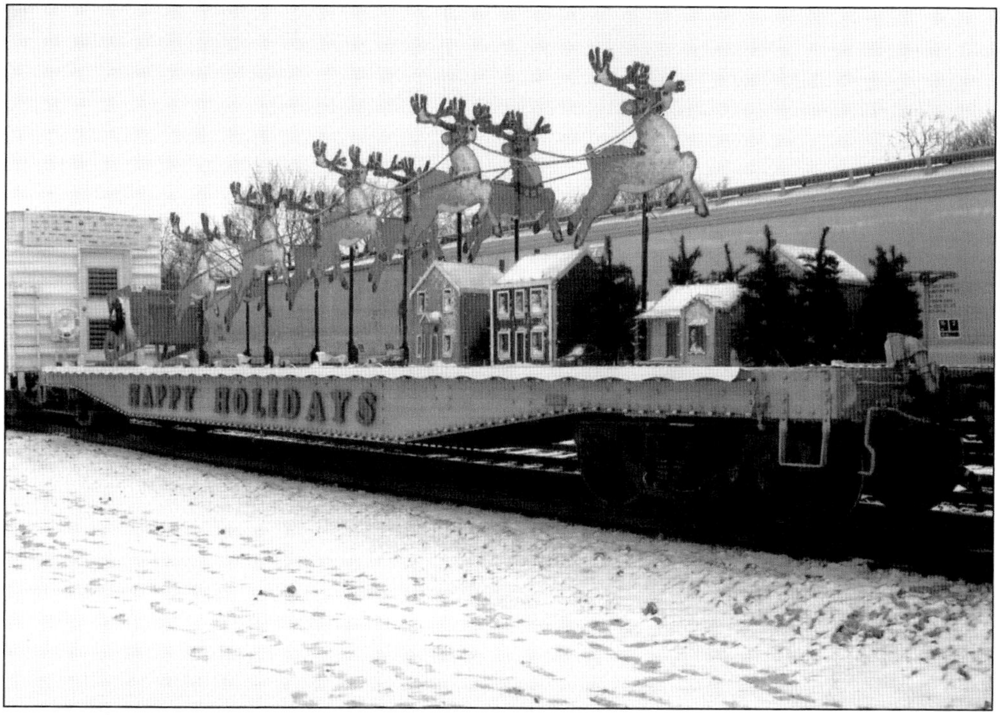

KCS employees do a great deal of volunteer work to make the *Holiday Express* a reality every year, as witnessed by this decorated flatcar. (Courtesy Gary Coates.)

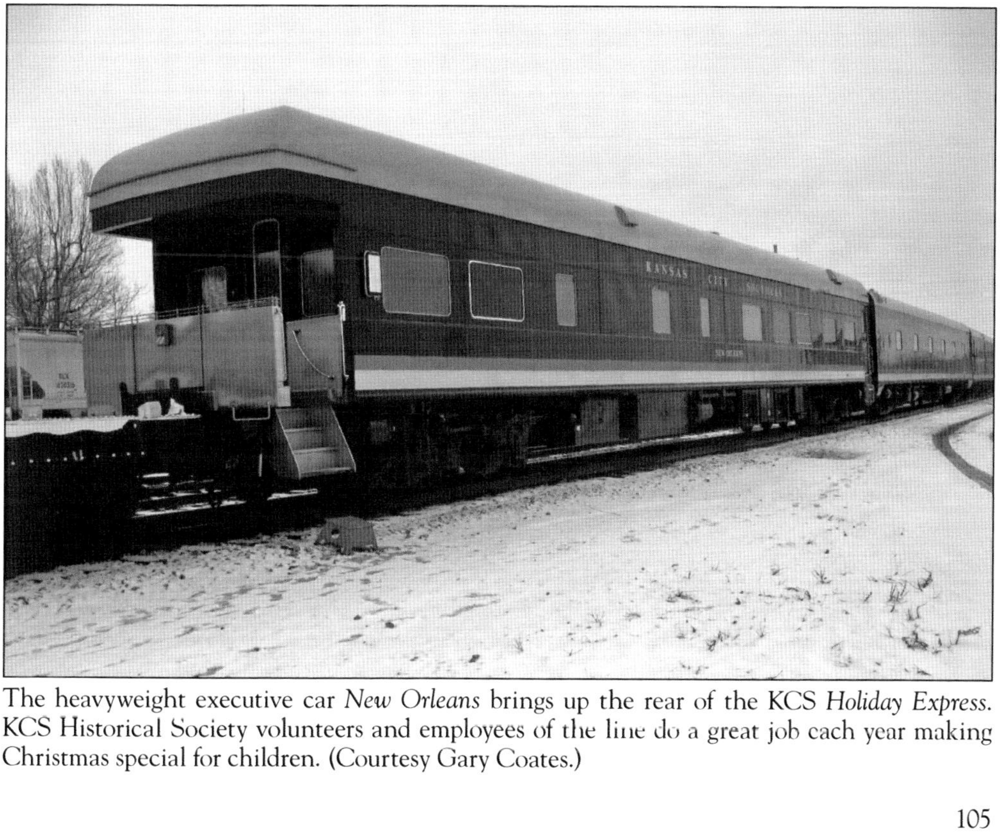

The heavyweight executive car *New Orleans* brings up the rear of the KCS *Holiday Express*. KCS Historical Society volunteers and employees of the line do a great job each year making Christmas special for children. (Courtesy Gary Coates.)

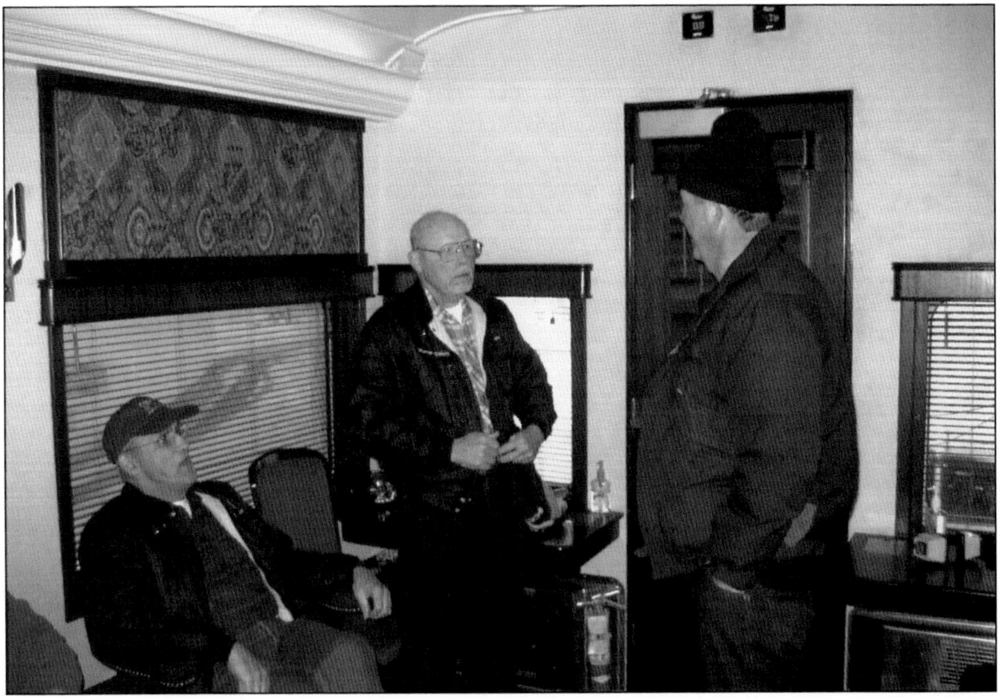

Jim Davis and KCS Historical Society members talk things over on board the KCS *Holiday Express*. It will not be long before the next stop where children will be waiting to see Santa. (Courtesy Gary Coates.)

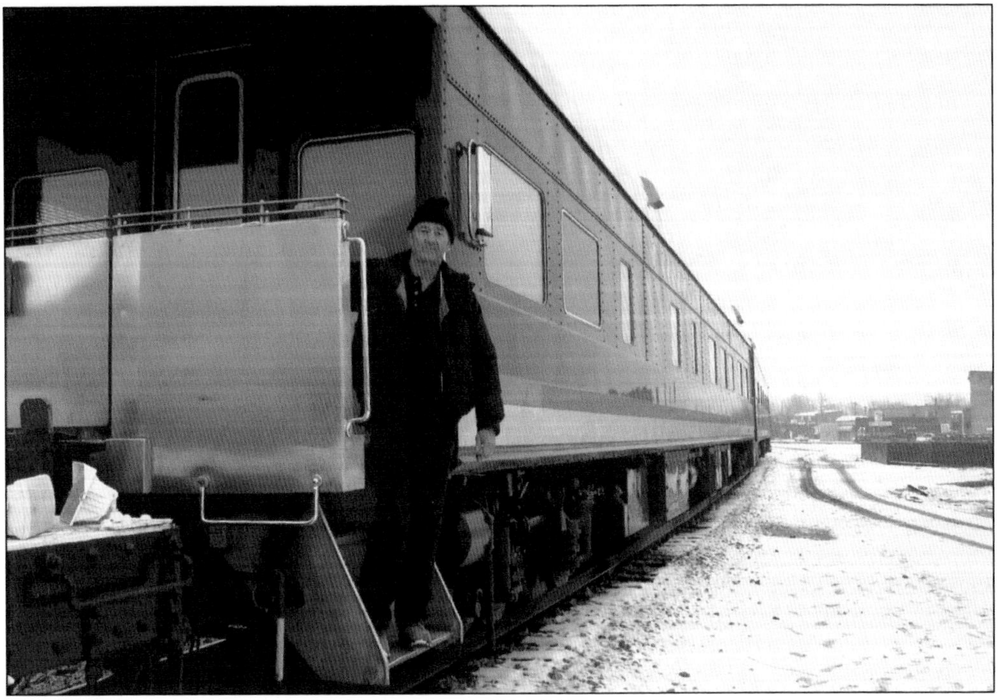

Jim Davis, a KCS employee, helps keep the *Holiday Express* rolling smoothly over its route each year. (Courtesy Gary Coates.)

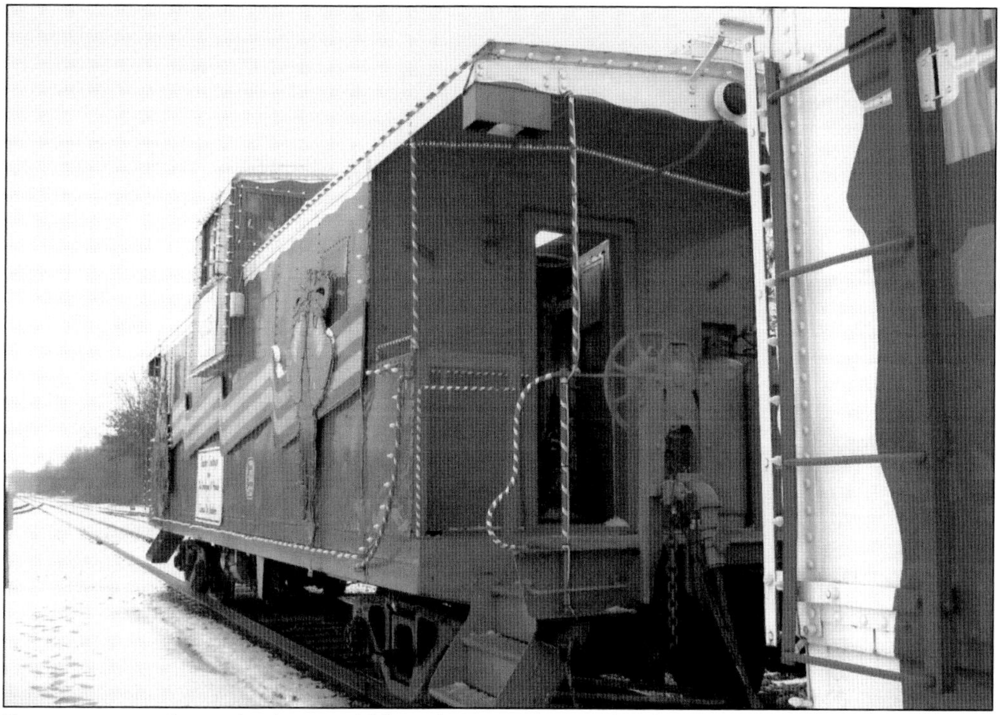

Every train needs a red caboose. Although most revenue freights no longer sport a caboose on the end of the train, the KCS *Holiday Express* is special and includes its very own caboose redone courtesy of the employees of the railroad. (Courtesy Gary Coates.)

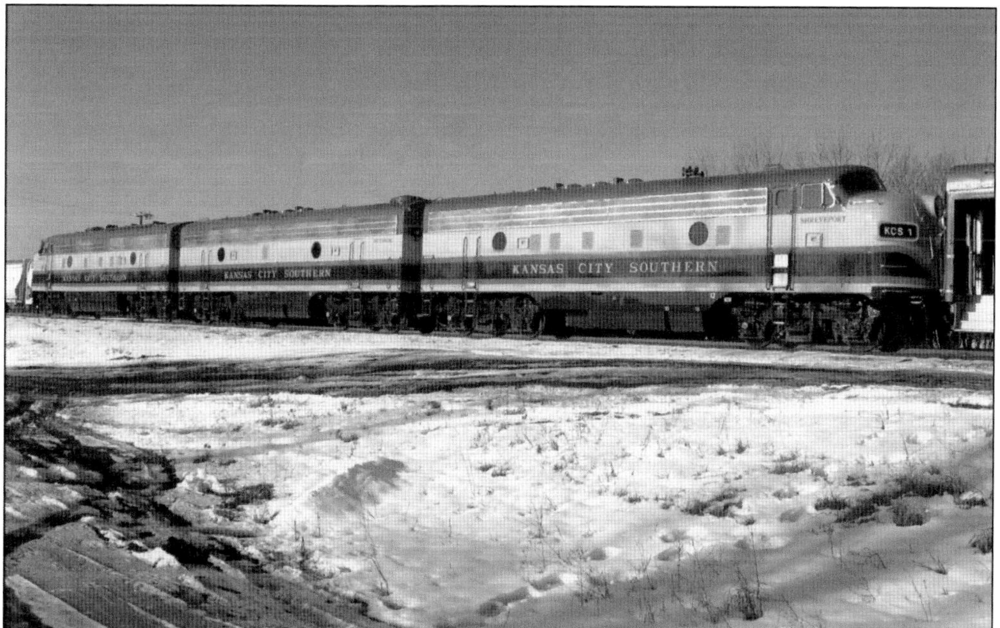

A beautiful A-B-A lash-up of diesel power pulls the KCS *Holiday Express* into Roodhouse, Illinois. These engines came from Canada and were rebuilt for KCS executive train service. (Courtesy Gary Coates.)

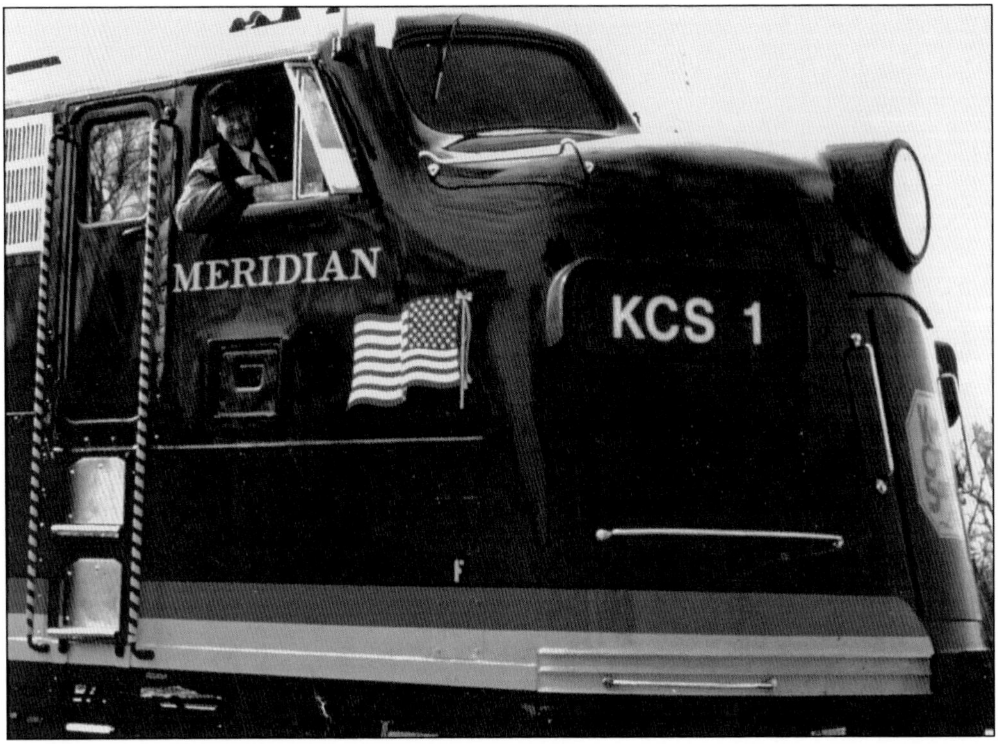

John Wettstein was engineer for the KCS *Southern Belle* executive train in the 1990s. Wettstein's years of experience as an engineer for the railroad helped qualify him to run the *Belle*. (Courtesy John Wettstein.)

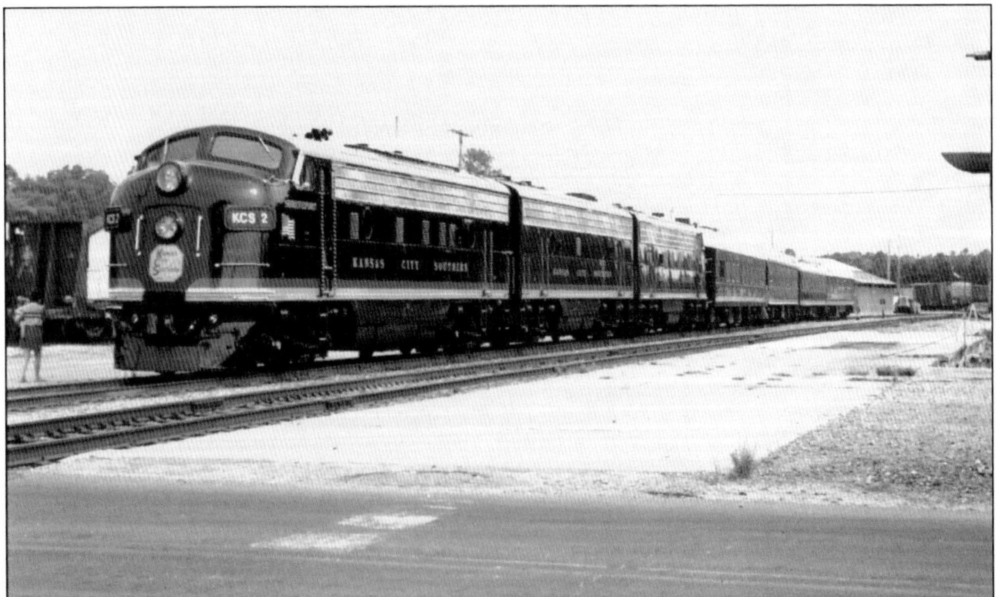

Here is KCS No. 2 on an inspection train on the DeQueen and Eastern Railway at DeQueen, Arkansas, some years ago. The youngster being carried by his mother is probably seeing his first passenger train. (Courtesy Philip L. Moseley.)

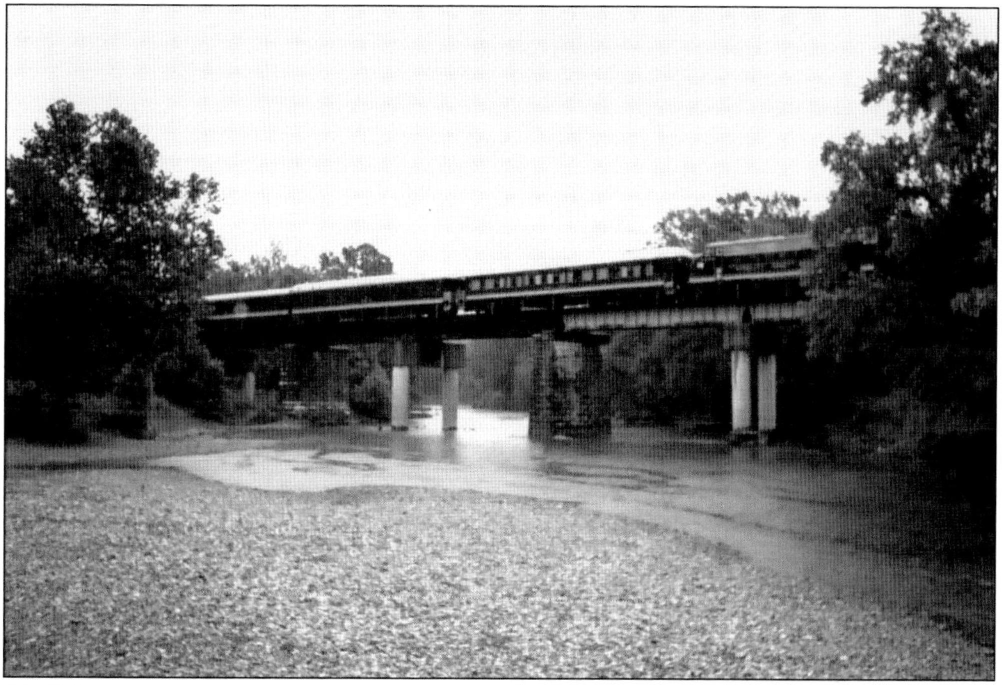

The KCS executive train continues its journey after a stop at Sulphur Springs, Arkansas. Note the trestle the train is traveling over has been updated with some modern supports. (Courtesy Glen Roark.)

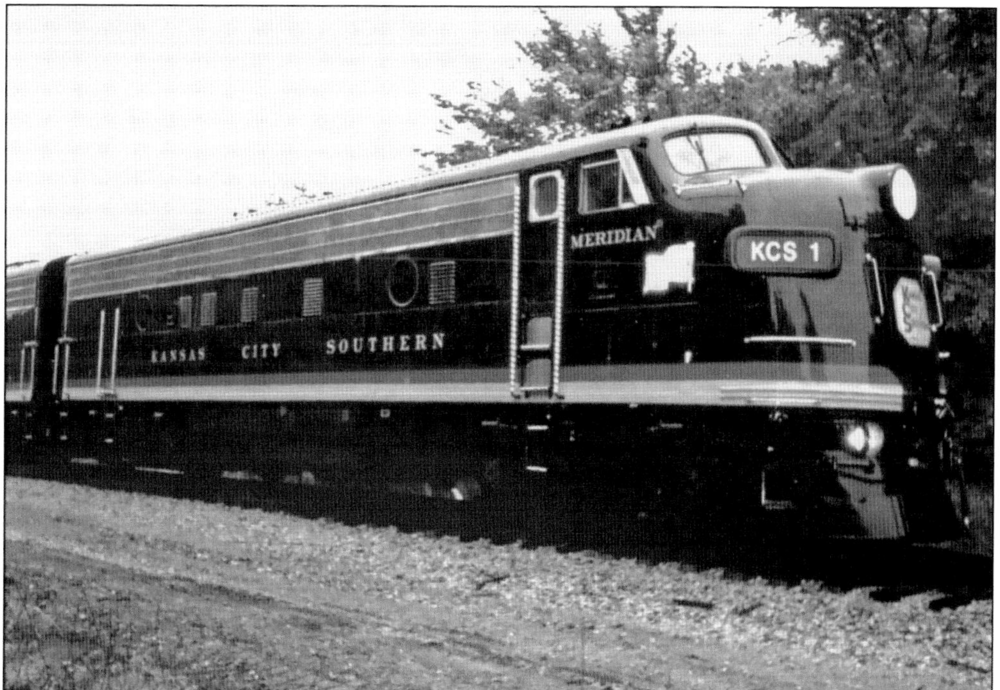

The diesel locomotive *Meridian* pulls the KCS executive train somewhere between Noel, Missouri, and Anderson, Missouri. The train is on an inspection trip. (Courtesy Glen Roark.)

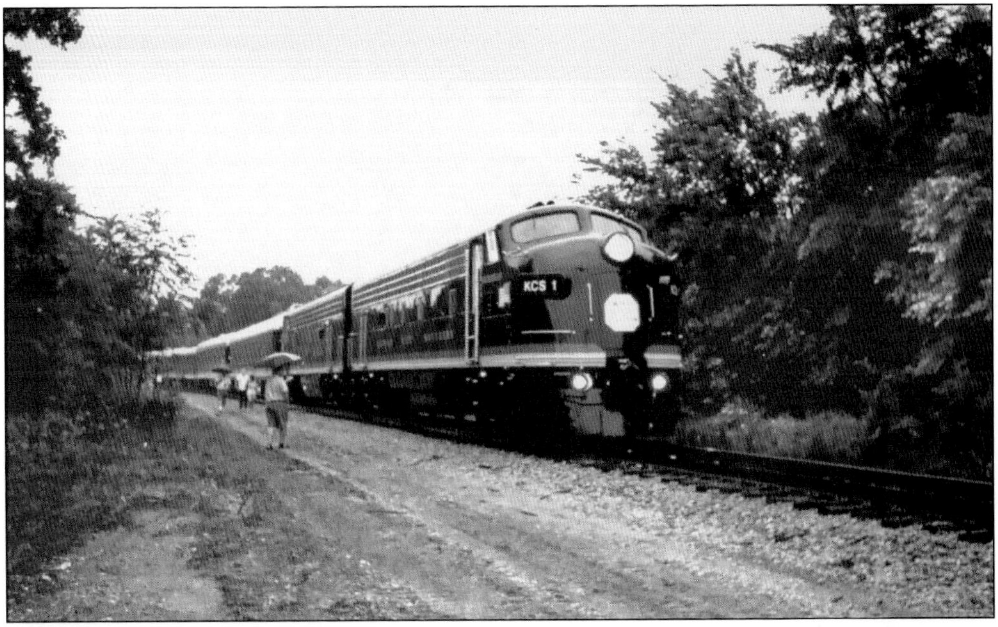

KCS chief executive officer Michael Haverty promoted the idea of a new *Southern Belle* in 1995. This train would be exclusively for executives and shippers. The units used to pull the train once belonged to VIA Rail Canada. Here at Sulphur Springs, Arkansas, the train has paused for a ceremony, and the crew awaits the return of the passengers before departing. It had been 26 years since the original *Southern Belle* last ran through here. (Courtesy Glen Roark.)

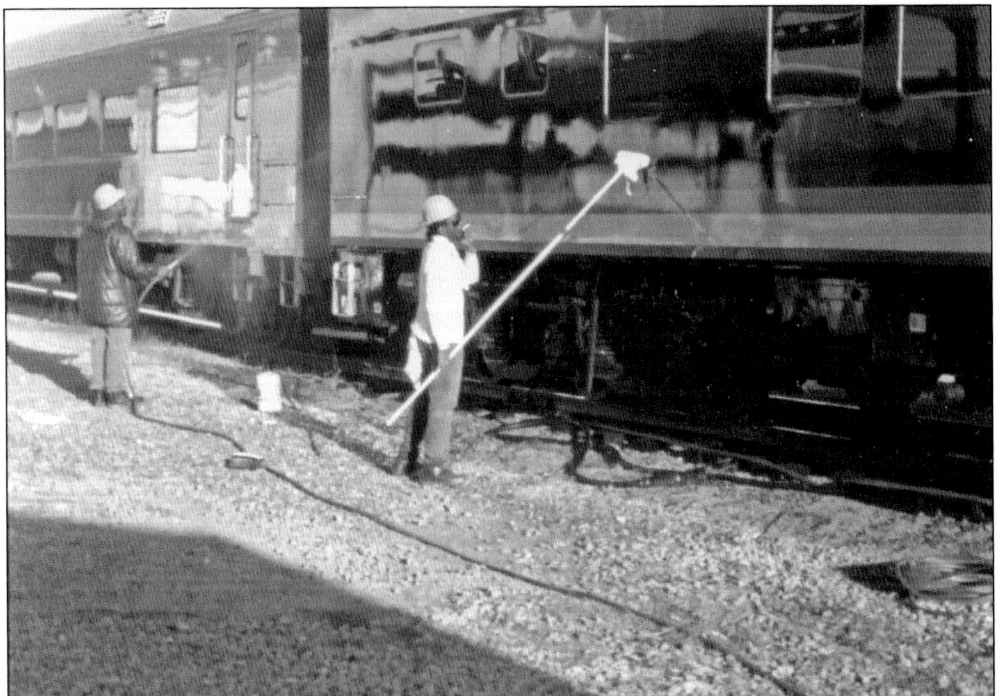

Part of the executive train's consist is the observation car *Kansas City*. Here the car receives a cleaning at the Deramus yard in Shreveport, Louisiana. (Courtesy Mary Jane McCrary.)

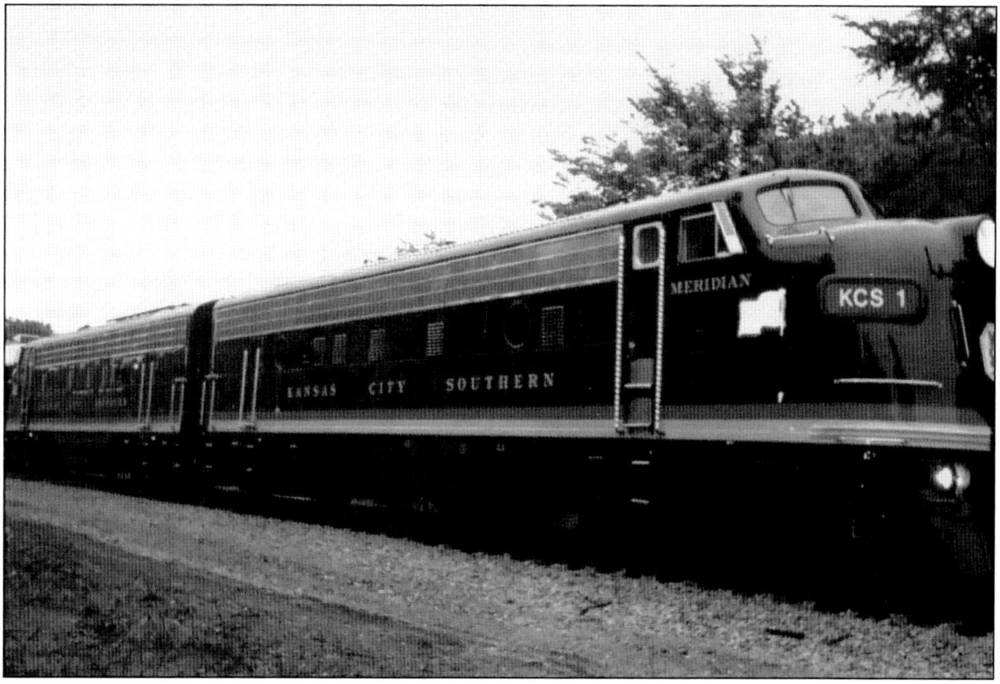

The new *Southern Belle* is parked at Sulphur Springs. (Courtesy Glen Roark.)

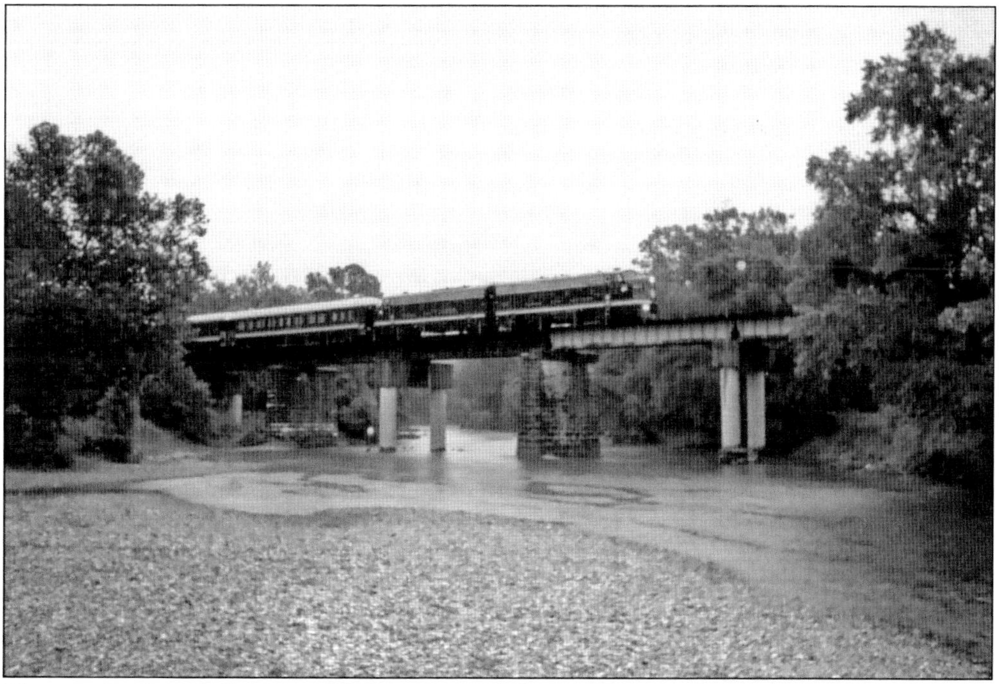

The new *Southern Belle* crosses Elk Springs trestle between Lanagan, Missouri, and Ginger Blue, Missouri, in early 1996. The original four-car consist has since been expanded to include a dormitory car, and a B unit has been added to the diesel lineup. (Courtesy Glen Roark.)

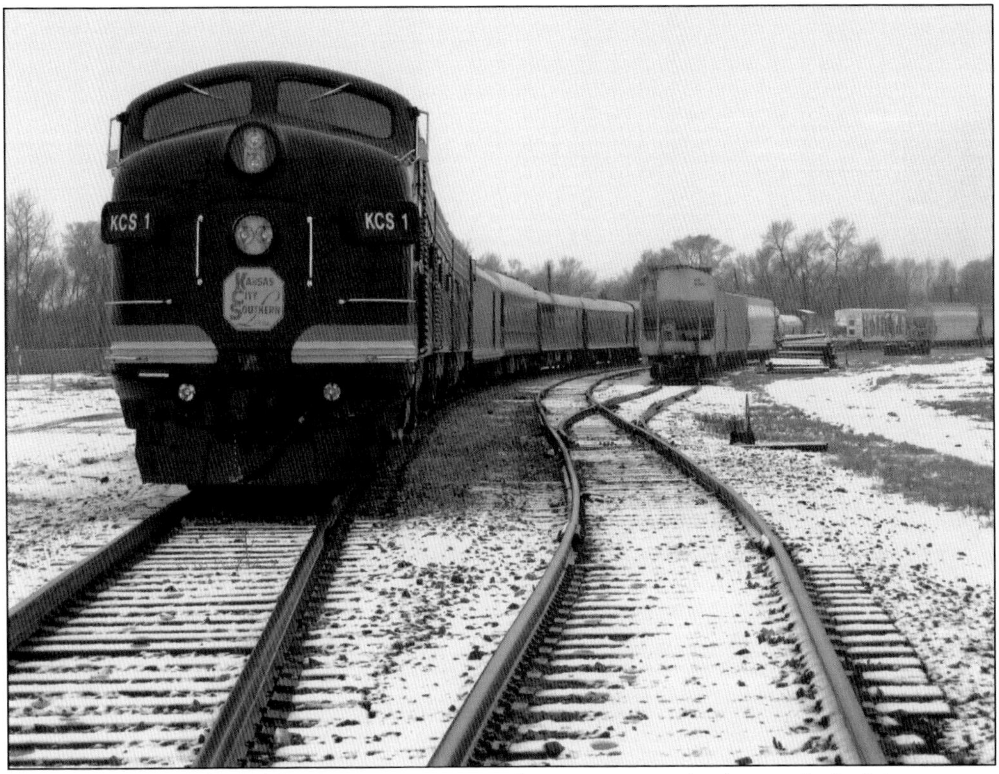

The lead unit on the KCS executive train stands out against a background of white snow at Roodhouse, Illinois, in 2005. Stormy weather did not stop the train from making its rounds to deliver gifts to children for Christmas. (Courtesy Gary Coates.)

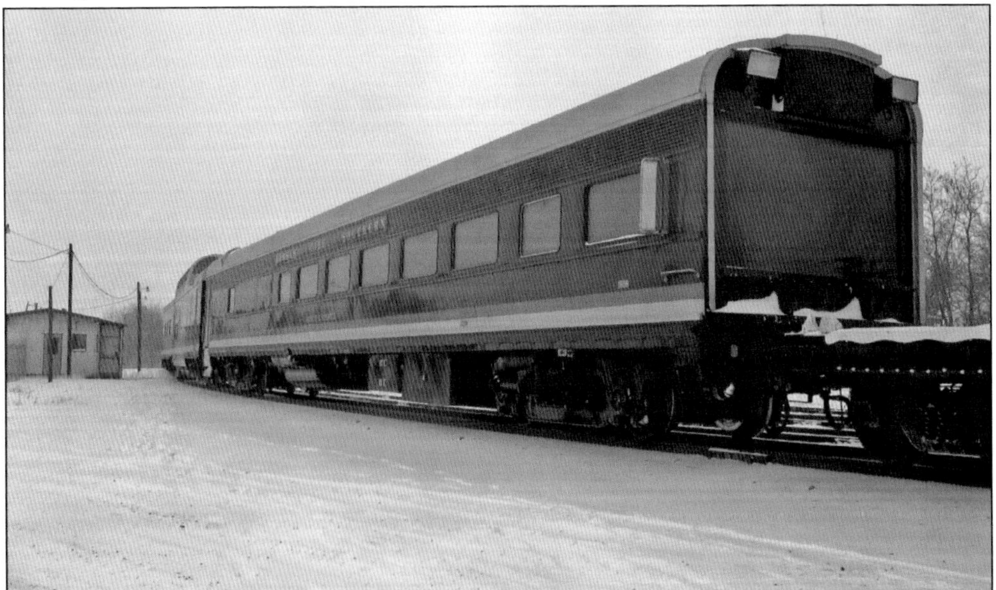

Another addition to the executive train is this restored passenger coach seen in the consist of the *Holiday Express*. (Courtesy Gary Coates.)

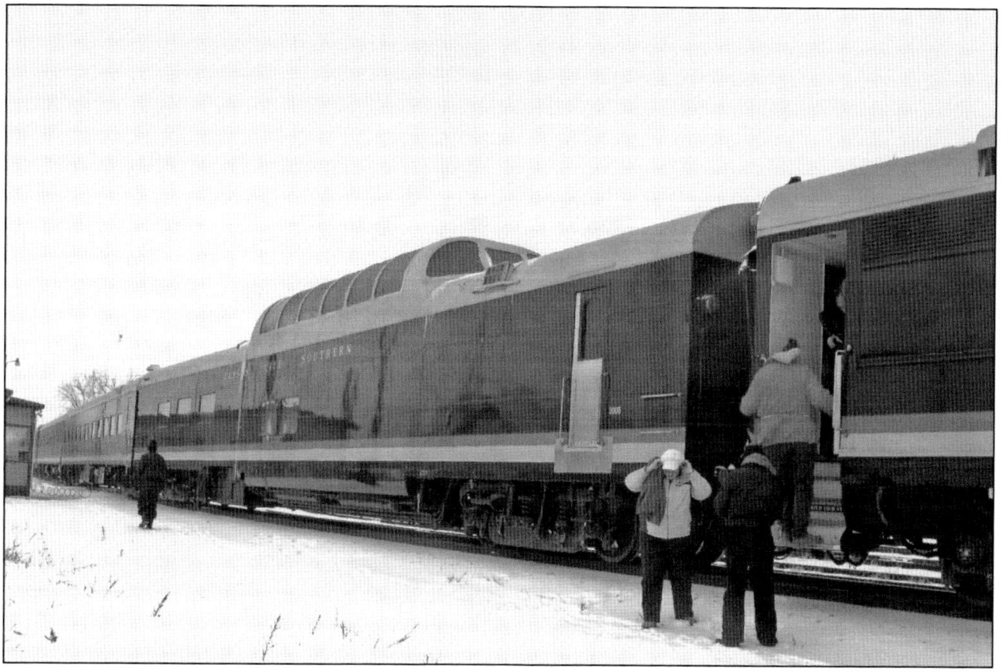

Once a Union Pacific Railroad dome diner from the 1950s, this beautifully restored dome car has been added to the *Southern Belle* executive train. Riders in the car will get a much better view of Rich Mountain. (Courtesy Gary Coates.)

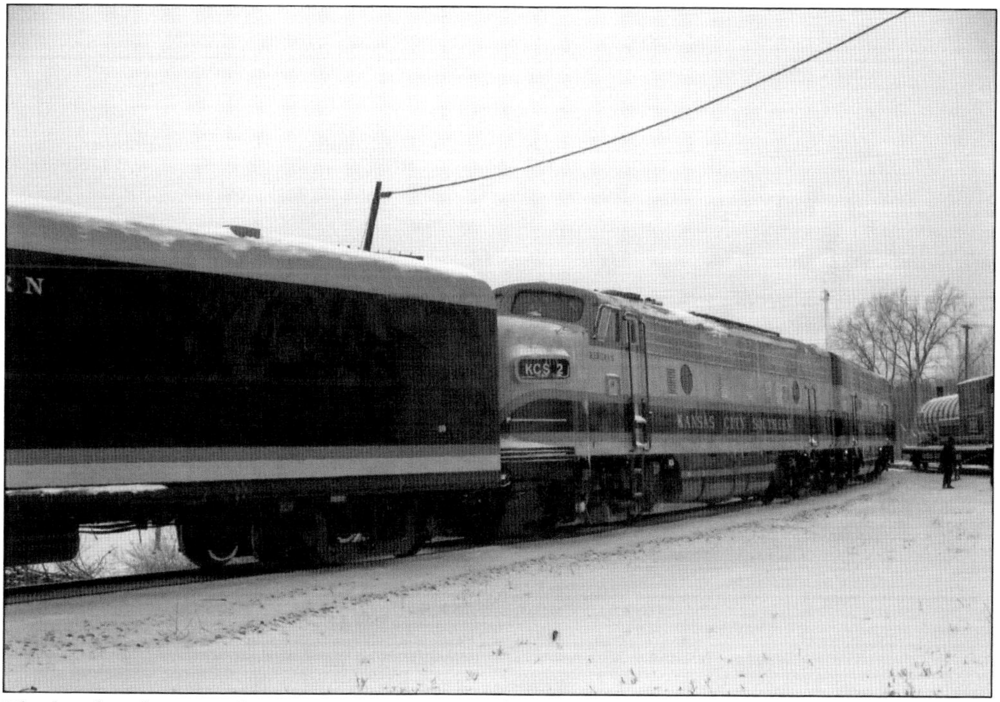

The head-end car on the executive train reminds one of the old smooth side baggage cars that once graced the front of the *Southern Belle* in the 1960s. The train has paused to bring some Christmas cheer to local residents of Roodhouse. (Courtesy Gary Coates.)

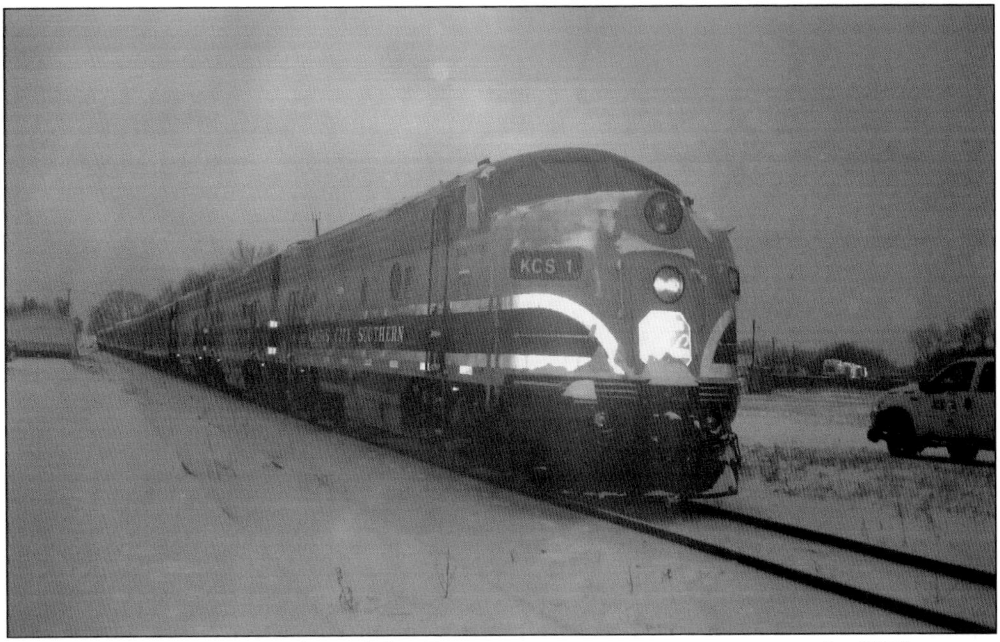

It is snowing at sunset as the *Holiday Express* continues its journey across the KCS system. Volunteers spend a month or more working on the train, helping out with gift distribution from town to town. (Courtesy Gary Coates.)

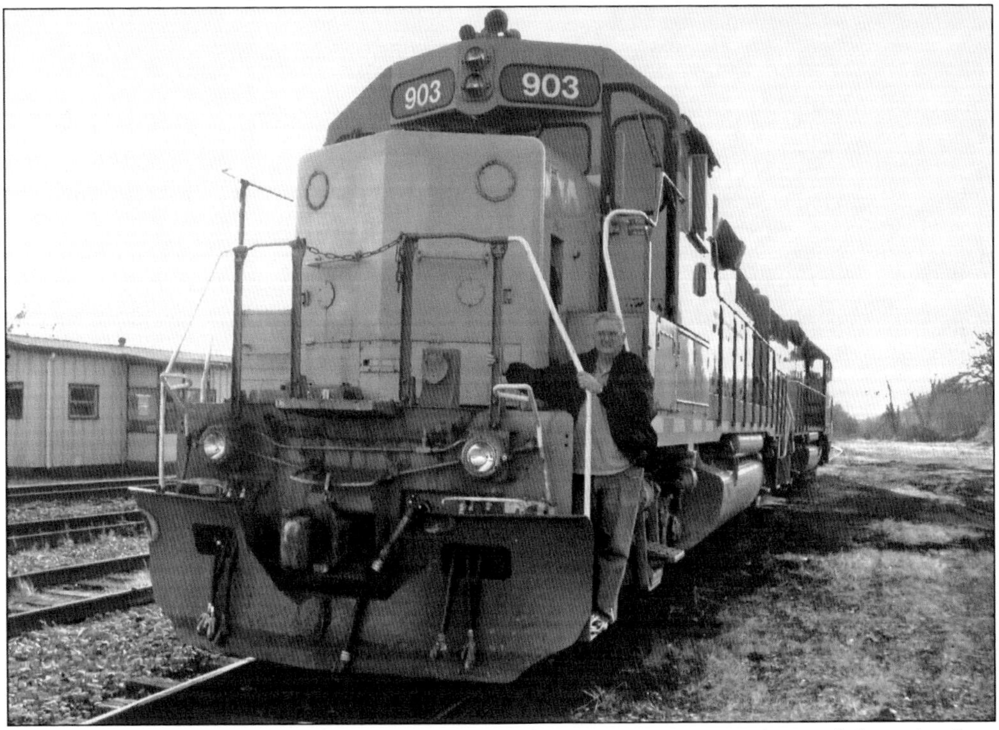

Southern Belle train photographer Gary Coates takes a turn posing in front of the cab of an ex–Union Pacific Railroad freight locomotive. Coates's love for railroads has taken him over much of the KCS line where he has photographed freight and passenger trains. (Courtesy Gary Coates.)

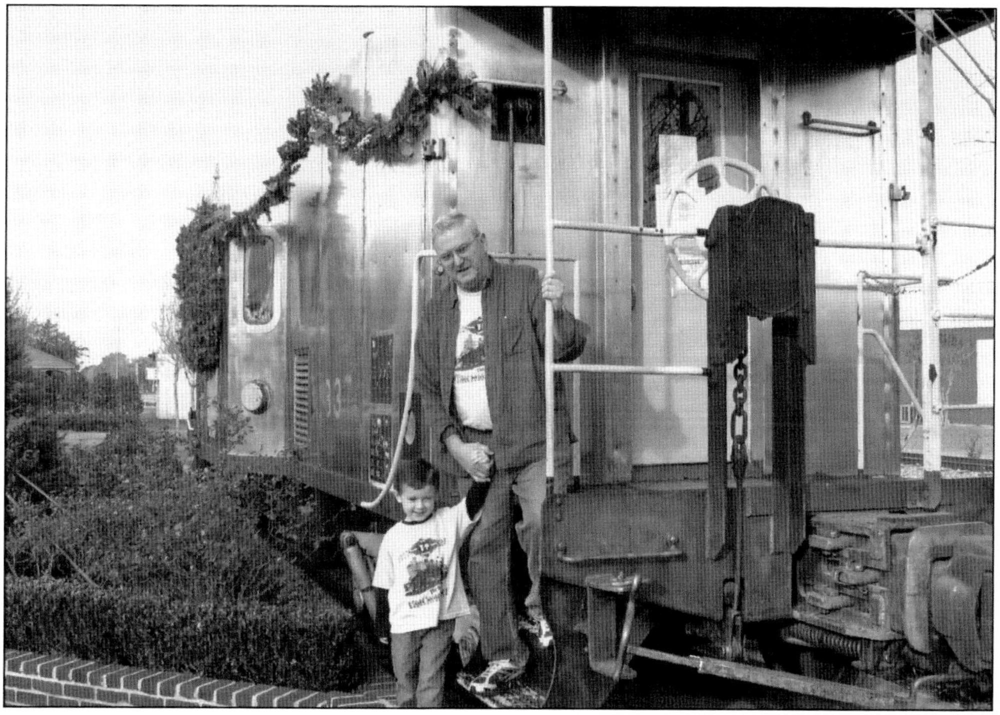

Perhaps awaiting the arrival of the *Holiday Express*, Coates and his grandson pose beside a KCS caboose on display at the DeRidder Museum in DeRidder, Louisiana. The young man has been a KCS stockholder since six months of age. (Courtesy Gary Coates.)

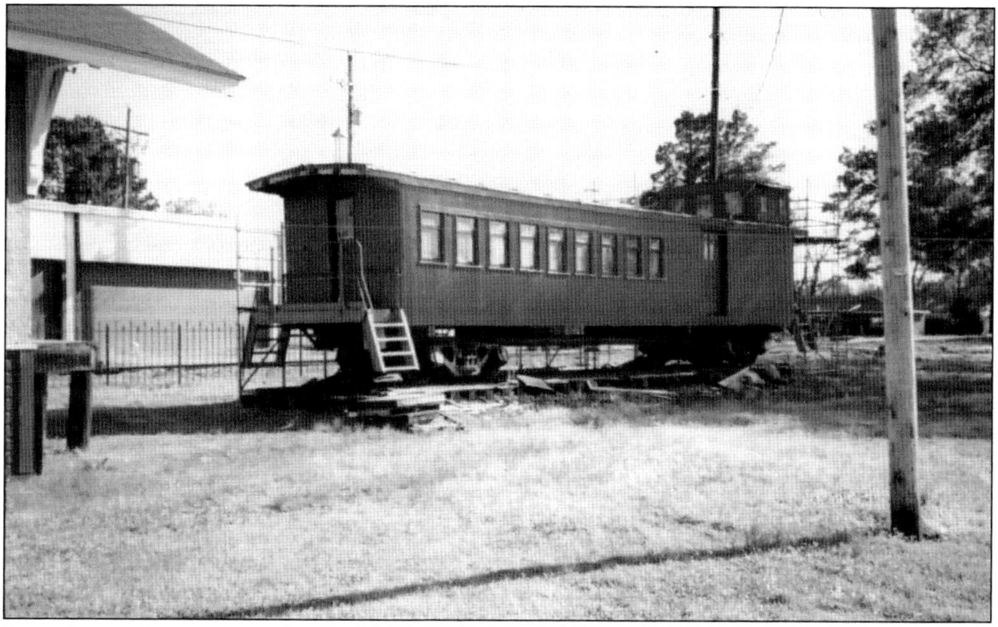

Just a few yards away from the KCS branch line at Ashdown, Arkansas, is this restored Drovers caboose. The old Cotton Belt caboose sat alongside Highway 71 for nearly 30 years before being brought to Ashdown where it was restored. It serves today as a local meeting site. (Courtesy Belinda S. Carter.)

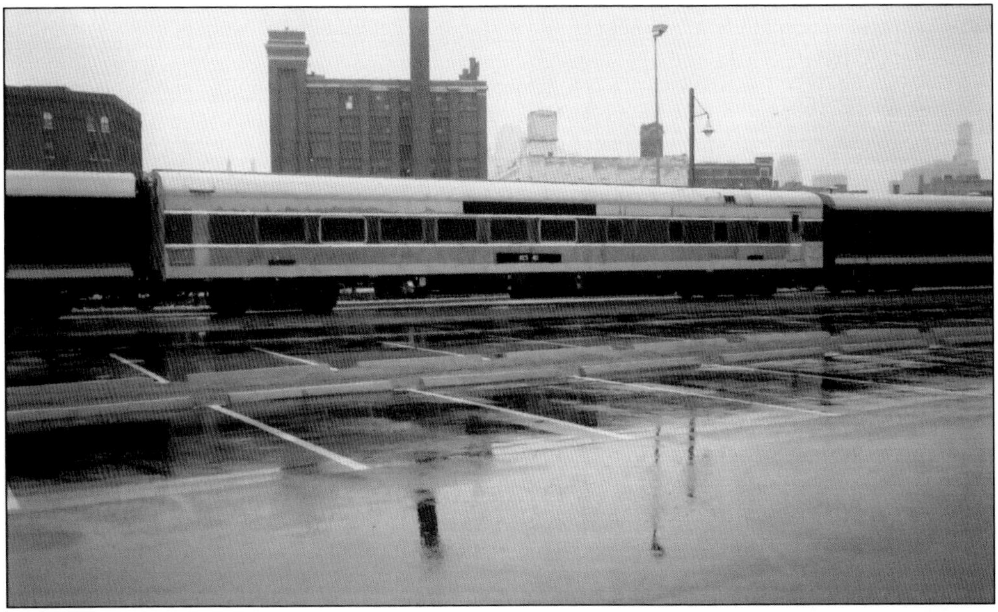

A recently acquired car for the *Southern Belle* business train is parked in the rain near the Kansas City Union Station. The KCS has continued to acquire cars for its private train over the last several years. (Courtesy Philip L. Moseley.)

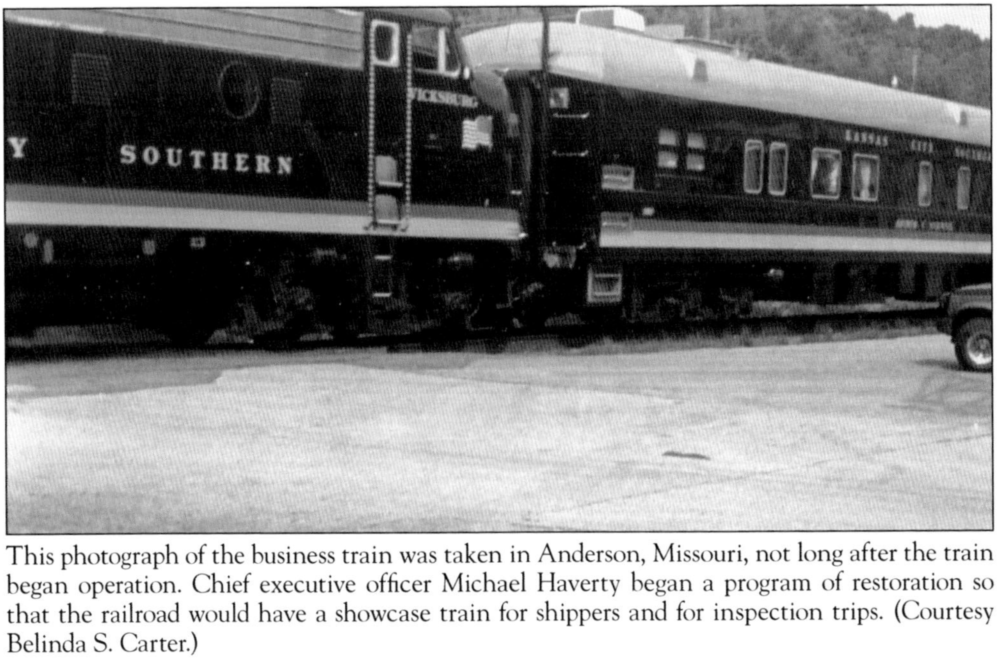

This photograph of the business train was taken in Anderson, Missouri, not long after the train began operation. Chief executive officer Michael Haverty began a program of restoration so that the railroad would have a showcase train for shippers and for inspection trips. (Courtesy Belinda S. Carter.)

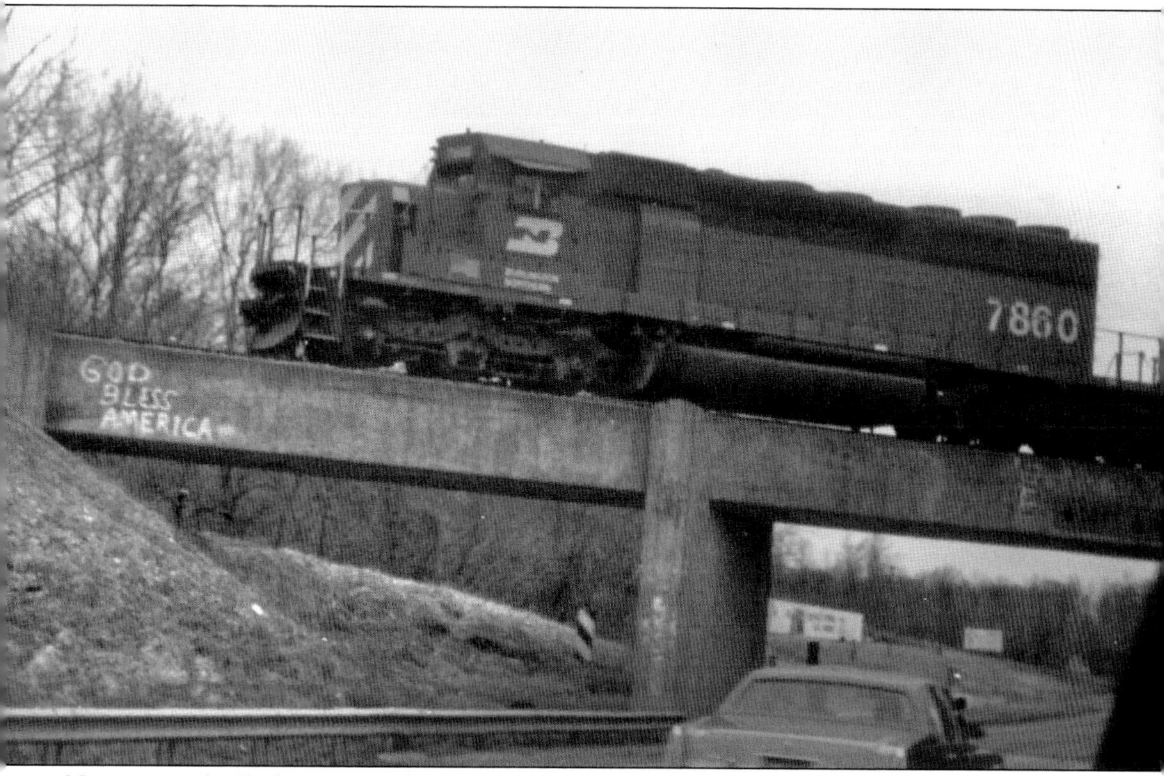

No, it is not the Burlington Northern Railroad. The locomotive is pulling a KCS coal train over the route of the *Southern Belle*. The train is headed north out of Anderson, Missouri. Notice the KCS emblem on the bridge. (Courtesy Belinda S. Carter.)

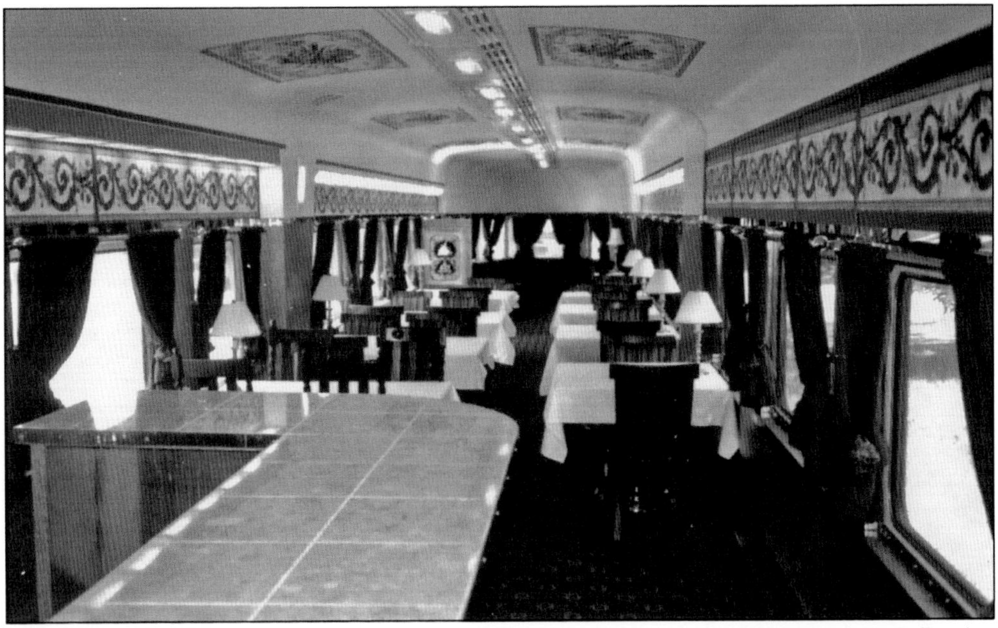

With a fancier interior than when it operated in food service on the KCS *Southern Belle*, this former New York Central Railroad observation car has found a home as a restaurant in Jackson, Louisiana. (Courtesy John Reed.)

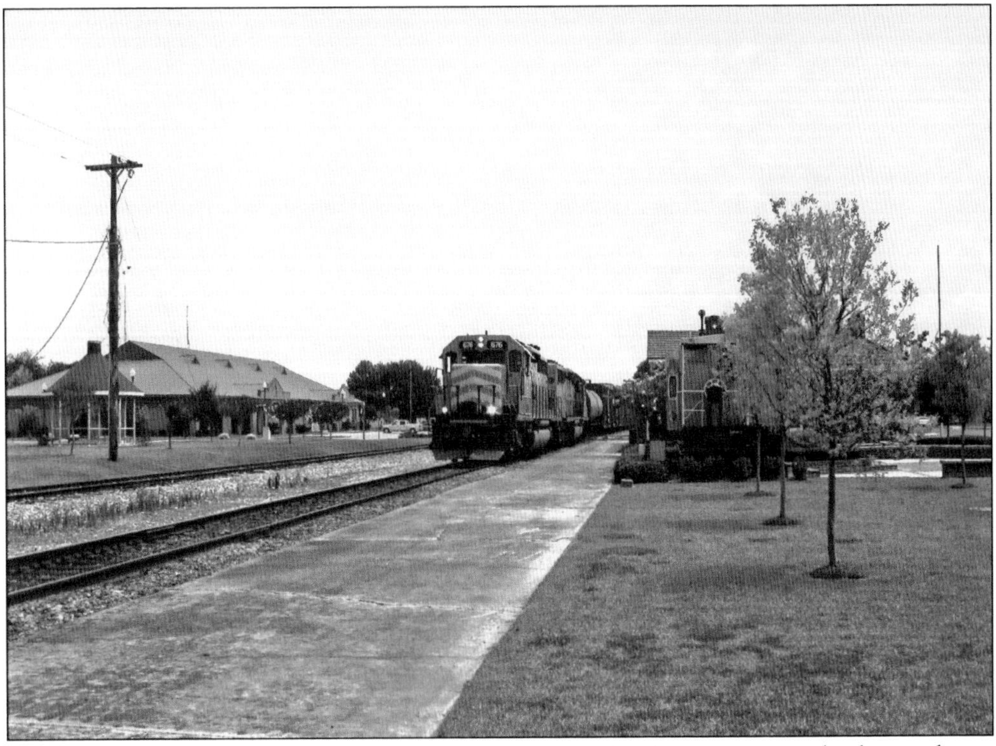

Going northbound through DeRidder, Louisiana, a KCS freight train passes the former depot, which now houses a museum and historical society. This was once a passenger train stop, but now only occasionally does the *Belle* executive go through. (Courtesy Gary Coates.)

Eight

Dining Car Menus

The original *Southern Belle* no longer runs, but one of the dining cars from the *Belle* is featured on the business train. Once upon a time, passengers ordered from specially prepared menus on the *Southern Belle*. The food selections were all prepared fresh in the dining cars on wood-fired cookstoves.

The author's earliest memories of eating in the dining car include waiting in line with his parents in the narrow hallway next to the kitchen. The aroma was fantastic as the chef and his helpers prepared meals on a wood-burning cookstove. They worked in a confined space, but still managed to turn out fantastic meals.

When it was time to be seated, the dining car steward would direct passengers to their table. Once they were seated, a waiter would bring out water and menus. Diners had to write their own food orders as the waiters were not permitted to do so. The meals were always worth the wait.

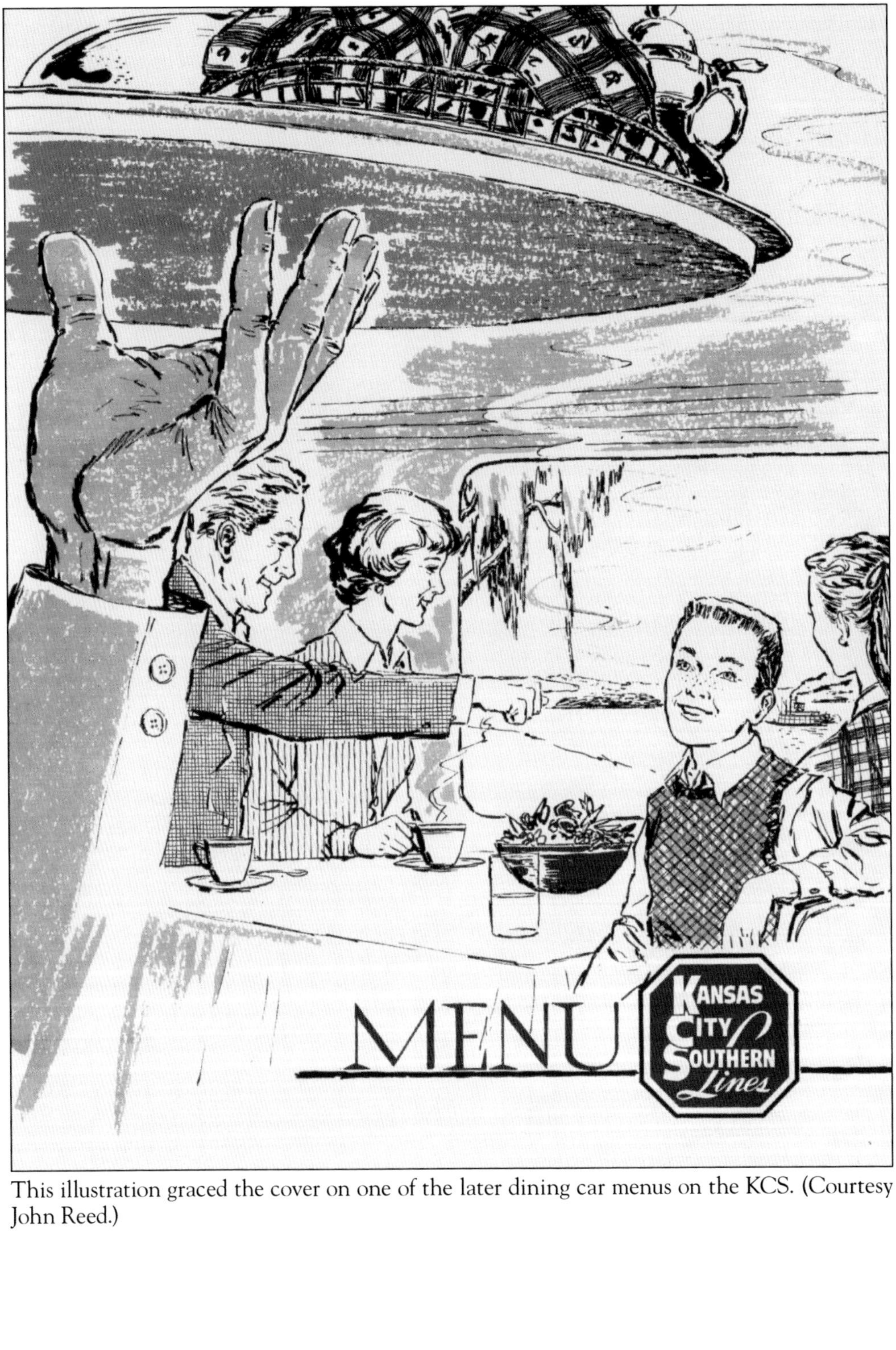

This illustration graced the cover on one of the later dining car menus on the KCS. (Courtesy John Reed.)

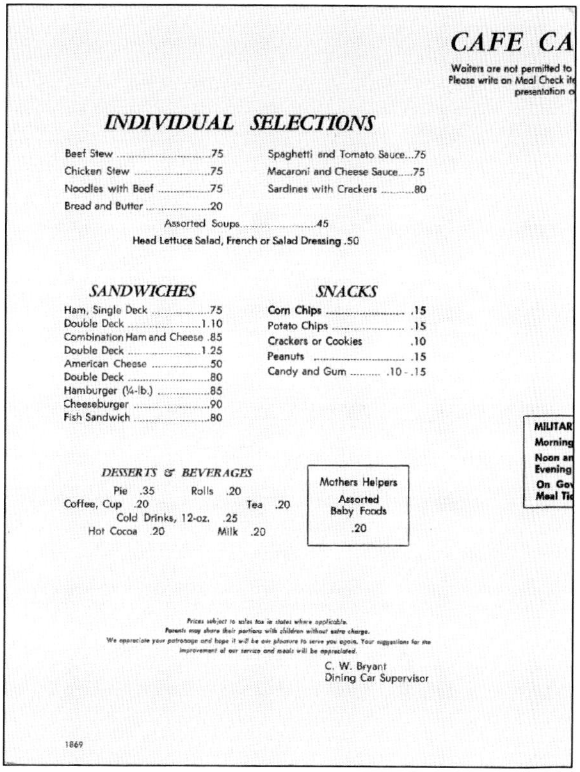

CAFE CA

Waiters are not permitted to
Please write on Meal Check ite
presentation o

INDIVIDUAL SELECTIONS

Beef Stew .75
Chicken Stew .75
Noodles with Beef .75
Bread and Butter .20
Spaghetti and Tomato Sauce .75
Macaroni and Cheese Sauce .75
Sardines with Crackers .80
Assorted Soups .45
Head Lettuce Salad, French or Salad Dressing .50

SANDWICHES

Ham, Single Deck .75
Double Deck 1.10
Combination Ham and Cheese .85
Double Deck 1.25
American Cheese .50
Double Deck .80
Hamburger (¼-lb.) .85
Cheeseburger .90
Fish Sandwich .80

SNACKS

Corn Chips .15
Potato Chips .15
Crackers or Cookies .10
Peanuts .15
Candy and Gum .10 - .15

DESSERTS & BEVERAGES

Pie .35 Rolls .20
Coffee, Cup .20 Tea .20
Cold Drinks, 12-oz. .25
Hot Cocoa .20 Milk .20

Mothers Helpers
Assorted Baby Foods
.20

MILITAR
Morning
Noon an
Evening
On Gov
Meal Tic

Prices subject to sales tax in states where applicable.
Parents may share their portions with children without extra charge.
We appreciate your patronage and hope it will be our pleasure to serve you again. Your suggestions for the improvement of our service and meals will be appreciated.

C. W. Bryant
Dining Car Supervisor

1869

Both inside pages of the menu feature items available for under $2, but the rib eye steak had been raised to $2.50. (Courtesy John Reed.)

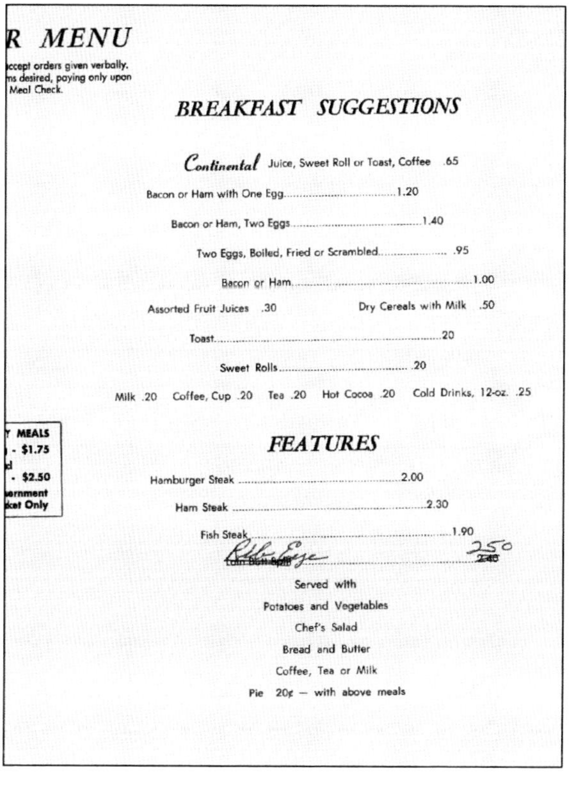

R MENU

ccept orders given verbally.
ms desired, paying only upon
Meal Check.

BREAKFAST SUGGESTIONS

Continental Juice, Sweet Roll or Toast, Coffee .65
Bacon or Ham with One Egg 1.20
Bacon or Ham, Two Eggs 1.40
Two Eggs, Boiled, Fried or Scrambled .95
Bacon or Ham 1.00
Assorted Fruit Juices .30
Dry Cereals with Milk .50
Toast .20
Sweet Rolls .20
Milk .20 Coffee, Cup .20 Tea .20 Hot Cocoa .20 Cold Drinks, 12-oz. .25

Y MEALS
) - $1.75
d
- $2.50
ernment
cket Only

FEATURES

Hamburger Steak 2.00
Ham Steak 2.30
Fish Steak 1.90
~~Loin Butt Split~~ Rib Eye ~~2.40~~ 250

Served with
Potatoes and Vegetables
Chef's Salad
Bread and Butter
Coffee, Tea or Milk
Pie 20¢ — with above meals

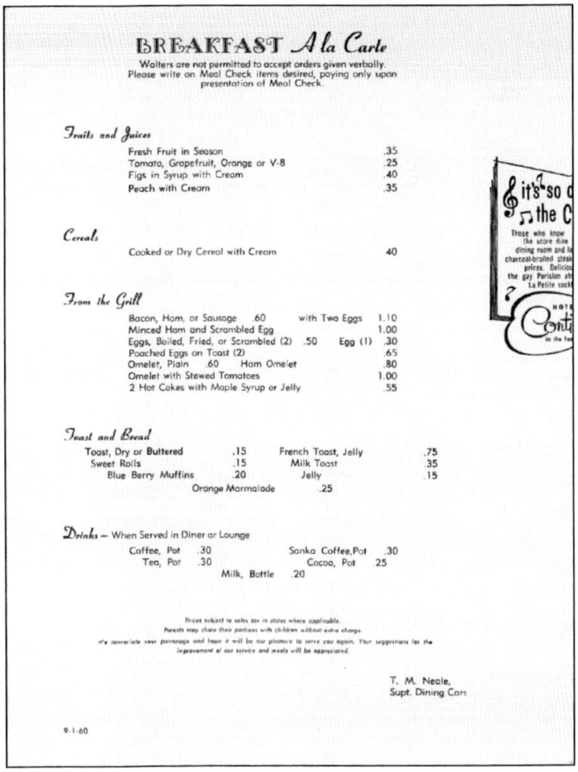

BREAKFAST *A la Carte*

Waiters are not permitted to accept orders given verbally.
Please write on Meal Check items desired, paying only upon presentation of Meal Check.

Fruits and Juices

Fresh Fruit in Season	.35
Tomato, Grapefruit, Orange or V-8	.25
Figs in Syrup with Cream	.40
Peach with Cream	.35

Cereals

Cooked or Dry Cereal with Cream	.40

From the Grill

Bacon, Ham, or Sausage .60 with Two Eggs	1.10
Minced Ham and Scrambled Egg	1.00
Eggs, Boiled, Fried, or Scrambled (2) .50 Egg (1)	.30
Poached Eggs on Toast (2)	.65
Omelet, Plain .60 Ham Omelet	.80
Omelet with Stewed Tomatoes	1.00
2 Hot Cakes with Maple Syrup or Jelly	.55

Toast and Bread

Toast, Dry or Buttered	.15	French Toast, Jelly	.75
Sweet Rolls	.15	Milk Toast	.35
Blue Berry Muffins	.20	Jelly	.15
Orange Marmalade	.25		

Drinks — When Served in Diner or Lounge

Coffee, Pot	.30	Sanka Coffee, Pot	.30
Tea, Pot	.30	Cocoa, Pot	.25
Milk, Bottle	.20		

Prices subject to sales tax in states where applicable.
Parents may share their portions with children without extra charge.
We appreciate your patronage and hope it will be our pleasure to serve you again. Your suggestions for the improvement of our service and meals will be appreciated.

T. M. Neale,
Supt. Dining Cars

9-1-60

The September 1960 dining car menu on the *Southern Belle* features a wide variety of choices for breakfast, including breakfast for military personnel for only $1.50. Diners were required to write their orders down on the check. (Courtesy John Reed.)

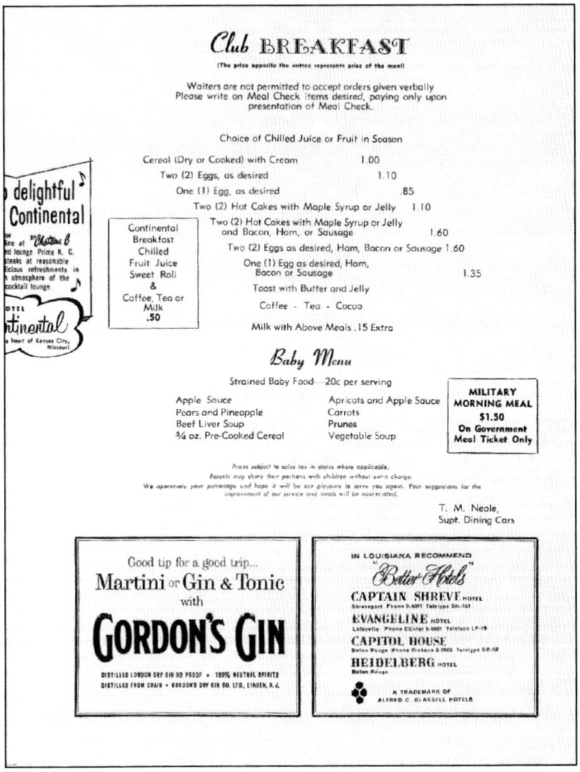

Club BREAKFAST

(The price opposite the entree represents price of the meal)

Waiters are not permitted to accept orders given verbally
Please write on Meal Check items desired, paying only upon presentation of Meal Check.

Choice of Chilled Juice or Fruit in Season

Cereal (Dry or Cooked) with Cream	1.00
Two (2) Eggs, as desired	1.10
One (1) Egg, as desired	.85
Two (2) Hot Cakes with Maple Syrup or Jelly	1.10
Two (2) Hot Cakes with Maple Syrup or Jelly and Bacon, Ham, or Sausage	1.60
Two (2) Eggs as desired, Ham, Bacon or Sausage	1.60
One (1) Egg as desired, Ham, Bacon or Sausage	1.35

Toast with Butter and Jelly
Coffee - Tea - Cocoa
Milk with Above Meals .15 Extra

Continental Breakfast
Chilled Fruit Juice
Sweet Roll
&
Coffee, Tea or Milk
.50

Baby Menu

Strained Baby Food—20c per serving

Apple Sauce	Apricots and Apple Sauce
Pears and Pineapple	Carrots
Beef Liver Soup	Prunes
¾ oz. Pre-Cooked Cereal	Vegetable Soup

MILITARY MORNING MEAL
$1.50
On Government Meal Ticket Only

Prices subject to sales tax in states where applicable.
Parents may share their portions with children without extra charge.
We appreciate your patronage and hope it will be our pleasure to serve you again. Your suggestions for the improvement of our service and meals will be appreciated.

T. M. Neale,
Supt. Dining Cars

Nine

MISCELLANEOUS

Signs of the KCS remain, even where the line does not. Today when driving from Westlake, Louisiana, to Lake Charles, Louisiana, over the old Calcasieu River Bridge, a quick glance off to the left reveals the Union Pacific railroad bridge. This is used by the Union Pacific and the KCS into Lake Charles. The old KCS railroad bridge is gone as is the right-of-way from Westlake into Lake Charles.

Although this small part of the KCS trackage is no longer in service, the railroad has survived into the 21st century as a healthy class-one line. Gone are the wood-sided boxcars pulled by steam locomotives. In their place are multimillion dollar diesel engines pulling freight cars filled with coal, grain, petroleum products, and piggyback cars. The caboose that once brought up the rear of the train has been replaced by a rear-end computer device. One reminder of *Southern Belle* days is the shiny diesel engines painted in the *Belle* scheme pulling 100-car freights. The KCS railroad is doing well and appears to have a very bright future.

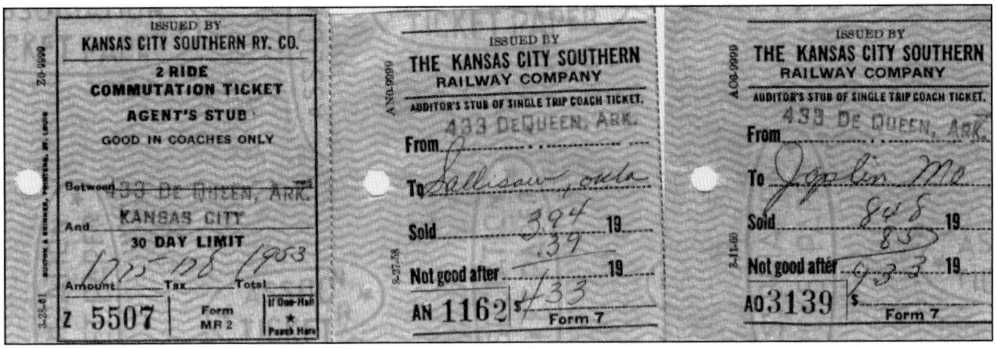

These three ticket stubs provide a clue as to why the KCS may have gone out of the passenger business. Fares ranged from $4.33 to $19.53 for a trip from DeQueen, Arkansas, to Kansas City. (Courtesy Philip L. Moseley.)

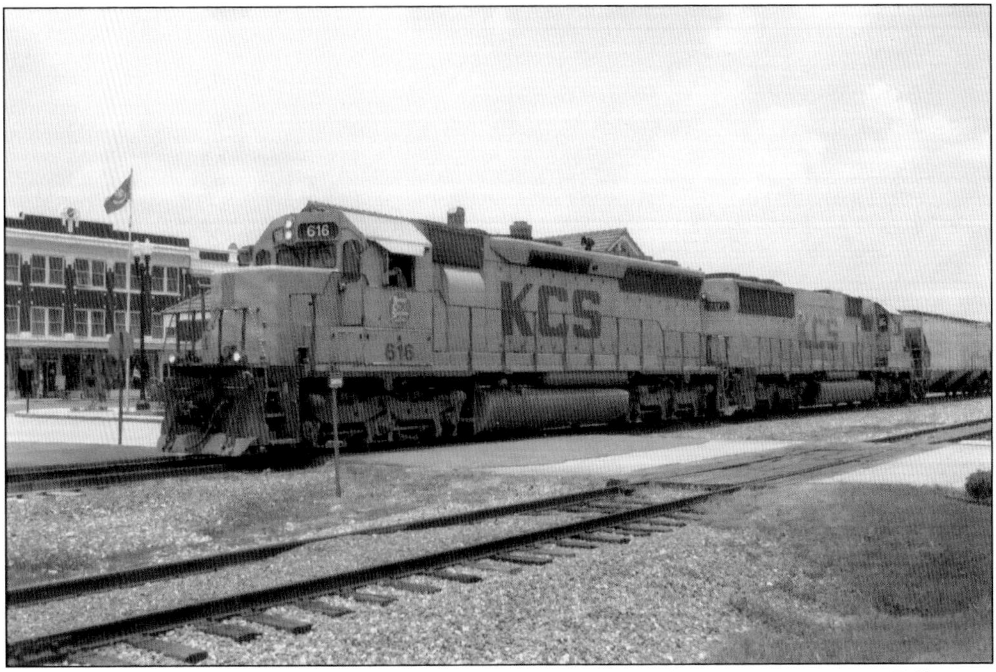

Headed south to Port Arthur, Texas, a KCS freight glides past the passenger station. Following the end of passenger service to DeRidder, Louisiana, the station was converted into a museum. (Courtesy of Gary Coates.)

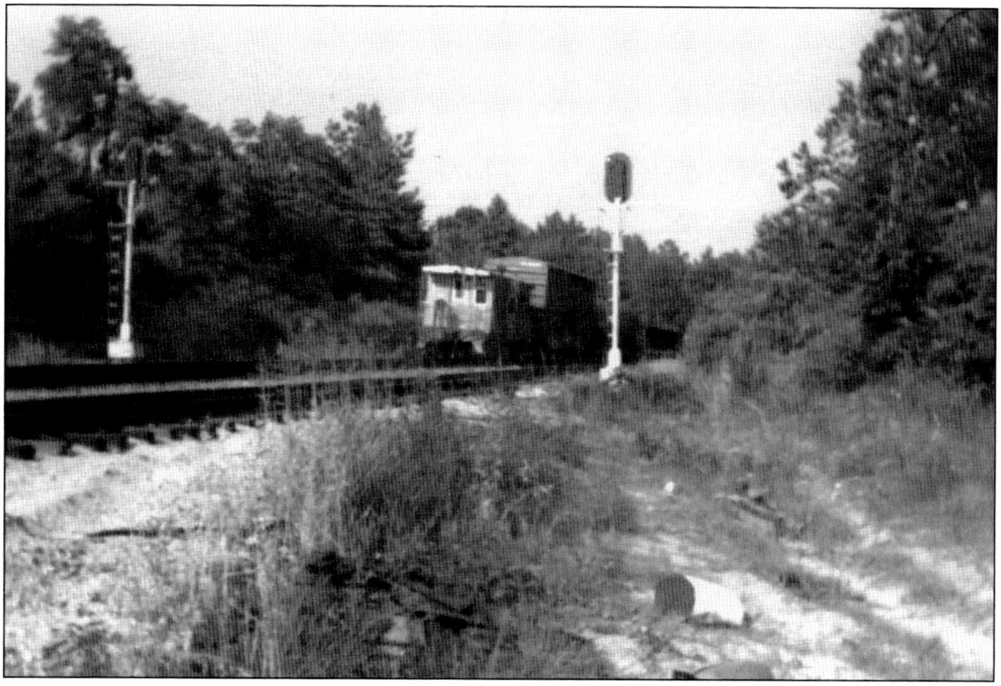

After going past a green block signal, a northbound KCS freight heads onward toward its destination in Kansas City. Scraps on the side of the roadbed indicate some possible track work. (Author's collection.)

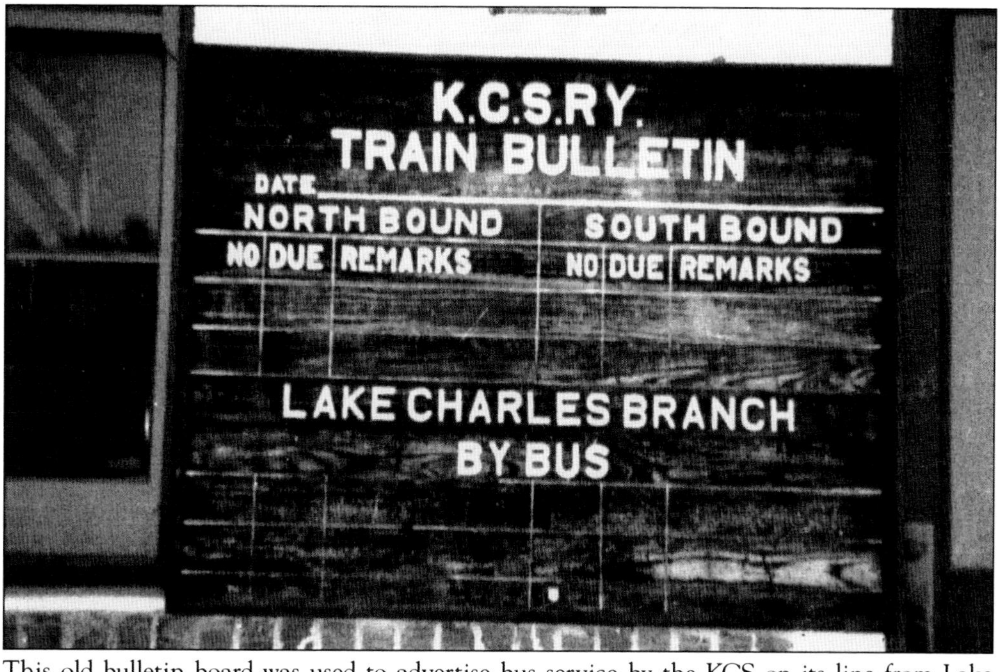

This old bulletin board was used to advertise bus service by the KCS on its line from Lake Charles, Louisiana, to DeQuincy, Louisiana. This picture was taken some years after service was discontinued. The driver of the bus, George Edwards, made a daily round-trip carrying passengers to the train at DeQuincy and back to Lake Charles. (Author's collection.)

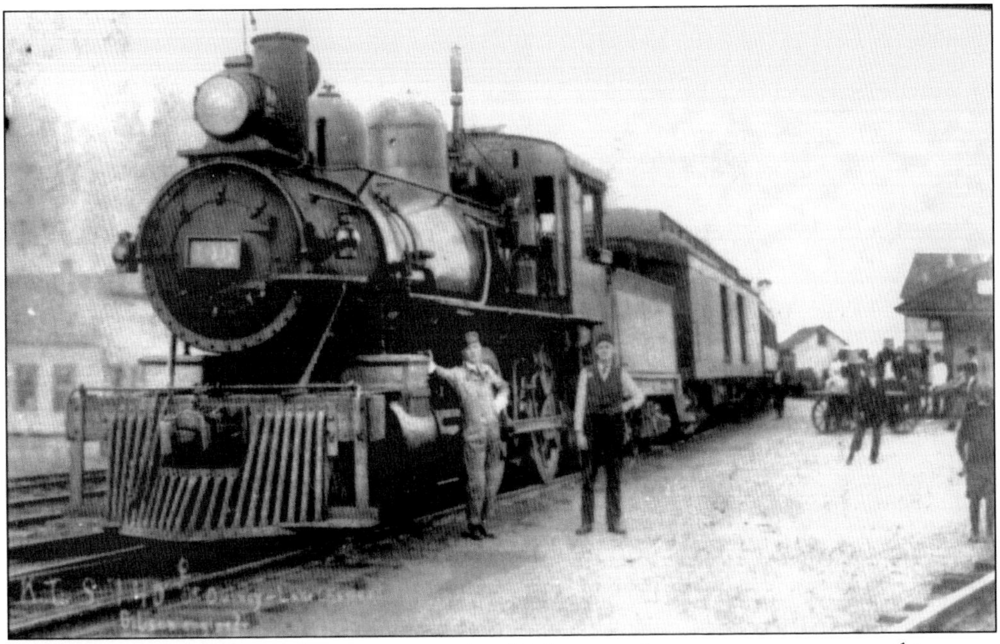

Over 100 years ago, when rail transport was the chief means of passenger conveyance, this steam train pauses at DeQuincy, Louisiana, to receive passengers for its run to Port Arthur, Texas. (Courtesy McNeese State University Archives.)

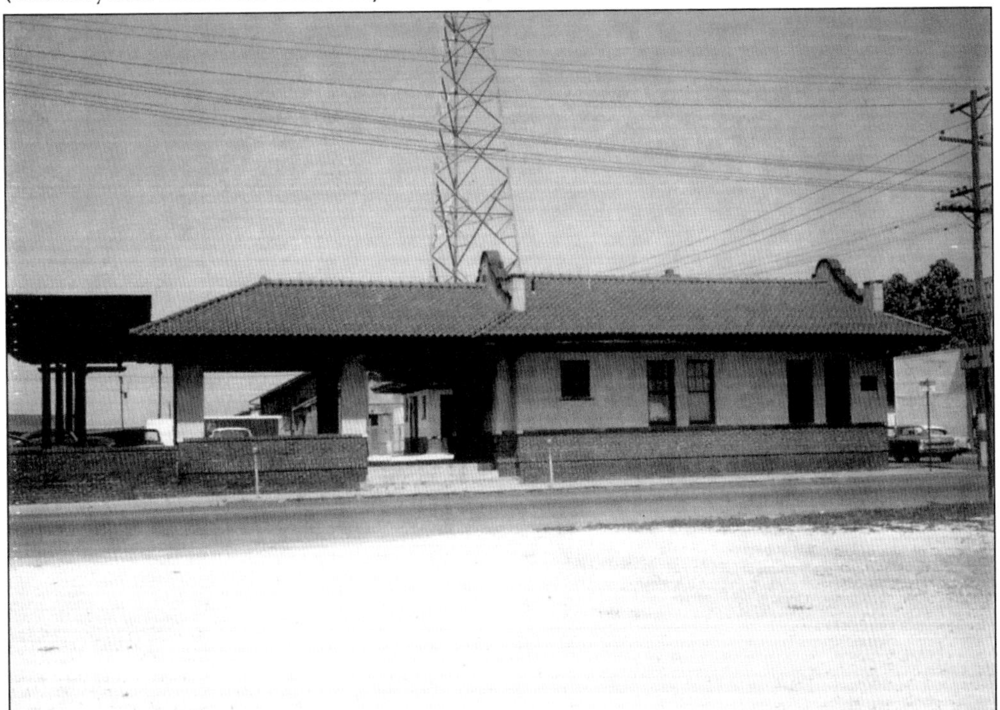

The KCS depot in Lake Charles, Louisiana, is shown about the time passenger service ended on the line in 1969. The building remained for a few more years before being torn down. (Courtesy McNeese State University Archives.)

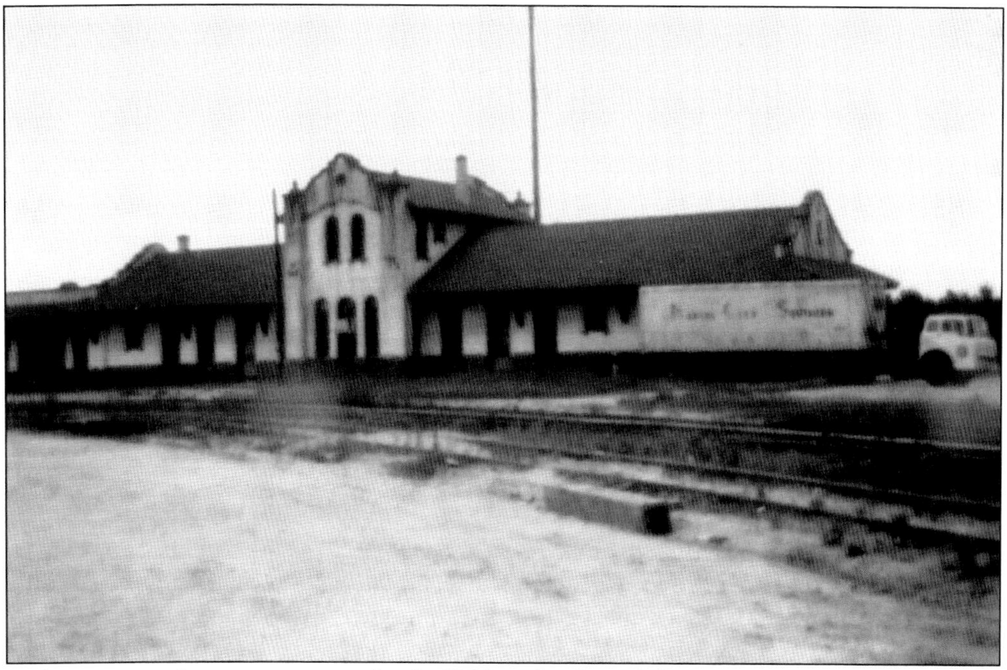

DeQuincy was the junction point for the KCS with a branch line going to Lake Charles. Here is the KCS depot, which later was converted into a history museum. (Courtesy McNeese State University Archives.)

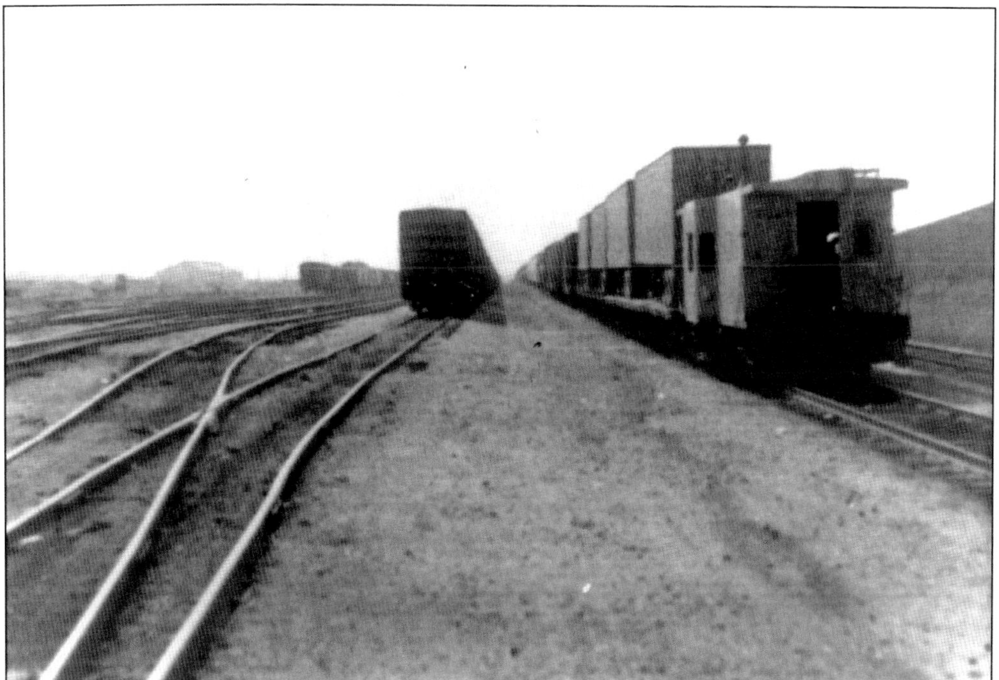

A misty fog covers the Deramus freight yard at Shreveport, Louisiana, in the early 1980s. KCS freights still sported a caboose on the end of each train. Soon after, cabooses were taken out of use and replaced by rear-end safety devices. (Courtesy Belinda S. Carter.)

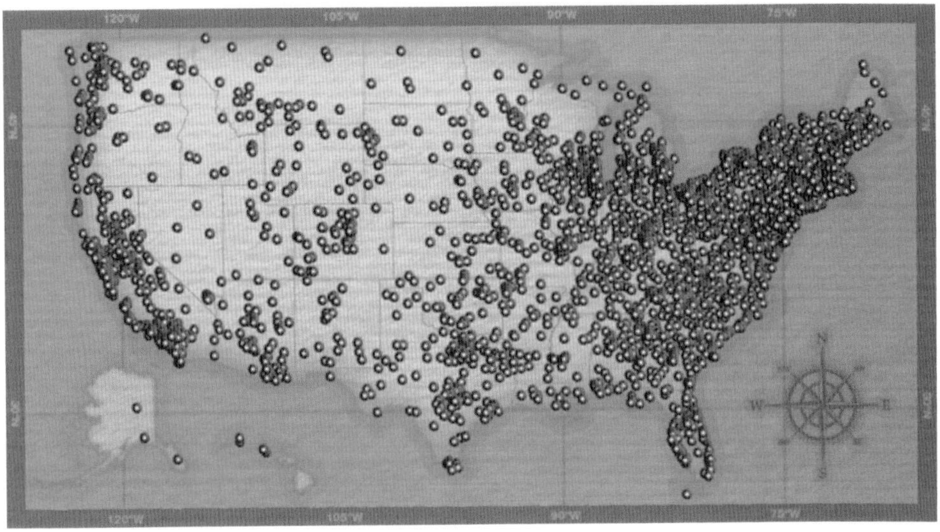

Consistent with our mission to preserve history on a local level, this book was printed in South Carolina on American-made paper and manufactured entirely in the United States. Products carrying the accredited Forest Stewardship Council (FSC) label are printed on 100 percent FSC-certified paper.

MADE IN THE USA